Best Educational Internet Sites
For English and Literature Students

Principal Site Reviewers
Victoria Chase
Heidi Frederick
Karen Hollingsworth

Additional Site Reviewers
Paxton Berardy
David M. Fortier
Linda M. Hawkes
Sharon Kurwelnz

Series Editor
Edward W. Knappman

Las Cruces, New Mexico, USA

NEW ENGLAND
PUBLISHING
ASSOCIATES

Copyright © by New England Publishing Associates, Inc.

All rights reserved. No part of this work may be reproduced or copied in any form or by any means — including, but not restricted to, photocopying or electronic data storage systems — without the express written permission of the publisher except for brief passages quoted for the purpose of review.

Produced by New England Publishing Associates, Inc. for SOFSOURCE, Inc.

Series Editor: *Edward W. Knappman*

Copy Editing: *Margaret Hogan and Mary Kate Hogan*

Editorial Administration: *Ron Formica and Chris Ceplenski*

Indexing: *Victoria Chase*

Design: *David Brackenbury and Teri Prestash*

Page Composition: *Teri Prestash*

Proofreading: *Margaret Heinrich Hand*

Library of Congress Cataloging-in-Publication Data
ISBN 1-57163-902-0
Library of Congress Catalog Card Number 98-84284
Printed in the United States of America
01 00 99 98   9 8 7 6 5 4 3 2 1

**Best Educational Internet Sites
for English and Literature Students**

Donated by Jorge Ortiz
Who loved to read books
Rest in eternal peace

Other Titles in the Series
Social Studies
Science & Math
French & Spanish

Table of Contents

vii	About This Book
1	Indexes, Search Engines & Resource Lists
21	Dictionaries & Reference
27	Words & Language
30	Grammar, Punctuation & Spelling
33	Writing Style & Composition Tips
38	Literature (General)
47	Mythology, Fairy Tales & Folk Tales
50	Poetry
58	Drama, Theater & Film
67	American & Canadian Literature
76	British & Irish Literature
80	World Literature
84	Pages Devoted to Specific Authors and Works
126	Journalism
130	Tips & Resources for Writers
135	Writing Opportunities for Students
139	Cyber & Web Writing
143	Books & Publishing
147	Miscellaneous Sites
151	Index

About This Book

This title is part of a series entitled Best Educational Internet Sites. Each title includes 500 or more brief evaluations of sites that assist students in a specific subject area such as English and literature, social studies, science and mathematics, and foreign languages (French and Spanish).

Our goal is to guide students — particularly those in high school — to sites on the Web that will help them complete homework or research assignments or help them hone skills in specific curricula areas. To insure the relevance of each site to high school students, all the sites were selected, evaluated, and reviewed by current or very recent teachers of the appropriate subject.

Of course, as all of us who use the Internet on a regular basis have learned, sites appear, disappear, and reappear with astonishing speed. Moreover, Web addresses (URLs) can and do change. That's why we can't promise that you'll find each and every site listed in this book at the URL we provide. We can assure you that these sites were alive and well and living at the address given in the summer and autumn of 1997. The address of each site was independently verified, by three different researchers over a period of several months. All sites that couldn't be verified were eliminated.

How We Selected & Evaluated Sites

Sites were selected on the basis of how useful and interesting they would be to high school students. In other words, our teacher/reviewers selected and evaluated sites by asking themselves the following questions:

- How relevant is the information to the core high school curriculum?
- How useful will the site be to students carrying out assignments?
- How interesting will the site be to student users? To teachers?
- How easy is it for high school students to access and use the site?
- How reliable/accurate is the information found at the site?
- How much depth and breadth of information is found at the site and linked sites?

How to Read a Site Abstract

Each site review consists of several elements.

- At the top, of course, is the site's name, which appears in bold type. Surprisingly, determining the actual name or title of a site is not as easy as it sounds! The home or welcome screen for some sites literally says "Welcome" and nothing else or something along the lines of "Welcome to Joan's Lizard Page." Others display one title on the home page and a radically different one in the browser's address bar. When the site lacked a formal name or was inconsistent about its name, we used a name that we thought was descriptive and clear.

- Directly underneath the name is the full Internet address for the site.

- Below the address in bold you'll find the name of the sponsor. A few sites do not list any sponsor at all. Others list so many sponsors that we were forced to select the ones that appeared to be primarily responsible for the site's content.

- Just below the sponsor's name, you'll find a gray dot ● followed by a listing of relevant courses.

- Next to the small symbol we've listed the grade appropriateness of the site. "All" means that students from grades 9 through 12 will find the site useful. "AP" means the site is most appropriate for advanced placement students.

- The text of the review follows describing what students will find on a visit to the site and indicating why it was chosen to be included.

- The bars to the left of the abstract, evaluate the site on a scale of 1 to 5 on the depth and breadth of information, the quality and accuracy of information, its relevance to the high school curriculum, its usefulness for students doing research or homework assignments, and its entertainment value — in other words is the site interesting and fun to visit.

- This symbol is used to indicate that the site includes information particularly relevant for multicultural studies.

How to Find Sites

Each volume in the series groups related sites into logical chapters [see the table of contents]. Within chapters, the sites are organized alphabetically by the first key word. At the end of most chapters, you will find a list of sites and page references found in other chapters that also contain information relevant to the chapter's theme. In the back of the book you will find a topical/subject index, which also lists all sites by name.

Where to Find the Latest Information

Check the publisher's Web site [http://www.sofsource.com] for updated information.

We're Still Looking for a Few Good Sites

If you find a site you would recommend for inclusion in future editions of this book, by all means let us know. You can E-mail us at **bestsite@sofsource.com**.

INDEXES, SEARCH ENGINES & RESOURCE LISTS

Athena: Authors & Texts
http://un2sg1.unige.ch/www/athena/html/authors.html
Pierre Perroud
- Art, Art History, English, Indexes and Resource Lists, Literature, Reference (General), Science (General), World History
- All

This site provides links to sources in many disciplines, from science to art, but the focus is on books and authors. You can search by categories or alphabetically by author. Books without authors have their own link. Books by French authors also are included. The electronic texts are free to students and teachers, but not for commercial use. Sometimes the books are available in HTML and, therefore, are immediately accessible on your screen. Other texts may have to be downloaded and opened using appropriate software.

Atlas to the World Wide Web
http://www.rhythm.com/~bpowell/Atlas/home.htm
Macmillan Publishing
- Computers, Indexes and Resource Lists, Reference (General)
- All

This on-line "atlas" is geared to the novice Web user and the more experienced Net surfer alike. The site is divided into two basic sections. Part I is an introduction to and history of the WWW, with information on hypertext, hypermedia, and HTML. Part II, organized by areas of interest from A to Z, includes lists of the "funniest, most informative, and useful" sites on the Web. The appendices alone include valuable information. This site is the on-line version of a print product.

Author's Pen
http://www.books.com/scripts/authors.exe
Book Stacks Unlimited, Inc.
- Current Events, English, Indexes and Resource Lists, Journalism, Literature, U.S. History, World History
- All

This resource page lists over 750 authors from all eras whose books are being offered through the Book Stacks Unlimited, Inc. Search for your author by using the alphabetized links at the top of the page or scroll down the page. Find the name of your author, click on the link, and go to a separate page with a biographical note and picture. From this page, choose from selections such as a bibliography or link to a page featuring the author. Also offered on this page is a link to famous speeches available through RealAudio.

Background Readings on Female Coming-of-Age Stories
http://www.scils.rutgers.edu/special/kay/ageback.html
Kay E. Vandergrift
- English, Literature
- AP

This resource page provides a list of books on feminism, feminist theory, and feminist literary theory. Twenty-eight books are listed. Titles include *African American Autobiography: A Collection of Critical Essays*, and *Feminist Fiction: Feminist Uses of Genre Fiction*. These titles are not linked. This is strictly a list.

1

English & Literature

1 2 3 4 5
DEPTH/BREADTH
QUALITY/ACCURACY
RELEVANCE
USEFULNESS
ENTERTAINMENT

Berkeley Digital Library SunSITE
http://sunsite.berkeley.edu/cgi-bin/welcome.pl
University of California, Berkeley, and Sun Microsystems
- Literature
- 11, 12

Sponsored jointly by Sun Microsystems and Berkeley, this site provides links to a wide variety of electronic text archives (largely of American authors), an "Image Finder," medieval and classical texts, and access to special collections of materials on Jack London and Emma Goldman. High school students may find this site difficult to use unless they know exactly what they are looking for or are experienced Net surfers.

1 2 3 4 5
DEPTH/BREADTH
QUALITY/ACCURACY
RELEVANCE
USEFULNESS
ENTERTAINMENT

Blue Web'N Applications: English References
http://www.kn.pacbell.com/cgi-bin/listApps.pl?English&WebReference
Pacific Bell Knowledge Network
- English, Grammar and Style, Indexes and Resource Lists, Literature, Writing
- All

This resource page lists links to popular sites on the study of English and literature. What's particularly helpful is that there is a brief description of each site and each has been rated. The best sites have five stars and the word "Hot" alongside them. You'll find on-line dictionaries, thesauruses, books of quotations, and books about grammar. In addition, there are a few popular sites for poetry, fiction, stories, and biography.

1 2 3 4 5
DEPTH/BREADTH
QUALITY/ACCURACY
RELEVANCE
USEFULNESS
ENTERTAINMENT

Books in Chains
http://www.uc.edu/~RETTBESR/Links.html
Scott Rettberg
- Drama and Theater, English, Grammar and Style, Indexes and Resource Lists, Journalism, Literature, Reading, Writing
- All

This is an extremely complete resource list devoted to literature, authors, drama, film, writing, and literary magazines on the Net. The site has three main divisions: General English Resources includes indexes, electronic texts, specific descriptive categories, libraries and institutions, booksellers, publishers, drama and film, journals, and reference tools. The Author division includes links to specific authors or schools of writing, arranged alphabetically and focusing on twentieth-century fiction writers. Literary Magazines is organized into 'zines, university-associated literary magazines, small press literary magazines, and commercial magazines.

✔ Bob's Cool Link of the Day, Novel Place of the Day, Useful Thing of the Day, Web Cite of the Week.

1 2 3 4 5
DEPTH/BREADTH
QUALITY/ACCURACY
RELEVANCE
USEFULNESS
ENTERTAINMENT

Book Lovers: Fine Books & Literature
http://www.xs4all.nl/~pwessel/
Piet Wesselman
- Art, Art History, English, Indexes and Resource Lists, Literature
- 11, 12, AP

Here you will find quality links to many sites on the Web on subjects related to fine books and art. To start your search for a book, click on general sites. If you have an unusual book in mind, click on rare books. You'll find literature from other countries, literary journals, authors who write for these publications, and more.

✔ Magellan 3 Star Site, Clearinghouse Approved, POINTCommunications Top 5% Web Site.

Canadian Literary Archive Services
http://canlit.st-john.umanitoba.ca/Canlitx/archive_Services.html

St John's College, University of Manitoba
- Literature, Writing
- All

At this site devoted to Canadian writers, students can find links not only to Canadian writers on the Web but also to writer's organizations and resources. There are other links to announcements of conferences, texts, a bibliography, images, and the University of Manitoba archives and publications.

Canadiana — The Canadian Resource Page
http://www.cs.cmu.edu/Unofficial/Canadiana/README.html

Carnegie Mellon University
- Current Events, Drama and Theater, Economics, Environmental Studies, French, Geography, Indexes and Resource Lists, Journalism, Literature, Political Science, Reference (General), Science (General), World History
- All

This exhaustive site lists links to virtually all things Canadian. The headings all contain a minimum of fifteen links and most many more. The nine major headings include News and Information; Facts and Figures; Travel and Tourism; Government Services and Information; Politics and History; Science and Education; Technology, Commerce, and Industry; Heritage, Culture, and Entertainment; and Other General Resources. The last area also links to Canadian-oriented newsgroups, Canadian information by subject, and the "Canuck Site of the Day," among others. For the adventurous visitor who wants to test their French, the site is available in that language.

Centre for Reformation and Renaissance Studies
http://citd.scar.utoronto.ca/CRRS/Index.html

University of Toronto
- Art History, Drama and Theater, English, Indexes and Resource Lists, Literature, Music and Dance, Religion, World History
- All

This resource site is extremely well-organized for research in the Reformation and Renaissance time periods. In the Resources category are links to sections on Classics, Medieval, Renaissance, Religion, and History of the Book. There are links to libraries in the United States and abroad, including the Vatican; institutions in the United States, Canada, and Europe; and journals. In the Miscellaneous category are links to exhibits and images.

Classroom Connect
http://www.classroom.net/

Classroom Connect
- English, Indexes and Resource Lists, Literature, Writing
- All

Although this site is more for teachers than students, the latter will find some useful information here such as Best K-12 Internet Links. The most useful information for English students will be found in "GRADES." Click on the button and you go to a search engine that allows you to initiate a search of your choosing or click on a list of categories such as literature or writing. At the bottom of the page is a button for A+ sites.

✔ "Everything an educator would ever want to know or need to plan, communicate or expand on any subject with students, parents, peers."—Gail L. DeCross, Sunnyslope High School, Phoenix, AZ

English & Literature

CM
http://www.mbnet.mb.ca/cm/home/about.html

CM

- English, Indexes and Resource Lists, Literature
- All

This site offers "book reviews, media reviews, web reviews, news, features and stories of interest to teachers, librarians, parents, and kids." The homepage has links organized under several categories: authors, books, media, bookshelf, search, order, and back issues. The link to Web reviews contains a treasure trove of information, but you've got to know what you are looking for in advance to really make maximum use of this site.

✔ *Top Canadian Web Site, Cool Canadian Web Site of the Day, EyeSite of the Day, EyeSite of the Week, Safe Surf's One of the Best Award, Compass for Schools Page of the Week, Scout Report Selection.*

ConnectED
http://www.mindspring.com/~fordp/pasha/Home.html

Pasha Souvorin

- English, Indexes and Resource Lists, Literature
- All

This site provides a listing of Internet resources for teachers and students. At present, the teacher resource list is much longer. The page sponsor promises to expand the student list soon. In addition, there is a list of Internet resource tools and an opportunity to submit new ideas. Among the resources are E-texts, links to regional literature sites, on-line schools, reference sources, and "teacher stuff."

Cool School Tools — Literature and Rhetoric
http://www.walker.public.lib.ga.us/cst/literatu.htm

Cherokee Regional Library

- English, Indexes and Resource Lists, Literature
- All

This resource site provides links to sites focusing on American literature and those of other cultures as well. Subject headings include Literature and Rhetoric, American Literature in English, English, Old English Literature, Literature of Germanic Languages, Romance Languages, Spanish and Portuguese Languages, Italian, Romanian and Rhaeto-Romantic Literature, Latin Literature, Hellenic Literature, and literature in other languages, including Russian, the Egyptian Book of the Dead, and the Bible in Swahili.

Eighteenth-Century Resources
http://www.english.upenn.edu/~jlynch/18th/

Jack Lynch, University of Pennsylvania

- Indexes and Resource Lists, Literature, Music and Dance, Philosophy, Religion, U.S. History, World History
- All

This no-nonsense text-only site is a quick loading set of links to resources on eighteenth-century subjects. The collection includes information on literature, history, art, music, religion, economics, and philosophy, as well as other links to groups and organizations devoted to eighteenth-century topics. Literature is this page's strong suit, and you can find many important documents in full text here. The site is fully searchable and is organized logically by topic as well.

✔ *Magellan 4 Star Site.*

Electric Library
http://www.elibrary.com/search.cgi

Infonautics Corporation

- Current Events, English, Geography, Indexes and Resource Lists, Journalism, Literature, Reference (General)
- All

This pay-for-use site offers the services you would expect from a library on-line. Search hundreds of newspapers and magazines, two international news services, 2,000 classic books, hundreds of maps, thousands of pictures, and reference major works of art and literature. You can subscribe as an individual, family, or educational institution.

	1	2	3	4	5
DEPTH/BREADTH					
QUALITY/ACCURACY					
RELEVANCE					
USEFULNESS					
ENTERTAINMENT					

English Language Resources
http://etext.lib.virginia.edu/english.html

The Electronic Text Center, University of Virginia

- English, Indexes and Resource Lists, Literature
- 11, 12, AP

This site provides access to on-line texts, including images, under many categories such as Old English Collection and Modern English Collection. There are also numerous links to special project pages. For example, one features Rita Dove; her project page has pleasant graphics, a photo, a poem, and an audio rendition of her reading the poem. One caveat: Many selections at English Language Resources are restricted by contract obligations. As a result, options such as the *Oxford English Dictionary* are unavailable to users unaffiliated with the university. Although somewhat eclectic, the selections that are available are exceptional.

✔ *NetGuide Platinum Site, Walking the World Wide Web Premiere Site, POINTCommunications Top 5% of All Web Sites, Magellan 4 Star Site, Web Crawler Select.*

The English Server
http://english-server.hss.cmu.edu/

Geoffrey Saucer, Carnegie-Mellon University

- Anthropology, Art History, Computers, Current Events, English, Environmental Studies, Indexes and Resource Lists, Journalism, Learning Disabilities, Literature, Music and Dance, Political Science, Reference (General), Science (General), Sociology, U.S. History, World History, Writing
- 11, 12, AP

This resource page is a cooperative venture offering more than 18,000 humanities texts and covering a wide range of interests. For example, click on the Fiction category and go to a page with the following: short fiction, novels, magazines, other sites, criticism, awards, drama, poetry, and search. Choose William Faulkner and you get a rich source of information and texts. The page sponsor encourages you to search the links, send your opinion about the page, telenet on the conference line, or join the mailing lists.

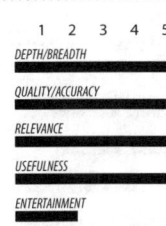

English & Literature

1 2 3 4 5
DEPTH/BREADTH
QUALITY/ACCURACY
RELEVANCE
USEFULNESS
ENTERTAINMENT

The English Teachers' Web Site
http://www.mlckew.edu.au/english/
Mark Dobbins

- English, Grammar and Style, Indexes and Resource Lists, Literature, Writing
- All

Everything the teacher of English would want in a resource site can be found here. The table of contents contains such categories as Useful Sites, Useful Files for the Computer-Based English Class, News and Information, Helpful Advice from Teachers, and Search Engines and Resource Sites. And just because the page is "advertised" as being for English teachers doesn't mean students cannot profit from it. Take the useful files for computer-based English classes: any student with a computer can call up "File Management for Students of English" and use it to get organized. The links to related sites can be used the same way—to your advantage.

✔ WebCrawler Select Site.

1 2 3 4 5
DEPTH/BREADTH
QUALITY/ACCURACY
RELEVANCE
USEFULNESS
ENTERTAINMENT

The European Enlightenment
http://www.wsu.edu:8080/~dee/ENLIGHT/ENLCONT.HTM
Richard Hooker

- Art, Art History, Indexes and Resource Lists, Literature, Math, Political Science, Reference (General), Religion, Science (General), World History
- 11, 12, AP

The visitor to this site will find a wealth of links to topics pertaining to the Enlightenment, both individuals and ideas. There are links to leading people of the period: Rene Descartes, Blaise Pascal, the Philosophes, and Jean-Jacques Rousseau. There are also links to topics: Pre-Enlightenment Europe; The Case of England; Seventeenth-Century Enlightenment Thought; The Scientific Revolution; The Eighteenth Century; Women: Communities, Economies, and Opportunities; Absolute Monarchy and Enlightened Absolutism; and the Industrial Revolution of the Eighteenth Century. There is also an Enlightenment Reader, a Glossary, a Gallery and links to other Internet resources.

1 2 3 4 5
DEPTH/BREADTH
QUALITY/ACCURACY
RELEVANCE
USEFULNESS
ENTERTAINMENT

FAQ Finder
http://ps.superb.net/FAQ/
Ras Jarborg, Philip Kallerman, and Superb Net

- Computers, Indexes and Resource Lists, Reference (General)
- All

The FAQ Finder is an inventive Web page that has links to hundreds of Frequently Asked Question pages or *FAQs* all over the Web. Organized into over a dozen subjects or keyword searchable, the FAQ Finder is easy to use and its text-oriented style makes it fast to load as well. Filled with real questions to real problems, the site isn't entirely composed of technical questions. Much of the site is dedicated to leisure-oriented questions, reference data, and general interest information; its section on politics and law is particularly helpful.

✔ WebCrawler Select, MSN Pick of the Day, NBNSoft's Content Award.

Great Writers
http://www.xs4all.nl/~pwessel/writers.html

Piet Wesselman

- English, Indexes and Resource Lists, Literature
- All

This is a resource page for writers and their homepages. The first area contains listings of Nobel Prize Winners with links and annotations, Literary Prize Lists, and Pulitzer Winners. The bulk of the site is an alphabetical listing of authors' homepages and pages that relate to them. Some of the entries have short notations that are helpful to identify their usefulness. The final area contains links to other author lists on the Web.

✔ *Starting Point Hot Site.*

Gutenberg Master Index
http://www.w3.org/pub/DataSources/bySubject/Literature/Gutenberg/

Frederick Roeber

- English, Indexes and Resource Lists, Literature
- 11, 12, AP

This resource page hasn't been updated since 1995, but it does have some worth in that it contains listings and links to classic works of literature that are now in the public domain. The database can be searched by author or title.

High School English Resource Page
http://www.bham.wednet.edu/ENGLISH2.HTM

Bellingham, WA, Schools

- Indexes and Resource Lists, Literature
- All

English teachers at the Bellingham (Washington) High School maintain this list of annotated resources for their own students, featuring links to writing and style guidelines and Net resources on British and American literature. While the site doesn't match the depth of some other resource lists, it is clean, simple to use, and closely tracks the high school English curriculum, making it a good starting place for high schoolers who might feel lost and overwhelmed exploring resource lists intended for college students.

Humanities Scholarship
http://www.wam.umd.edu/~mlhall/scholarly.html

Michael L. Hall

- Art History, Computers, Drama and Theater, English, Literature, Religion, U.S. History, World History
- All

This resource index of links covers topics in the humanities. The categories include General Humanities Resources, Humanities Computing, Humanities Scholarship, Humanities Centers, and English Department links. The largest listing is within Humanities Scholarship, which has over ninety links, including the Vergil Home Page, Medieval Resources, Galileo Project, the Victorian Web, Poetry Search, and Art History resources.

The HUMBUL Gateway

http://info.ox.ac.uk/oucs/humanities/international.html

Chris Stephens, Oxford University

- Anthropology, Art, Drama and Theater, English, Grammar and Style, Literature, Music and Dance, Philosophy, Religion, U.S. History, World History
- All

This resource page of international resources for humanities would benefit students in many areas. Specific subject areas covered are Anthropology, Archaeology, Classics, Electronic Text Centers, Text Archives, Literature, Film, Drama, Media Studies, History, Hypermedia and Multimedia, Language and Linguistics, Medieval Studies, Music, Philosophy, Religious Studies, Visual Arts, Art History, and Museums and Exhibitions. You can also link to general resources such as dictionaries and reference works and libraries on the Internet.

✔ *Magellan 4 Star Site.*

An Index of Web Sites on Modernism

http://www.modcult.brown.edu/people/Scholes/modlist/Title.html

Malcolm S. Forbes Center for Research in Culture and Media Studies, Brown University

- Art History, English, Indexes and Resource Lists, Literature, Music and Dance, Philosophy
- All

This page offers links to Web pages and gopher files on artists, poets, novelists, musicians, critics, and philosophers who wrote, created, and composed in the first half of the twentieth century. The listing is done alphabetically and includes links to What's New, General Resources on Modernism, and Electronic Journals and Reading Groups.

Infomine: Scholarly Internet Resource Collections

http://lib-www.ucr.edu/rivera/

Regents of the University of California

- Anthropology, Art History, Drama and Theater, English, Indexes and Resource Lists, Literature, Political Science, Religion, Sociology, U.S. History, World History
- All

This Web site is a search index for scholarly resources. The visitor can enter a query in the search engine by keyword, subject, or title. In addition, you can also browse, visiting What's New, a table of contents, a subject listing, a keyword listing, or a title listing. There are links to Help, the Library, Featured Resources, Educational Resources, and other Internet search tools.

Inter-Play

http://www.portals.org/interplay/

Robert Westover and Jane Wright

- Drama and Theater, English, Indexes and Resource Lists, Literature
- All

Inter-Play is an "on-line index to plays in collections, anthologies, and periodicals." It promises to be a good source of assistance for students who have chosen a dramatist for a research paper and simply cannot find much material. Sure, it's easy to find popular plays. But there are many more good plays that never became popular enough to be included in the standard anthologies. Sources range from the nineteenth century to the current year.

Internet 1996 World Exposition
http://amsterdam.park.org:8888

Sun Microsystems, IBM, and Quantum

- Computers, Indexes and Resource Lists, Reference (General)
- All

This Web site calls itself a world's fair for the information age. The fair consists of "pavilions" that contain pages of resources for topics such as education, science and technology, animals, and sports. Regions includes links to all areas of the world. There is a page of real locations where people can have access to the Internet and the fair. Viewers can vote for the pavilions they like best. The site includes many animations and audios and is fun as well as informative.

The Internet Classics Archive
http://classics.mit.edu/

Daniel C. Stevenson

- English, Indexes and Resource Lists, Literature
- All

This site maintains a searchable collection of four hundred classic Greek and Roman texts in English with commentary from people who have used the text. Easy to use but if you encounter problems, click on the help button. If you can't find what you are looking for at this site, consult its list of other classics and electronic databases. The homepage offers a featured selection, notable works, and an ongoing trivia game.

✔ PC Magazine's Top 100 Web Sites, POINTCommunications Top 5% Web Site, WebCrawler Select Best of the Net, Yahoo! Cool Link, Magellan 4 Star Site, Iway 500 Site, Jammin' Cool Site of the Week, Resource One Awesome Site, QuickClue QuickLinks.

Internet Public Library
http://www.ipl.org/

IPL

- Reference (General)
- All

Librarians set up this site to offer the public free quality resource information. Aside from general categories that you would find in any library, organized by the Dewey Decimal system, which is explained in a link of its own, this site offers special sections for youth and teens. Follow the links to entire books. Click on the Say Hello link and learn how to say hello in any number of languages. Also learn about these cultures. Special exhibits and reference section provide quality information.

✔ PC Magazine Top 100 Web Sites, MacUser 101 Must-see Sites, POINTCommunications Top 5% Web Site, and many other awards.

Internet Resources in Literature
http://www.vanderbilt.edu/AnS/english/flackcj/LitIndex.html

Christopher J. Flack, Vanderbilt University

- Indexes and Resource Lists, Literature
- 11, 12

An evaluative overview of the major English language resources to be found on the Web. In effect, this is an annotated list of resource lists. While far from exhaustive, it's a good first stop if you have never before researched an English literature project on the Web. It offers a clear and coherent overall perspective. The site also provides links to lists of college and university English department sites in the United States and abroad, archives of electronic texts, and lists of writing centers and other writing resources.

Journalists' Resource List

http://www.mediasource.com/links.html

MediaSource

- Art, Geography, Indexes and Resource Lists, Journalism, Reference (General), Religion, Science (General), U.S. History, World History, Writing
- All

This comprehensive site will help students access Internet sites on a wide range of topics. There are twenty categories of topics listed, among them Art and Architecture, Business, Fifty States, Geography, History, Humanities, International Law, Medicine and Health, Religion, Search Engines, and Sports. Many of these categories are further broken down into classifications for ease of use.

Kathy Schrock's Guide for Educators

http://www.capecod.net/schrockguide/

Kathy Schrock

- Computers, Indexes and Resource Lists
- All

Originally designed as a guide to curricula resources for educators, this site is useful for students as well. The site is clearly laid out and well-organized with more than one hundred links categorized by subject in over a dozen areas. In addition to its links to research-oriented Web pages, the site also has links to several very powerful search engines, a set of instructions on how to properly cite Web resources, and several Web-based slide shows, which teach the basics of the Internet, how to create Web pages, and how to properly use search engines.

✔ *Argus Clearinghouse Seal of Approval, NetGuide 3-Star Site, A+ Site from Classroom Connect.*

Kay E. Vandergrift's Special Interest Page

http://www.scils.rutgers.edu/special/kay/kayhp2.html

Kay E. Vandergrift, School of Communication Information and Library Sciences, Rutgers University

- English, Grammar and Style, Indexes and Resource Lists, Literature, Reading, Writing
- 9, 10

Students, notwithstanding first impressions, this page is not solely for teachers. Stick with it, page down, and skim the endless list of resources. When it seems impossible to find an interesting book for a classroom assignment, click on Vandergrift's 100: List of Young Adult Authors and Titles. Another site for young writers is the Children's Writing/Publishing link. Features of the page include young adult literature, feminism, research, and links to many sites with similar interests.

✔ *Electronic Resources for Youth Services Site of the Week, Blue Web'n Learning Application Library Award, Free Speech Online Blue Ribbon Campaign, 5-Star Internet, Underground Web Site.*

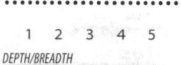

Librarians' Index to the Internet

http://sunsite.berkeley.edu/InternetIndex/

Carole Leita with Digital Library SunSITE

- Indexes and Resource Lists
- All

This site features a subject directory of more than 2,600 Internet resources under 43 subject headings, primarily from the point of view of the public library user. A special "New This Week" heading provides a list of new subjects and evidence that the page gets updated regularly. Under the "Kids" subject heading, there are subheadings for homework, fun, and health. The "Literature" category provides links to book reviews, full-text copies of a wide variety of books, and tips for better writing.

The Literary Menagerie
http://sunset.backbone.olemiss.edu/~egcash/

Eric Cash and Erin Campbell

- English, Indexes and Resource Lists, Literature
- All

This site touts itself as "Your resource for links to the best of the author-based sites on the Web." Click on a letter and get an alphabetical listing, or scroll down the page for an author's name.

✔ *Free Speech Online Blue Ribbon Campaign.*

Literary Resources—Ethnicities and Nationalities
http://www.english.upenn.edu/~jlynch/Lit/ethnic.html

Jack Lynch

- English, Indexes and Resource Lists, Literature
- 11, 12, AP

This resource site provides links to sites about literary traditions with an emphasis on nationality or ethnicity. The obvious choices are African American, Native American, and Chicano/Latino links. Also included are women of color, Canadian, and post-colonial links.

Literature and Language Arts Resources
http://molebio.iastate.edu/js/lit.htm

Jefferson/Scranton, PA, High School Media Center

- English, Grammar and Style, Indexes and Resource Lists, Literature, Writing
- All

This resource site is an English literature Mecca for students and teachers. Links from the homepage to the first two links—WWW Language Arts page and WWW High School English—are invaluable resources with many links of their own. They are an indication of the quality of the links to follow. Curriculum-based and relevant—if not necessarily exciting—this site offers students and teachers an opportunity for more advanced study at all levels through college.

Literature and Medicine
http://mchip00.med.nyu.edu/lit-med/lit-med-db/literature.html

Hippocrates Project, New York University School of Medicine

- English, Literature, Indexes and Resource Lists, Science (General)
- 11, 12, AP

This resource page assists in the search of works of literature that involve medicine and vice versa. Click a hyperlinked phrase to search by a keyword, an author, genre, title, era, or gender. The search takes you to a list where you make your next choice, and, finally, to a page with a summary of the work with biographical information. Some pages offer links to the actual works, if they are available on the Net to read or listen to. Works are offered under three categories: art, literature, and film.

English & Literature

Literature Hotlist
http://sln.fi.edu/tfi/hotlists/literature.html
The Franklin Institute
- English, Indexes and Resource Lists, Literature
- All

This is strictly a list of links to sites with information about or electronic texts of pertinent literature. The variety of links is wide, but the depth is a bit shallow.

Literature Resources for the High School and College Student
http://www.teleport.com/~mgroves/index.shtml#Home
Michael Lee Groves
- Drama and Theater, English, Grammar and Style, Indexes and Resource Lists, Literature, Writing
- All

This site is organized into six separate areas: Literature, broken down by century; Indices; Books (On-line); Writer's Resources, such as on-line writing centers; Magazines; and "!?!." The last category includes links to entertaining sites such as the Insult Server (which generates a literary insult with every reload of the page), the Literary HyperCalendar, Puzzles and Timelines, and others. The visitor can also search the site by an alphabetical listing of authors.

LSU Libraries Author Webliography
http://www.lib.lsu.edu/hum/authors.html
Steven R. Harris, Louisiana State University Libraries
- English, Indexes and Resource Lists, Literature
- All

This site is a self-proclaimed "index of indexes" because it contains pointers to individual author guides or documents that deal with specific writers. The writers included are generally considered to be "literary," as science fiction, romance, and other genre authors are excluded. The visitor can search by an alphabetical listing or use the alphabet graphics to go to a specific writer. The authors included range from Jane Austen to William Butler Yeats.

Mitsuhara Matsuoka's Home Page [English Literature on the Web]
http://ernie.lang.nagoya-u.ac.jp/~matsuoka/index.html
Mitsuhara Matsuoka, Nagoya University
- Indexes and Resource Lists, Literature
- All

An eclectic list of English literature resources on the Web assembled by a professor at a Japanese university. The focus is on Victorian literature with special features on Charles Dickens and Elizabeth Gaskill. Attractive graphics but slow loading.

Ms. Smith's English Page
http://home.earthlink.net/~jesmith/

Janice E. Smith

- English, Indexes and Resource Lists, Literature
- 9, 10

Famous authors and student authors are two of the links from this page. You'll also find links to writing resources, notes about novels, and biography and autobiography. Ms. Smith lists her favorite sites, sites where you can play games with words, and sites to check out when your homework is done. The site is for both students and teachers.

✔ LookSmart Editor's Choice, Brain Bait Golden Times Award, Safe Surf Rated All Ages, Argus Clearinghouse Seal of Approval, Education Index Top Site.

My Virtual Reference Desk
http://www.refdesk.com/facts.html

Bob Drudge

- English, Grammar and Style, Indexes and Resource Lists, Literature, Reference (General), Writing
- All

This page provides links to numerous resources in many categories. In the English and literature category, there are connections with dictionaries, encyclopedias, virtual libraries, biographies, and more.

The National Writing Project
http://www-gse.berkeley.edu/Research/NWP/nwp.html

Richard Sterling

- English, Grammar and Style, Indexes and Resource Lists, Literature, Writing
- All

This is a valuable site for teachers, but there is also something here for students: in particular, the section titled Other WWW Sites for Teachers and Learners. There are lots of links to chatrooms and news groups. The purpose of the site is to tap resources, people, and networks of teachers nationwide to "improve the teaching and learning of writing in the nation's classrooms."

NetSERF: The Internet Connection for Medieval Resources
http://www.cua.edu/www/hist/netserf/home.htm

Department of History, Catholic University of America

- Art History, Indexes and Resource Lists, Literature, World History
- All

At many Web pages about the Middle Ages, the contents are too dry and academic for high school students. NetSERF is an exception, connecting visitors to resources on the medieval era that often have a quirky and even irreverent feel to them. There are over a dozen categories of information about the Middle Ages including cooking, clothing, and medieval games. More traditional medieval resources include full text transcripts of classic literature (e.g., *Beowulf*) and links to pages on medieval history, culture, and art. A collection of medieval fonts and clip art that can be integrated into school reports or multimedia presentations is another example of what makes this site so useful and interesting for students.

English & Literature

1 2 3 4 5
DEPTH/BREADTH
QUALITY/ACCURACY
RELEVANCE
USEFULNESS
ENTERTAINMENT

NM's Creative Impulse
http://www.evansville.net/~nbmautz/index.html

Nancy Mautz
- Art History, Drama and Theater, Indexes and Resource Lists, Literature, Music and Dance, U.S. History, World History
- All

This unusual social studies Web site looks at history through the eyes of each historical era's artists. Based on the principle that the art, music, drama, and literature of a period offer unique insights into its people and culture, Creative Impulse gathers hundreds of links from the Web that accentuate these connections. Organized by historical era, with special sections detailing each period's art, Mautz's eclectic collection of links and content provides a unique perspective.

✔ *LookSmart Editor's Choice, Wise Owl Site of the Month, Education Index Top Site.*

1 2 3 4 5
DEPTH/BREADTH
QUALITY/ACCURACY
RELEVANCE
USEFULNESS
ENTERTAINMENT

On-line Books Page
http://www.cs.cmu.edu/books.html

John Mark Ockerbloom
- English, Indexes and Resource Lists, Literature
- All

This resource page provides links to quality literary sites (such as "Celebration of Women Writers"), connections to electronic versions of thousands of titles that can be read right on the Web, and good instructions on its use. You can search by category, author, or title. This easy-to-use site is updated regularly.

1 2 3 4 5
DEPTH/BREADTH
QUALITY/ACCURACY
RELEVANCE
USEFULNESS
ENTERTAINMENT

On-Line Literary Resources
http://www.english.upenn.edu/~jlynch/Lit/

Jack Lynch, University of Pennsylvania
- Indexes and Resource Lists, Literature
- 11, 12

Although this is essentially only a list of resources for literary research on the Net, it is one great site! Professor Jack Lynch's selection of sites is discriminating, well-organized, and often annotated. It contains extensive links to categories with information ranging from classical and biblical, through modern theater and drama and literary theory. There are also categories for women's literature, ethnic literature, mailing lists, foreign languages, and resources for writing. The only problem is that the site has so many links that poor Professor Lynch apparently can't keep them all up-to-date, resulting in some links to sites that are no longer maintained or have changed Web addresses.

✔ *Magellan 4 Star Site.*

1 2 3 4 5
DEPTH/BREADTH
QUALITY/ACCURACY
RELEVANCE
USEFULNESS
ENTERTAINMENT

Pitsco's Ask an Expert
http://www.askanexpert.com/askanexpert

Pitsco, Inc.
- Art, Economics, Indexes and Resource Lists, Music, Political Science, Reference (General), Religion, Science (General), U.S. History, World History
- All

This site will prove a boon to students who need an answer to a question on almost any topic. The page is set up in an attractive fashion that encourages visitors to question experts, first via their Web pages or by direct E-mail if a page is not available. Over three hundred Web site links are provided in twelve categories: Science and Technology, Health, Recreation and Entertainment, International and Cultural, Money and Business, Law, Career and Industry, Internet and Computer, Education and Personal Development, Resources, Arts, and Religion.

✔ *An* Education World *Education Site, Ten Cool Sites from Exploratorium, Scout Report Selection, and recognition from Classroom Connect and the* Washington Post, *among others.*

Public Domain Modern English Search
http://www.hti.umich.edu/english/pd-modeng/

Humanities Text Initiative, University of Michigan

- Literature
- All

This site provides access to several hundred electronic texts of novels, poems, and other literature. The site grows, adding new texts by leaps and bounds. The range of E-texts found here is indicated by this selection of authors whose names begin with "c" or "d": James Branch Cabell, Lewis Carroll, Willa Cather, Joseph Conrad, Stephen Crane, Charles Darwin, Charles Dickens, Rita Dove, and Arthur Conan Doyle. Generally, the bibliography search is the easiest way to access the text if you know the name of the author. A boolean search engine also is available.

Science Fiction Resource Guide
http://sflovers.rutgers.edu/Web/SFRG/

Chaz Boston Baden

- Drama and Theater, English, Indexes and Resource Lists, Literature, Music and Dance, Writing
- All

An extremely comprehensive resource site devoted to the science fiction genre. Here you will find links to: art, comics, fiction, movies, music, games, television, and zines devoted to the topic. There are also links organized alphabetically under authors, bibliographies, conventions, mailing lists, publishers, and writer's resources. The popularity of this resource is demonstrated by the nine mirror sites where it can be found.

✔ Magellan 4 Star Site, NetGuide Gold Award, Delos Site of the Month.

SIRS: The Knowledge Source: Arts and Humanities
http://www.sirs.com/tree/artshum.htm

SIRS, Inc.

- Art, Drama and Theater, English, Indexes and Resource Lists, Journalism, Literature, Music and Dance, Religion
- All

A site sponsored by SIRS, a well-known publisher of print research materials for libraries, this site lists links in the following areas: Architecture and Design, Culture, Film, Radio, Television and Video, Literature, Music, Performing Arts, Philosophy and Religion, Visual Arts, and Museums. The links in each category are basic and good starting points for research.

Texts and Contexts
http://paul.spu.edu/~hawk/t&c.html

Haakon's Computer Consulting

- Economics, English, Literature, Math, Music and Dance, Philosophy, Political Science, Religion, World History
- All

This resource page provides information on a cross-section of influential texts and authors throughout history. Choosing one of the thirty-four links listed under Subjects will bring the visitor to a page of links and on-line texts relating to that topic. There are philosophers and writers such as Aquinas and Kierkegaard, political writers such as Karl Marx and Machiavelli, and general topics such as the Enlightenment and predestination.

16 *English & Literature*

1 2 3 4 5
DEPTH/BREADTH
QUALITY/ACCURACY
RELEVANCE
USEFULNESS
ENTERTAINMENT

Ultimate Science Fiction Web Guide, The
http://www.magicdragon.com/UltimateSF/SF-Index.html

Magic Dragon Multimedia

- English, Indexes and Resource Lists, Literature
- All

This resource page offers more than 3,000 hotlinks, from timelines indicating when a book was published to authors in different countries to items of general interest to categories such as "Aliens." This information is presented in alphabetical order for easy access.

✔ "This incredible Web resource maintains a list of 5,235 authors' names and/or hotlinks and/or pseudonyms. While all of this information is fascinating, you'll find 1,913 names listed with hotlinks." —Kristyn Rose, editor, who gave this site the "Suite 101 Top 5" award in the category "Authors on the Net." Many other citations and awards.

1 2 3 4 5
DEPTH/BREADTH
QUALITY/ACCURACY
RELEVANCE
USEFULNESS
ENTERTAINMENT

Using Young Adult Fiction and Non-Fiction to Produce Critical Readers
http://scholar.lib.vt.edu/ejournals/ALAN/winter94/Kaywell.html

Joan Kaywell

- English, Literature
- 9, 10

This resource page argues for the use of young adult reading materials in the classroom, especially for students with reading-related special needs. Included is a long list of interesting books by topic, including abuse, eating disorders, homosexuality, teenage pregnancy, and stress and suicide.

1 2 3 4 5
DEPTH/BREADTH
QUALITY/ACCURACY
RELEVANCE
USEFULNESS
ENTERTAINMENT

Vassar CoolSchool: The Best Sites on the Web for Teens and Teachers
http://vassar.coolschool.edu

Vassar College

- Indexes and Resource Lists
- All

This site was launched by Vassar College to showcase outstanding educational sites on the Web. It's intended for high school students and their teachers. The attractive and well-designed site is divided into four sections. "Go to Class" includes a list of academic subjects with links to selected sites; "Hang Out" is an index of sports and entertainment sites; "SAT, etc." lists college and university homepages, College Board Online, and more; and "Teachers' Lounge" is loaded with resources for teachers. This is a useful index of well-chosen sites.

1 2 3 4 5
DEPTH/BREADTH
QUALITY/ACCURACY
RELEVANCE
USEFULNESS
ENTERTAINMENT

Voices from the Gaps: Women Writers of Color
http://www-engl.cla.umn.edu/lkd/vfg/VFGHome

Department of English and Program in American Studies, University of Minnesota

- English, Indexes and Resource Lists, Literature
- All

This resource page links to lists of writers and finally to a page about each author with biographical information designed to introduce the author and her works and selective bibliographies of works and works about the author. You can find writers by name, birth date, racial/ethnic background, or significant dates. The page offers links to a discussion room (Help, I'm writing a paper on Alice Walker and can't find anything!), a search engine for the site, and related sites.

✔ *Mining Company Best of the Net, Los Angeles Times* Pick, *Scout Report Selection, WebCrawler Select.*

Indexes, Search Engines & Resource Lists **17**

WebCrawler Guide: Arts: Literature
http://www.webcrawler.com/select/art.histlit.html

WebCrawler

- English, Indexes and Resource Lists, Literature
- All

This resource page provides lists of sites under five headings: author pages, short fiction, indexes and reference, on-line book collections, and news groups.

1 2 3 4 5
DEPTH/BREADTH
QUALITY/ACCURACY
RELEVANCE
USEFULNESS
ENTERTAINMENT

WebLit
http://www.rust.net/~rothfder/weblit.html

Eric Rothfeder

- English, Indexes and Resource Lists, Literature
- All

This resource page has links for authors and poets, search engines, four-star pages, downloadable texts, and other links, which make it a valuable place to search for information on authors and other literary topics. It's especially surprising how useful this site is when you discover that a sixteen-year-old came up with the idea and maintains the site in his spare time. Included in his listings is a rating system that grades the content of the sites, use of graphics, etc.

✔ POINTCommunications Top 5% Web Site.

1 2 3 4 5
DEPTH/BREADTH
QUALITY/ACCURACY
RELEVANCE
USEFULNESS
ENTERTAINMENT

Western Canon, The
http://www.geocities.com/Athens/Acropolis/6681/index.html

Paul J. Barnette Jr.

- English, Indexes and Resource Lists, Literature, Philosophy
- 11, 12, AP

This site enables you to access some of the basic texts of the classical Western canon without leaving your chair. The most valuable contribution of this page, aside from providing avenues to get electronic texts and basic lists of canonical literature, is the mailing list — it allows anyone to comment on these great books. Search for authors and works by era, alphabetically, or by subject.

✔ WebCrawler Select Site, Mining Company Best of the Web.

1 2 3 4 5
DEPTH/BREADTH
QUALITY/ACCURACY
RELEVANCE
USEFULNESS
ENTERTAINMENT

The Wiretap Electronic Text Archive
http://wiretap.area.com/

Thomas Dell and Area Systems

- Indexes and Resource Lists, Literature, Political Science, U.S. History, World History
- All

This is one of the early repositories of government documents and other electronic texts on the Internet. Accessible via the World Wide Web but still in Gopher text format, Wiretap has links to thousands of electronic documents. Many are government documents taken from around the world. One especially interesting area is the world constitution pages which allows you to compare and contrast the U.S. Constitution with many others. The full texts of hundreds of classic books, poems, myths, and essays by the likes of Mark Twain, Francis Bacon, and Aesop can all be found using the links found at this page.

1 2 3 4 5
DEPTH/BREADTH
QUALITY/ACCURACY
RELEVANCE
USEFULNESS
ENTERTAINMENT

Women Romantic-Era Writers

http://www.ccc.nottingham.ac.uk/~aezac/craciun.womrom.html

Adriana Craciun, University of Nottingham

- English, Indexes and Resource Lists, Literature
- All

This site provides a comprehensive listing of texts by eighteenth-century women writers available on-line. Over forty women are represented on the list, including such well-known writers as Mary Wollstonecraft and Mary Robinson and such less well-known writers as Joanna Baillie and Lucretia Maria Davidson. The page also includes a helpful listing of Other Women Writers On-line Resources as well as an interesting link called Contemporary Responses to Women Writers, which has reviews by S. T. Coleridge and Richard Polwhele.

Women Writers of the Middle Ages

http://www.millersv.edu/~english/homepage/duncan/medfem/medfem.html

Bonnie Duncan

- English, Indexes and Resource Lists, Literature, World History
- 11, 12, AP

This appealing resource page has links to everything about women writers of the Middle Ages and loads of information about other subjects of interest about the Middle Ages, such as alchemy. The page is the offering of a college professor who teaches a course on women writers of the period. It is incredibly erudite yet lots of fun, pleasing in design with separate categories to explore, and features eclectic artwork from the era. The categories with many links to quality resources are secular women writers, saints and women in religious vocations, materials concerning women, and secondary hypertexts.

Writing Black

http://www.keele.ac.uk/depts/as/Literature/amlit.black.html

Andrew L. Graham

- Drama and Theater, English, Indexes and Resource Lists, Literature
- All

5   4   4   4   2   4

This site offers a Web resource list of literature and history written by and on African Americans. In the section Text and Resources on the Web, the materials are listed alphabetically by author, from Maya Angelou through Malcolm X. The Historical Texts link includes *Confessions of Nat Turner*, *The Emancipation Proclamation*, and several *Atlantic Monthly* articles. The final area, Other Libraries and Indexes, provides links to the English server at Carnegie-Mellon, the African American Bibliography at the University of Michigan, and the African American Mosaic at the Library of Congress.

Yahoo! Arts: Humanities: Literature: Authors

http://www.yahoo.com/Arts/Humanities/Literature/Authors/

Yahoo! Inc.

- English, Indexes and Resource Lists, Literature
- All

Be prepared to browse before selecting a link, and then to browse some more. Stick with it and the search will pay off. Immediate categories featured on this resource page include the Beat Generation, Playwrights, and Romance, among others. Below these generic categories are more specific links to Canadian authors and modern writers. In the end, interviews, resource materials, photos, and sometimes audio recordings are the reward.

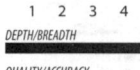

Indexes, Search Engines & Resource Lists **19**

Young Adult Librarian's Help/Homepage
http://www.kcpl.lib.mo.us/ya/

Patrick Jones, Kansas City Public Library

● English, Indexes and Resource Lists, Literature, Reference (General)

♛ All

This site provides a resource for librarians serving teenagers. It is not a tool that reviews or recommends materials, but teachers and students can make use of the links provided. Some are more specific, for example, the Judy Blume Homebase page; others are more general, for example, the On-line Educator. A search engine is linked to the site for more specific or detailed searches.

Young Adult Services
http://docker.com/~whiteheadm/yaread.html

Murray Whitehead

● English, Indexes and Resource Lists, Literature

♛ 9, 10

This resource page promises more than it delivers, but the book lists and links to related sites are worth a look. Each recommended reading list indicates the suitability of the material and lets you know if it there are contents of a graphic nature.

Young Adult Literature Library
http://www.uiowa.edu/~english/litcult2097/tlucht/lit-yalib.html

Thorven Lucht

● English, Indexes and Resource Lists, Literature

♛ 9, 10

This resource page contains links to summaries and critiques of individual novels appropriate for the junior high and high school English classroom. The books are organized into categories. There are also links to essays about the genre, bibliographic resources, and young adult authors who are not represented on the page. Teachers, students, and parents will find the material presented here useful.

The Zuzu's Petals Literary Resource Homepage
http://www.lehigh.net/zuzu/index.htm

Zuzu's Petals Literary Resource

● Drama and Theater, English, Indexes and Resource Lists, Literature, Writing

♛ All

With over two thousand organized links to helpful resources, this site can be very useful to writers, artists, performers, and researchers. The most prominent feature of the first page of the site is a search feature — a good starting point for research. Other links go to Zuzu resources, literary news and notes, a Web site overview, links, writers' guidelines, information on poetry contests, and back issues as well as the latest issue of *Zuzu's Petals Quarterly*.

✔ Magellan 4 Star Site, USA Today *Hot Site*, NetGuide Gold Site, POINTCommunications Top 5% Web Site, and many other awards.

See Also

DICTIONARIES & REFERENCE chapter (p. 17)

PAGES DEVOTED TO SPECIFIC AUTHORS AND WORKS chapter (p. 86)

British Poetry 1780-1910: A Hypertext Archive of Scholarly Editions
   http://etext.lib.virginia.edu/britpo.html (p 51)

eZines: Ultimate Magazine Database http://www.dominis.com/Zines/ (p. 126)

Guide to Theater Resources on the INTERNET http://www-old.ircam.fr/divers/theatre-e.html (p 59)

Home Page of Theater http://www.cs.fsu.edu./projects/group4/theatre.html (p 60)

English & Literature

Hyperbibliography to American Poetry
http://www.hti.umich.edu/english/amverse/hyperbib.html (p 52)

Irish Literature, Mythology, Folklore, and Drama
http://www.luminarium.org/mythology/ireland/ (p 78)

Native American Authors http://www.ipl.org/ref/native/ (p 72)

Native Lit-L: A Mailing List for Native Literature http://www.uwm.edu/~mwilson/lit.htm (p 73)

Newseum http://www.newseum.org/ (p 127)

North American Native Authors Catalog
http://nativeauthors.com/search/home.html (p 73)

Richard's Poetry Library http://itpubs.ucdavis.edu/richard/library/ (p 55)

Ron's On-line ESOL Classroom http://www.vcu.edu/cspweb/,gram/grammar.html (p 32)

Snagged Links: On Modern World Drama
http://www.stetson.edu/~csata/snaglnk1.html (p 63)

South Asian American Literature
http://alumni.EECS.Berkeley.EDU:80/~manish/index.html (p 75)

Spondee http://www.execpc.com/~jon/ (p 56)

Victorian Web, The http://www.stg.brown.edu/projects/hypertext/landow/victorian/victov.html (p 45)

DICTIONARIES & REFERENCE

AwardWeb: Collections of Literary Award Information
http://www.city-net.com/~lmann/awards/

AwardWeb and Laurie D. T. Mann
- English, Indexes and Resource Lists, Literature
- All

This resource page lists mostly science fiction books that have won prestigious awards from around the globe. There are brief descriptions of the awards with links to the winners. Promises are made that the range of the site will be expanded to include awards for a greater variety of books.

1 2 3 4 5
DEPTH/BREADTH
QUALITY/ACCURACY
RELEVANCE
USEFULNESS
ENTERTAINMENT

Barr's English Class
http://www.capecod.net/~bbarsant/class/

Robert P. Barsanti, Nantucket, MA, High School
- English, Grammar and Style, Literature, Reading, Writing
- All

This busy site is designed as a resource for secondary students and teachers. For students, there are student essays, exam questions, and class pictures. Teachers get lessons for such courses as The Wounded Male, American Giants, Power and Utopia, and That's Right, The Women Are Smarter. Links provide connections to resources about books, such as J. D. Salinger's *Catcher in the Rye*, and writing resources.

✔ USA Today *Hot Site*, Yahoo Award.

1 2 3 4 5
DEPTH/BREADTH
QUALITY/ACCURACY
RELEVANCE
USEFULNESS
ENTERTAINMENT

The Brown University Women Writers Project
http://www.stg.brown.edu/projects/wwp/wwp_home.html

Brown University
- English, Indexes and Resource Lists, Literature,
- AP

The sponsors of this site state their mission is to create a state-of-the-art electronic database of writing by women before 1830. They appear well on their way to accomplishing this feat. However, there is one problem: rights to the two hundred or more texts must be purchased, generally for three to fifteen dollars. This requirement is necessary because Brown University is in a unique arrangement with Oxford University Press. Resources linked from this page allow access to discussion groups and essays on some of the works, directly through a link. For students, this is a good place to locate an obscure work to impress your teacher. For teachers, this is a good place to uncover a unique work testifying to the broad range of writing by women from an era textbook publishers have largely ignored.

1 2 3 4 5
DEPTH/BREADTH
QUALITY/ACCURACY
RELEVANCE
USEFULNESS
ENTERTAINMENT

Dictionary of Literary Terms
http://www.bell.k12.ca.us/BellHS/Departments/English/Literary.Terms.html

Bell High School
- Drama and Theater, English, Literature
- All

This site is a dictionary of terms relevant to various aspects of the literary genre. An alphabetical listing of terms provides their definitions. This page would be a useful source for a student studying almost any aspect of drama or literature.

1 2 3 4 5
DEPTH/BREADTH
QUALITY/ACCURACY
RELEVANCE
USEFULNESS
ENTERTAINMENT

A Glossary of Rhetorical Terms with Examples
http://www.uky.edu/ArtsSciences/Classics/rhetoric.html#related
Kentucky Classics
- Debate, English, Literature, Speech, Writing
- All

This site provides a list of rhetorical terms with examples and links to other sites that explore rhetoric or literary devices that have been used throughout history to embolden speech and writing. The familiar metaphor is defined as "implied comparison achieved through a figurative use of words; the word is used not in its literal sense, but in one analogous to it." Here's the definition of the not-so-familiar paraprosdokian: "surprise or unexpected ending of a phrase or series." There are examples of each if the definition is less than enlightening. Links lead to a fairly scholarly bunch of Web sites.

Great Books Overview
http://www.mala.bc.ca/~mcneil/matrix.htm
Malaspina University College
- English, Indexes and Resource Lists, Literature, Reading
- All

This site is based on the Great Books concept of Mortimer Adler and Charles Van Doren. It contains several different search methods, the most prominent being the Interdisciplinary Matrix, which allows the visitor to search by topic (Science, Art, Books, Theater, Music) or by time period (Antiquity, Medieval, Renaissance, Baroque, Classical, Romantic, or Modern). One can also browse the Great Books Database or view a list of Five Star Sites on the Great Books List.

✔ *Web Counter Top-Ten Site, All-in-One Site Pick of the Day, Scout Report Selection, Education First Blue Web'n Learning Application, and others.*

Homework Help
http://www.startribune.com/stonline/html/special/homework/
The Star Tribune
- English, Current Events, Indexes and Resource Lists, Literature, Math, Reference (General), Science (General), U.S. History, World History, Writing
- All

Sponsored by the daily newspaper of the St. Paul/Minneapolis area, this site offers homework assistance for several high school subject areas. Individuals seeking help with their homework submit a question to a pool of teachers who respond directly. Questions and answers are listed for students who may seek the same information. The page is updated regularly and the list of subjects is considerable. A Web Links button on the attractive homepage—it features a brain with buttons for the different subject areas—provides plenty of connections to other quality Web sites for additional homework help.

The Johns Hopkins Guide to Literary Theory and Criticism
http://www.press.jhu.edu/books/hopkins_guide_to_literary_theory/g-index.html
The Johns Hopkins University Press
- English, Indexes and Resource Lists, Literature
- 11, 12, AP

This resource page is a useful reference for all things literary. Click on a name, term, or school of criticism and a comprehensive, factual, well-written essay appears on your screen. Within the essay, hyperlinked words lead to further information. At the bottom of the page are cross-referenced terms closely identified with the subject of the essay. No graphics, but plenty of information nicely organized and easy to follow under the following categories: "Contents," "List of Entries," "Special Listings," "Index of Names," "Index of Topics," and "Ideas, History and Theories Entries." Features the ability to perform a full-text search.

Merriam-Webster OnLine
http://www.m-w.com/

Merriam-Webster, Inc.

- English, Grammar and Style, Writing
- All

This on-line version of *Merriam Webster's Collegiate Dictionary, Tenth Edition* allows a visitor to look up a definition, pronunciation, etymology, spelling, or usage in the WWWebster Dictionary. One can also check the Word of the Day, transcripts of the "Word for the Wise" radio program, or visit the Merriam-Webster OnLine Bookstore.

✔ Los Angeles Times *Pick*.

The New York Public Library Home Page
http://www.nypl.org/index.html

New York Public Library

- Art, Literature, Music and Dance, Reference (General), Science (General), Social Studies
- All

You could begin research on almost any topic at this site which provides access to several key divisions of the New York Public Library system. Here the visitor can access Catalogs and Indexes, Resource Guides, Exhibitions and Programs, and Publications. There are also links to the Research Libraries, the Center for the Humanities, NYPL for the Performing Arts, the Schomburg Center for Research in Black Culture, and the Sciences, Industry, and Business Library.

Nobelstiftelson: The Nobel Foundation
http://www.nobel.se/index.html

The Nobel Foundation

- Biology, Chemistry, Current Events, Economics, English, Indexes and Resource Lists, Literature, Physics, Political Science, Reference (General), Science (General), Spanish, U.S. History, World History
- All

The official site of the Nobel Foundation, this site is classic and thoughtful. At first glimpse, it may not appear to have much to offer. But the deeper you probe, the more information you find. The homepage leads to lists of Nobel winners, the official press release, bibliographical information, biographies, and lists of works. There are photos, an electronic Nobel Museum, and a searchable database.

On-Book: An Introduction to the Study of Literature
http://www.uwm.edu/People/jat/

Jane Thompson

- English, Indexes and Resource Lists, Literature, Writing
- All

This intelligently conceived and thoughtfully laid out site offers help to high school and college level students who are involved in the study of literature. As the introductory page states the page "does not contain papers for students to copy. It does contain definitions, literary terms, brief explanations of a variety of literary theories, directions for doing various kinds of literary analysis, and links to other resources on the Web." Among the various kinds of literary aids provided are detailed instructions for the writing of essays.

One Look Dictionaries: The Faster Finder

http://www.onelook.com

Stonehenge Internet Communications

- English, Grammar and Style, Writing
- All

This reference page allows the visitor to search 121 indexed dictionaries. One can search by Special Subject, General Words, Pronunciation Only, Spelling Word Lists, or All Dictionaries. There are also links to related sites, FAQs, and hints to aid in searching the dictionaries.

✔ The Best 500 Award by Epicurus, PRN Radio Network Award of Excellence, Groovy Site Award.

Reference Shelf

http://alabanza.com/kabacoff/Inter-Links/reference.html

Rob Kabacoff

- Current Events, English, Geography, Grammar and Style, Indexes and Resource Links, Reference (General), Science (General), Writing
- All

The Reference Shelf provides quick access to facts and figures on a number of topics. Under Geographic, the visitor can access Postal Abbreviations, the MapQuest Atlas, U.S. Census Information, and World Maps, among other topics. Phone Numbers provides airline toll-free numbers, area code lookup, and on-line phonebooks. Under Words are links to Bartlett's Quotations, Roget's Thesaurus, Webster's Dictionary, and Computer Jargon as well as an Acronym Lookup and the On-line Dictionary of Computing. The visitor can also access scientific links to the periodic table and weights and measures.

Roget's Thesaurus

http://ecco.bsee.swin.edu.au/text/roget/index.html

Alex A. Sergejew

- English, Grammar and Style, Writing
- All

This Web version of the Project Gutenberg E-text thesaurus allows visitors to search Roget's Thesaurus. The main page also includes thesaurus headings, a synopsis, and a facsimile of the first page of the original. There are links to other implementations of the volume both at U.S. locations and abroad.

A Semantic Rhyming Dictionary

http://www.cs.cmu.edu/~dougb/rhyme.html

Doug Beeferman

- English, Grammar and Style, Writing
- All

This is a practical site for anyone who need to find rhyme words to use in their own writing. The visitor has the option of putting in a word and choosing whether to find a perfect rhyme, partial rhyme, or homophone. The results for the search are sorted alphabetically by syllable count. A unique benefit is that the page can sort the output based on how near in meaning a word is to the target word provided.

Dictionaries & Reference   **25**

The Virtual Reference Desk
http://thorplus.lib.purdue.edu/reference/index.html

The Libraries of Purdue University

- English, Geography, Grammar and Style, Indexes and Resource Lists, Political Science, Reference (General), Science (General)
- All

At this extremely useful reference site, you can link to Selected Government Documents, Information Technology Sites, Dictionaries, Thesauri and Acronyms, Phone Books and Area Codes, Maps and Travel Information, Science Data, Time and Date, and ZIP and International Country Codes. The final link will take the visitor to other Reference Sources.

✔ NetGuide 4-Star Site, POINTCommunications Top 5% Web Site, The Best of the Internet by Progressive Farmer Online.

Wired Style
http://www.hotwired.com/hardwired/wiredstyle/

HardWired, Inc.

- Computers, English, Grammar and Style, Literature, Writing
- 11, 12, AP

Having trouble keeping up with all the new technology terminology? Better yet, sick of all the crazy jargon out there? Here's a site for you. Not only are there definitions, but there are also discussions about the use of this jargon and its impact on our language. This site offers examples from Wired Style, outtakes (pieces that never made the magazine), and an on-going discussion of these new terms and their proper use.

See Also

INDEXES, SEARCH ENGINES & RESOURCE LISTS chapter (p 1)

Bibliomania, The Network Library http://www.bibliomania.com/ (p 143)

***Booklist*: Books for Youth** http://www.ala.org/booklist/002.html (p 144)

BookTalks—Quick and Simple
http://www.concord.k12.nh.us/schools/rundlett/booktalks/ (p 144)

Campus Writing Program's Resources for Writers
http://www.missouri.edu/~writcwp/resource.html (p 30)

Chapter One http://www1.psi.net/chapterone/ (p 145)

Electronic Archives for the Teaching of American Literatures
http://www.georgetown.edu/tamlit/tamlit-home.html (p 68)

English Language Resources http://etext.lib.virginia.edu/english.html (p 5)

For Young Writers http://www.inkspot.com/young/ (p 135)

Freedom of Information Center http://www.missouri.edu/~foiwww/ (p 127)

Home Page of Theater http://www.cs.fsu.edu./projects/group4/theatre.html (p 60)

Kairos: A Journal for Teachers of Writing in the Webbed Environment
http://english.ttu.edu/kairos/1.1/index.html (p 140)

Luminarium http://www.luminarium.org/lumina.htm (p 42)

National Library of Canada http://www.nlc-bnc.ca/ (p 72)

Natural Language Playground, The http://bobo.link.cs.cmu.edu/dougb/playground.html (p 32)

Perseus Project, The http://medusa.perseus.tufts.edu/ (p 48)

PHRASEOLOGY: A Catalogue of Multilingual Resources on the Internet
http://info.utas.edu.au/docs/flonta/PHRASEOLOGY/ (p 28)

REAL McCoy African American Phat Poetry Book, The
http://members.aol.com/bonvibre/rmp0a.html (p 55)

Researching American Literature on the Internet
http://www.sccd.ctc.edu/~sbeasley/mais/amlittoc.html (p 74)

English & Literature

Texts and Contexts http://paul.spu.edu/~hawk/t&c.html (p 15)

Videomaker's Glossary of Terms http://www.videomaker.com/edit/other/GLOS-SAZ.HTM (p 64)

Young Adult Literature Library
http://www.uiowa.edu/~english/litcult2097/tlucht/lit-yalib.html (p 19)

WORDS & LANGUAGE

American Slanguages
http://www.slanguage.com/
Mike Ellis, Valley Forge Publishing
- English, Grammar and Style, Writing
- All

At this site, the visitor can choose a city and see a list of terms that are unique to that area—its "slanguage." Some of the areas represented in mid-1997 were Atlanta; Bar Harbor, Maine; Chicago; Dallas; New Orleans; the Philadelphia Main Line; Portland, Orgeon; San Diego; and Washington, DC. The site is still evolving, adding more cities on a regular basis. The visitor can also add slanguage terms, take a Slanguage Quiz, and link to the Slanguage Time Tunnel.

✔ USA Today *Hot Site*, Yahoo *Cool Site of the Week*, cool@infi.net *Cool Site of the Day*.

Bohemian Ink
http://www.levity.com/corduroy/index.htm
Dan Levy
- Indexes and Resource Lists, Literature
- All

Dedicated to keeping alive the Alternative/Spoken Word on the Web, this site consists of articles, a coffeehouse, Writings from the Web, and a link to Water Row Books. Under the Literary Section area you'll find the following categories: Modern Boheme, Beat Generation, Historical Canon, and Global Affluence. There is also a search feature, a link to contact authors, and a link to the Bohemian News Archives.

The Cool Word of the Day Page
http://130.63.218.180:80/~wotd/
Faculty of Education, York University
- English, Grammar and Style, Writing
- All

This small site offers a word of the day and includes links to the definition, past words, and credits. You are also encouraged to submit a cool word of your own to be used at a future date.

EXCHANGE
http://deil.lang.uiuc.edu/exchange/
LinguaCenter
- English, Grammar and Style, Literature, Writing
- All

Exchange stands for Electronic, Xross Cultural, Hypertextual Academy of Non-native Gatherings in English. This site is for non-native speakers who would like to improve their writing ability, enhance their ability to learn English, and learn more about their own cultures. So what do you get? Examples of English works by non-native speakers from across the globe, unique insights from these writers about their own heritages, and self-study materials.

✔ Magellan 4 Star Site and Blue Web'N Site.

English & Literature

Flappers 2 Rappers
http://www.m-w.com/flappers/flaphome.htm
Merriam Webster

- English, Indexes and Resource Lists, Reference (General)
- All

This resource page contains information from the book of the same name. If you are interested in language as it has evolved here in the United States, this is a good place to visit. You get slang from the time of F. Scott Fitzgerald to the contemporary hip hop: for example, there is a long section on "phat." Links on the page include Intoxicated Flappers, Rock 'n Roll, Dude Sport, among others.

PHRASEOLOGY: A Catalogue of Multilingual Resources on the Internet
http://info.utas.edu.au/docs/flonta/PHRASEOLOGY/
University of Tasmania

- English, Literature, Writing
- All

This site provides interesting and informative links to multilingual resources on the Net. There are links here to a number of catalogues of electronic journals, but the most fruitful resource for students is the Home Page, which has links to a number of proverb pages—Japanese, African, Kurdish, and Palestinian to name a few — as well as slang from other cultures and quotation links. There is another category of links to books on-line, which also includes sites on proverbs, idioms, slang, and quotations.

Puzzle Depot
http://www.puzzledepot.com/puzzles.shtml
Pinnacle Solutions

- English, Writing
- All

This site offers loads of word puzzles, from acrostics to crosswords and more. Click on the education button and you go to a page designed with your curriculum and studies in mind. This site requires downloading some software to take full advantage of the offerings. There is also a puzzle newsletter available free and delivered through E-mail.

Susie's Place—The Word Games Page
http://www.primenet.com/~hodges/susplace.html
Sue Hodges

- Grammar and Style, English
- All

This fun site has three word games to improve vocabulary and provide entertainment. The three games at this site — crambo, stinky-pinky, and doggerel — provide examples, a chance to play, and other people's responses to the game. Susie's Place also provides links to fifteen other word-lovers' sites such as Ambigrams, Vocabulary Stretcher, and Anagram Insanity.

✔ Genie Hotspot on the Web, Net Junkie's Pick of the Day.

Where's That From?
http://www.intuitive.com/origins/

Intuitive Systems

- English. Grammar and Style. Writing
- All

Devoted to making words fun, this site provides ten randomly selected word origin or word definition puzzles to solve. For each word presented, the visitor must choose the correct explanation for its origin from a list provided. Some of the false answers may seem quite logical and the true answers may stretch the imagination, but documentation is provided for all answers.

✔ *Education First Blue Web'n Learning Application.*

Word a Day, A
http://www.wordsmith.org/awad/index.html

Anu Garg

- English, Writing
- All

This site offers a new word a day and an archive of past words of the day. Each entry includes pronunciation, definition, and an example from a reputable source, such as a book or newspaper.

See Also

Deciphering Old Handwriting http://www.firstct.com/fv/oldhand.html (p 147)

Literature and Language Arts Resources http://molebio.iastate.edu/js/lit.htm (p 11)

Natural Language Playground, The http://bobo.link.cs.cmu.edu/dougb/playground.html (p 32)

Virtual Reference Desk, The http://thorplus.lib.purdue.edu/reference/index.html (p 25)

Wired Style http://www.hotwired.com/hardwired/wiredstyle/ (p 25)

GRAMMAR, PUNCTUATION & SPELLING

Advanced Grammar and Composition
http://www.vcu.edu/cspweb/,961/9513.html

Ron Corio and ESLoop
- English, Grammar and Style, Indexes and Resource Lists, Writing
- 11, 12, AP

This resource page lists links to reference and class materials for an on-line writing class. Among the useful links are model essays, research tools, references and grammar help. A few other links give additional information for writing essays, but you have to be willing to wallow through explanations of classroom assignments. The most helpful is the link to essay assignments. If you don't quite get what your classroom teacher means when she talks about "the essay," tune in here and you'll find a good explanation.

Ask Miss Grammar
http://www.protrainco.com/info/noframes/grammar.htm

Professional Training Company
- English, Grammar and Style, Writing
- All

This site provides help in writing and editing. Visitors can send queries to Miss Grammar by E-mail; however, you may get a quicker answer by using the on-line sources and reference books linked to this site. There are also on-line articles that may answer some common questions. Among the articles are "The Passive Engineer," "Problematic Pronouns," and "How—and Why—to Get Rid of Acronyms."

Campus Writing Program's Resources for Writers
http://www.missouri.edu/~writcwp/resource.html

University of Missouri-Columbia
- English, Indexes and Resource Lists, Writing
- AP

Several features of this sophisticated repository of high falutin' grammatical studies may interest high school students. There is help with the rules of grammar and capitalization and many links to other writing programs, such as the Purdue Online Writing Laboratory, and to several dictionaries. Other links take you to sites on English as a second language, composition and rhetoric, computers and writing, and HTML programming.

Common Errors in English
http://www.wsu.edu:8080/~brians/errors/index.html

Paul Brians
- English, Grammar and Style, Writing
- All

This page helps students of English avoid the common errors of usage that occur in the English language. Examples on the page include proper use of such phrases as "close proximity," the difference between "it's" and "its," and the correct usage of "pray" and "prey." There is also a link to a page of "non-errors," forms of usage that are actually standard in English. Another link takes you to a list of the most commonly misspelled words and another to other grammar sites.

✔ Recommended by Yahoo! as an "Incredibly Useful Site" and by Internet Life magazine.

Grammar, Punctuation & Spelling

31

Digital Education Network Home Page
http://www.edunet.com/english/grammar/index.html

Digital Education Network
- Grammar and Style, Writing
- All

Be warned, this site originates in Britain where the rules of spelling, punctuation, and capitalization are slightly different from those followed in the United States. A quasi-commercial site, basically intended for students of English as a second language, its On-Line English Grammar page is simple and easy to use and covers all the primary grammatical rules. Starting with the alphabet in English sound files, topics covered range from adjectives, their form and function, adverbs, nouns, possessives with "'s" and "s,'" determiners, pronouns, and verbs. There are also links to an English Grammar Clinic, an English Language Practice Page, and a student-produced magazine.

Grammar and Style Notes
http://www.english.upenn.edu/~jlynch/grammar.html

Jack Lynch, University of Pennsylvania
- Grammar and Style
- All

University of Pennsylvania Professor Jack Lynch has put together a user-friendly, low-key grammar and style guide broken into 23 short files, organized alphabetically, to make for faster loading. The grammatical rules and explanations, comments on style, and suggestions on usage are clearly written, quick to find, illustrated by examples, and generally sound — although some sticklers for the formal rules of grammar may regard Lynch's advice as a bit too soft.

✔ Magellan 3 Star Site.

Grammar Lady, The
http://www.grammarlady.com/

Mary Newton Bruder
- English, Grammar and Style, Writing
- All

This is the home page of The Grammar Lady. There are four sections: columns written for newspapers, a biography, tips on English grammar, and the Grammar Hotline. There is some useful information here, but it appears most of the information is available in grammar bulletins for a nominal fee of $2.

Grammar Safari
http://deil.lang.uiuc.edu/web.pages/grammarsafari.html

LinguaCenter
- English, Grammar and Style, Indexes and Resource Lists, Reading, Writing
- All

Although created as part of a program to teach English to speakers of other languages, this site offers solid support to anyone who takes English seriously. The idea behind the safari is to search for and locate examples of grammatical constructions specified by the activity. The homepage provides links to suggestions, safari journal assignments, and safari activities. Safaris are divided into common hunts and exotic hunts. Beginners as well as more advanced students may profit from this page since the site has been designed to encourage the development of new skills at each level of competency.

English & Literature

Natural Language Playground, The
http://bobo.link.cs.cmu.edu/dougb/playground.html

Doug Beeferman

● English, Grammar and Style, Indexes and Resource Lists, Literature, Writing
♛ AP

This interesting resource page offers links to unique sites such as The Natural Language Typechecker, which checks entire sentences for grammar, syntax, and semantics. There are a number of dictionaries, including a reverse dictionary. This playground is fairly sophisticated, but if you like words and how they work, you will have some fun here.

OnLine English Grammar
http://www.edunet.com/english/grammar/

Anthony Hughes

● English, Grammar and Style, Literature, Writing
♛ 11, 12, AP

Here is a grammar site that goes one step further — or is it farther — than the others. It even provides an opportunity for graded tests to help you focus on your weaknesses. The introductory page has links to information about the author, instructions on how to use the grammar, a table of contents, an alphabetical index, a grammar clinic (although part of the clinic is restricted to members, the nonrestrictive section is very informative), and practice pages—where the tests can be found.

Ron's On-line ESOL Classroom
http://www.vcu.edu/cspweb/,gram/grammar.html

Ron Corio and ESLoop

● English, Grammar and Style, Indexes and Resource Lists, Writing
♛ 11, 12, AP

This resource page provides links to top sites, such as the Purdue On-line Writing Lab. It is a plain page with direct links to subjects: gerunds and infinitives, articles, developing an outline, etc. Farther up on the page are links to exercises that are part of the writing program associated with the page. Some of the exercises link you to sites such as Fluency Through Fables, which are worth checking out.

See Also

WRITING STYLE & COMPOSITION TIPS chapter (p 135)

Blue Web'N Applications: English References http://www.kn.pacbell.com/cgi-bin/listApps.pl?English&WebReference (p 2)

My Virtual Reference Desk http://www.refdesk.com/facts.html (p 13)

National Writing Project, The http://www-gse.berkeley.edu/Research/NWP/nwp.html (p 13)

WRITING STYLE & COMPOSITION TIPS

11 Rules of Writing
http://www.concentric.net/~rag/writing.shtml
Junket Studies
- English, Grammar and Style, Writing
- All

This site provides a concise guide to commonly violated rules of writing. Each rule is stated briefly, hyperlinked to examples of correct and incorrect usage, and linked further to references with more thorough explanations with examples such as those found in Strunk's *Elements of Style*. A word of the day frame appears beneath the rules frame. Helpful comments for classroom instruction and off-site references are additional links.

✔ Fledge Approved by McGraw-Hill Home Interactive.

Advice on Academic Writing
http://utl1.library.utoronto.ca/www/writing/advise.html
Margaret Procter and Will Buschert
- English, Grammar and Style, Indexes and Resource Lists, Literature, Writing
- 11, 12, AP

This resource page was designed with college students in mind, but it contains some practical information for high school students. Categories and links include: background or general information; reading and using sources; writing in a specific discipline or form; style and editing, with pointers for using the word processor; grammar and punctuation; some pointers for those in English-as-a-Second-Language programs; and related resources. Among the interesting links are Jack Lynch's grammar and style notes and the Purdue On-line Writing Center.

Archeus: Worksearch Resources
http://www.golden.net/~archeus/worksrch.htm
Garry Will
- English, Grammar and Style, Indexes and Resource Lists, Writing
- 11, 12

This site offers helpful tips on resume and cover letter writing, on how to conduct yourself during a job interview, and on how to network. The visitor is presented with several sources of information, beginning with articles written by the sponsor, and links to more than seventy-five relevant articles from across the Web. The page includes titles of books on the topic, a Resume Service Guide, and links to Canadian Worksearch Resources. There are also links to other sites that offer job search and resume preparation information. While offered as a job search site, the page has much to offer the student assigned to write a resume or who is looking for a job and wants to prepare the best possible presentation.

✔ Argus Clearinghouse Site of the Month.

Basic Prose Style and Mechanics

http://www.rpi.edu/dept/llc/writecenter/web/text/proseman.html

Craig Waddell

- English, Grammar and Style, Writing
- All

This site provides a straight-forward, terse, clear presentation of solid information about writing well. You get twelve writing rules with examples as well as eighteen grammar and punctuation rules. Follow these and you will write well. Also included is a bibliography of works that are cited on the page.

The CalRen Project

http://128.32.89.153/CalRENHP.html

Pete Alvarez, Student Learning Center, University of California at Berkeley

- English, Math, Reading, Reference (General), Science (General), U.S. History, World History, Writing,
- All

A site devoted to offering a series of tips and exercises to help develop better study strategies and habits. Topics listed include When to Study, Techniques to Avoid Procrastination, Learning by Listening, Effective Note-Taking, and Ideas on Taking Essay, Problem-solving, and Objective Tests. A helpful site for a student to brush up on skills or get ideas for developing better study habits.

Cela: A+ Research and Writing for High School and College Students

http://www.albany.edu/cela/linkindex.html

Center on English Learning and Achievement

- English, Grammar and Style, Indexes and Resource Lists, Literature, Writing
- 11, 12, AP

After you get to the CELA home page, scroll down the page to K-12 resource and click on the link to A+ Research and Writing. At the A+ page, you get instructions on how to become an expert research paper writer. In fact, if you like what you see here, you can download the entire guide. In the guide, you'll find step-by-step instructions on how to search for information and links to "great on-line resources for research and writing." Click on the Table of Contents and you are off and writing.

Erik's Quick Style Sheet: Better Writing in Only Twenty Minutes a Day!

http://www.english.upenn.edu/~esimpson/Teaching/style.html

Erik Simpson

- English, Grammar and Style, Writing
- All

This page contains straightforward advice for improving your writing. Here you'll find ten tried-and-true rules, such as using the active voice, with examples. Each rule begins with an example of poor writing, which breaks the rule that it addresses.

The Fundamentals of a Research Paper
http://history.hanover.edu/fund.html
Hanover College
- English, Grammar and Style, Reference (General), Writing
- All

This site is devoted to helping students plan and write a basic research paper. The steps are clearly laid out and explained. The first step, The Structure and Content of the Paper, contains information on developing a thesis, defining your argument, and following through to the conclusion. Other steps are Sources, Scope, Selecting a Topic, Redefining and Refining, and Guides to Historical Research. This is a very useful site for students to visit.

Model Essays
http://www.vcu.edu/cspweb/,961/,96113/models.html
Ron Corio and ESLoop
- English, Literature, Writing
- 11, 12

This site provides three model essays from an English-as-a-Second-Language site. It provides students with a standard for measuring their own efforts.

Paradigm Online Writing Assistant
http://www.idbsu.edu/english/cguilfor/paradigm/
Chuck Guilford
- English, Grammar and Style, Writing
- All

A visitor to this site will find help for virtually any kind of essay writing. The links provide access under such headings as Discovering What to Write, Organizing Your Writing, Revising Your Writing, and Editing Your Writing. Specific information is then provided on types of essays—informal, thesis/support, exploratory, and argumentative. An additional link is provided to Documenting Sources, which provides the necessary guidelines for the student.

✔ WebCrawler Select Site, Scout Report Selection, Education First Blue Web'n Learning Application.

The Purdue Online Writing Lab (OWL)
http://owl.english.purdue.edu/
Jonathan Bush with Purdue University Writing Lab
- English, Grammar and Style, Indexes and Resource Lists
- All

For students with personal initiative, this site will prove useful. Teachers, however, will find a hundred handouts and exercises on grammar and writing to drive home points about these subjects. There is an on-line tutorial service for students. Additional links are to search tools and directories on the Internet and resources for teachers.

Research Paper Page
http://www.researchpaper.com
Infonautics Corp.

- Grammar and Style, Reference (General), Writing
- All

The Research Paper Project is a comprehensive writing and research center. It is a collection of topics, ideas, and assistance for school research projects. You can choose a topic in any major subject area and launch a search. The Writing Center helps with organization, writing tips, and techniques, and provides answers to questions about punctuation and grammar. In the Discussion Area you even can meet people working on similar projects.

Roane State Community College On-line Writing Lab
http://www2.rscc.cc.tn.us/~jordan_jj/OWL/owl.html
Jennifer Jordan-Henley

- English, Grammar and Style, Writing
- 11, 12, AP

This site is an on-line writing center for a community college. Some of the content has limited relevance beyond the college's own programs. (For example, there is a section on technical writing and home health care.) Aside from these, the material focuses on general writing skills. You get information about how to write different types of essays and practical information on grammar and punctuation, style, and editing on a computer. Several links from the page deal specifically with the use of computers, such as keyboarding tips and how to choose a typeface.

Stephen's Guide to the Logical Fallacies
http://www.assiniboinec.mb.ca/user/downes/fallacy/fall.htm
Stephen Downes

- Debate, English, Grammar and Style, Indexes and Resource Lists, Speech, Writing
- 11, 12, AP

Trying to make a point with style and conviction? Forge an invincible argument to get that "A" on your next essay. This page features links to an index of terms as well as substantive references and resources. The latter are bibliographies and are not linked to sites on the Web, so you'll have to pester the librarian or visit the bookstore to make a special order. What's the point? Writing is more than grammar. Time spent on this type of activity will make you a better writer.

✔ Links I Like Citation, Link Madness Categorically Cool Winner.

University of Victoria Writer's Guide
http://www.maclab.uvic.ca/writersguide/Pages/StartHere.html
Department of English, University of Victoria

- English, Indexes and Resource Lists, Literature, Writing
- 11, 12, AP

This resource site provides information to help with writing assignments. The categories on this page are broad, for example "Essays" and "Grammar" or lists of literary terms (alphabetically or by category). These take you to longer lists of links in more specific categories. For example, clicking Essays takes you to another page with links to types of essays, getting started, organizing essays, etc.

Useful Resources for Composition
http://www.usd.edu/engl/resources_ac.html
Dakota Writers Project
- English, Grammar and Style, Indexes and Resource Lists, Writing
- 11, 12, AP

This resource page contains links to sites under three categories: reference, useful writing sites, and on-line writing lab on the Web. It is sponsored by the Dakota Writers Project. At the bottom of the page, there are two links: one to a research page for teachers and students, and a second to an advanced composition page.

Writing Argumentative Essays
http://cougar.vut.edu.au/~dalbj/argueweb/frntpage.htm
Bill Daly
- Debate, English, Grammar and Style, Indexes and Resource Lists, Writing
- 11, 12, AP

This resource site helps you improve your ability to write argumentative essays. When you enter the site, you are greeted with a long list of linked sites that will take you step by step through the process of writing your own essay. Each linked site has an introductory paragraph that, for example, explains using connectives or transitions. (This program was designed for students in Canada so the terminology is slightly different.) Then, you can do exercises to test your understanding. As you proceed through the program, you get a very good idea of how to argue your point.

Writing Practice
http://www.uakron.edu/english/heath/practice.html
Cheryl Malgay Heath
- English, Grammar and Style, Writing
- All

This site contains an essay that discusses writing. The intended audience consists of students in a college-level composition course, but don't let that scare you off. The message is clear, and the essay is short. Find ideas to help you get started on your writing assignment; read about rough drafts; and pick up some good pointers about final editing.

See Also
GRAMMAR, PUNCTUATION & SPELLING chapter (p 30)
TIPS & RESOURCES FOR WRITERS chapter (p 130)
American Literature Survey Site
   http://www.cwrl.utexas.edu/~natasha/316/index.html (p 67)
Barr's English Class http://www.capecod.net/~bbarsant/class/ (p 21)
Books in Chains http://www.uc.edu/~RETTBESR/Links.html (p 2)
Classroom Connect http://www.classroom.net/ (p 3)
English Server, The http://english-server.hss.cmu.edu (p 5)
High School English Resource Page
   http://www.bham.wednet.edu/ENGLISH2.HTM (p 7)
Learning About Poetry http://tqd.advanced.org/3721/poems/forms/learn.html (p 53)
Mothers Who Think: Word by Word — Annie Lamott's On-line Diary
   http://www.salonmagazine.com/july97/mothers/lamott.html (p 104)
My Virtual Reference Desk http://www.refdesk.com/facts.html (p 13)
National Writing Project, The http://www-gse.berkeley.edu/Research/NWP/nwp.html (p 13)
On-Book: An Introduction to the Study of Literature
   http://www.uwm.edu/People/jat/ (p 23)
Roget's Thesaurus http://ecco.bsee.swin.edu.au/text/roget/index.html (p 24)

LITERATURE (GENERAL)

19th Century Woman's Place, A
http://www.digisys.net/users/zsk/welcome.htm
Zsuzsa Sztaray and DigiSys
- English, Indexes and Resource Lists, Literature, U.S. History, World History
- All

Students studying the Victorian period and/or its literature will find helpful background information on this page. The page has delightful Victorian icons as links to places such as Tid Bits, Decorative Arts, Household Issues, Readings, Women's Issues, and Holidays and Amusements. The Readings link includes articles women of the period would have read, and Women's Issues lets visitors read about issues that concerned women of the late-nineteenth century. There are also links to an Archive section and other Victorian Web sites.

A&E — Behind the Scenes
http://www.aetv.com/scenes/
A&E Television Network
- Drama and Theater, English, Literature
- All

This Web site changes with the programs being shown on the A&E network, so it is worth a visit on a regular basis. In mid-1997, the network was featuring five performances, three of which were behind the scenes looks at literary masterpieces *Ivanhoe*, *Emma*, and *Pride and Prejudice*. For *Ivanhoe* and *Emma*, the student could find what life was like in the England of that period; the *Pride and Prejudice* segment had information from the cast and crew on the making of the movie.

The Alsop Review
http://www.hooked.net/users/jalsop
The Alsop Review
- English, Literature
- All

This site is devoted to poets and writers — established and up-and-coming — who are on the cutting edge of their genres. The visitor can access information under the following headings: Poets, Writers, The Literary Life, Useful Reference Sources, A Commonplace Book, and a list of favorite poets and poems of editorial board members. There is also a FAQ, which provides background on the site.

✔ *Magellan 4 Star Site*, Windows Magazine *Hot Spot of the Day*, Golden Web Award for Excellence in Design, and some thirty other awards.

Artsedge
http://artsedge.kennedy-center.org
Kennedy Center, National Endowment for the Arts, U.S. Department of Education
- Art, Art History, Current Events, Drama and Theater, English, Indexes and Resource Lists, Literature, Music, Speech
- All

This site is dedicated to arts education information, with a national focus. Directed toward a broad audience of teachers and students, it features sections on arts education news, grants and job listings, calendars for conferences and workshops, and curriculum design resources. Students are encouraged to participate in on-line discussions and to link to other arts-related sites. An arts education search engine can direct viewers to resources outside the site. Links galore!

✔ *"Superb site—clean links for kids—research pages of use to students and teachers alike." —Steven J. Klass, G. C. Marshall High School, Falls Church, VA.*

Literature (General)

BookRadio
http://www.BookRadio.com/

BookRadio.com
- English, Literature, Writing
- All

Choose to listen to an interview with and reading by a contemporary author in many categories—fiction, music, film, politics, mystery, poetry, and nonfiction—or go right to a list of interviews or reviews.

A Brief Guide to the Romance Genre
http://www.rwanational.com/subgen.html

Romance Writers of America
- Literature
- All

This brief guide in the form of a grid identifies and describes each romance sub-genre and lists publishers and award-winning authors in that category. This site will help students identify significant contributors to the genre. The major subdivisions of the romance genre are given as Historical Romance, Regency Romance, Traditional Series Romance, Short Contemporary Series Romance, Long and Single Title Romance, Romantic Suspense, Multicultural Romance, Futuristic Romance, Time Travel Romance, and Paranormal Romance.

Celebration of Women Writers, A
http://www.cs.cmu.edu/People/mmbt/women/writers.html

Mary Mark Ockerbloom
- Indexes and Resource Lists, Literature
- 11, 12

This plain but exhaustive site provides access through links to the rich history of women authors found on the Web. The principal feature of the site is an alphabetical listing of several hundred women authors—from Abigail Adams to Marguerite Yourcenar. Click on an author's name and you are linked to sites devoted to that author, which may include the full text of novels such as *Little Women*, biographies, bibliographies, diaries and letters, or photographs. Other features include links to topical bibliographies (e.g., feminist science fiction, fantasy and utopian writing), sites on women in history (e.g., women in the American West), and specialty collections (e.g., literary women of the Left Bank). The developers hope to encourage many people to contribute texts and supporting information about women writers. New links are added one or two times each month.

CyberSchool Magazine
http://www.cyberschoolmag.com/

CyberSchool Magazine
- Drama and Theater, English
- All

CyberSchool Magazine is a monthly on-line magazine offering selected Web sites, on-line books, author biographies, and museum selections for students and teachers. Departments include Science, Literature, World Reviews, Xtra Files, History, Teachers, Commentary, and Library. The Surfin' Librarian area also references Web sites for students and educators. The Spring 1997 edition included the article "Shakespeare and the Real Henry V" by Pat McArthur.

✔ POINTCommunications Top 5% Web Site.

Female Coming-of-Age Stories
http://www.scils.rutgers.edu/special/kay/age.html
Kay E. Vandergrift
- English, Literature
- All

This site contains a bibliography of recent books that feature female coming-of-age stories. This list is fairly comprehensive, and its contents are dictated by the opinions of the page's knowledgeable sponsor.

Feminist Science Fiction, Fantasy and Utopia
http://www.uic.edu/~lauramd/sf/femsf.html
Laura Quilter
- English, Literature, Writing
- All

A resource page devoted to the feminist influence in science fiction and related genres. The visitor—whether a reader, a researcher, or a writer—can find numerous useful links. For readers there are many listings of Feminist SFFU bibliographies (by author or theme), anthologies, and recommended readings. Researchers can access Literary Criticism, Journals, Newsletters and 'Zines, Conferences, Meetings, and Symposia. Writers can find a list of publishers and venues for publication of feminist science fiction. This last area provides links to other sites, Trivia, Quotes, a Bulletin Board, and Fan Clubs. The size of this site makes the search engine that is included particularly helpful.

✔ Sci-Fi Site of the Week.

A Guide to Christian Literature on the Internet
http://www.iclnet.org/pub/resources/christian-books.html
Institute for Christian Leadership
- Indexes and Resource Lists, Literature, Religion
- All

A site for anyone who wishes to find Internet-accessible literature related to classical Christianity. The contents of the page include Bibles with links to all major translations, Bible study aids with links to FAQs, a Bible dictionary, and other sites. There are also books, listed by title, including works by Augustine, John Donne, John Calvin, and many others. Finally, there are links to collections of Christian books including Books Online from the Bruderhof Community and the Christian Classics Ethereal Library.

A Guide to Classic Mystery and Detection
http://members.aol.com/mg4273/classics.htm
Michael E. Gross
- Literature
- All

An educational resource site of reading lists and essays on great mysteries, primarily for the period before 1960. Visitors can search an alphabetical list of mystery writers or browse the articles organized under the following headings: Nineteenth Century Mystery Fiction, Turn of the Century Mystery Fiction, The Golden Age (including the Intuitionist School), the Van Dine School, the Realist School and the Bailey School, Pulp Fiction, Contemporary Mystery Fiction, and General Discussion. The page also includes a link to the Mysterious Home Page, which claims to have links to nearly all mystery Web sites.

Hola! (Hello) Oh What a Book! Science and More!!
http://tqd.advanced.org/3240/
ThinkQuest
- English, Indexes and Resource Lists, Literature, Spanish, Science (General)
- All

This site offers a smattering of information in three areas: English, Spanish, and Science. For the English student, there are summaries of works by Shakespeare, Homer, and Hemingway, among others. Links take you to more information about a limited number of authors, each likely to be covered in class. An interesting feature is a chart that rates modern authors. For the student of Spanish, there is some basic vocabulary. For the science student, there are links to NASA, endangered species, science experiments, and Superscience sites.

An Inquirer's Guide to the Universe
http://www.fi.edu/planets/planets.html
Franklin Institute, Philadelphia
- Astronomy and Space, Literature, Writing
- All

Students interested in science fiction will enjoy this site. The Space Science Fact section allows the visitor to investigate what we already know about planets and the universe; Space Science Fiction resources provide additional background information. You can then visit the Imaginary Planet Gallery where imaginary planets are awaiting exploration. After visiting these new planets, it is on to the Space Story Studio to write a story or the Space Story Portfolio to read other stories about an imaginary universe.

John's Nautical Literature Page
http://www.cyber-dyne.com/~jkohnen/naut-lit.html
John Kohnen
- English, Literature
- All

Anyone interested in fiction or nonfiction with a nautical theme will find many choices on this page. The page includes an extensive nautical fiction list that is updated monthly except in January and July. A short Reader's Guide to Nonfiction Books on the Age of Fighting Sail, Joseph McWilliams's nautical nonfiction adventure list, nautical books available on the Internet, mail order sources for nautical books, book reviews by readers, and a selection of short articles are other options from which the visitor may choose.

The Libyrinth
http://www.microserve.net/~thequail/libyrinth/libyrinth.html
Allen Ruch
- Drama and Theater, English, Indexes and Resource Pages, Literature,
- 11, 12, AP

This page covers twentieth-century authors whose prose style employs shifting realities or who write in the "magic realism" genre. At the Omphalos, the center of the Web site, there is an alphabetical list of authors. The listing provides links and summaries of some of the major works; among those listed are Jorge Luis Borges's *The Garden of the Forking Paths*, Umberto Eco's *Porta Ludovica*, and Thomas Pynchon's *Spermatikos Logos*.

✔ *Tapertry Web Viewers Library Site Award, Literary Research Award, Mining Company Best of the Net, "Novel Place" by Book Stacks Unlimited, and several other awards.*

The Literature and Poetry Page

http://www.netten.net/~bmassey/

Bill Massey

- English, Indexes and Resource Lists, Literature
- All

This Web page is based on the sponsor's personal likes and dislikes. However, it offers an extremely good framework on the authors it covers, giving a short biography and links to works available on-line. Authors included are Austen, Blake, Bacon, Browning, Carroll, Coleridge, Conrad, Cooper, Dante, Dickinson, Dickens, Donne, Dostoevsky, Frost, Hawthorne, Holmes, Houseman, James, Kipling, Longfellow, Melville, Milton, Plutarch, Poe, Sandburg, Shakespeare, Stevenson, Tennyson, Twain, and Whitman.

Luminarium

http://www.luminarium.org/lumina.htm

Anniina Jokinen

- English, Indexes and Resource Lists, Literature
- 11, 12, AP

This site offers extensive information on writers and writing from the medieval and Renaissance eras and the seventeenth century. Beautifully conceived pages with pictures of the authors and outstanding resources—from quotes, biography, and bibliographies to texts and essays about the writer and the works of any number of writers—are featured at this page. You even get music from the era of the writer. Also, in association with Amazon.com, you may order many of the books cited.

✔ Digital Library Award, Kaplan Student Choice, Yahoo's Cool Pick of the Day, Visit CityScapes, Cool Site of the Week.

Male Coming-of-Age Stories

http://www.scils.rutgers.edu/special/kay/male.html

Kay E. Vandergrift

- English, Indexes and Resource Lists, Literature
- All

This resource site contains a list of male coming-of-age stories. The books listed are fairly recent releases. For example, Frank McCourt's *Angela's Ashes* is included.

The Michigan State University Celebrity Lecture Series

http://hs1.hst.msu.edu/~cal/celeb/index.html

College of Arts and Letters and Dean's Community Council, Michigan State University

- Current Events, English, Literature
- All

This resource page provides links to information pages about contemporary authors of fiction and nonfiction who have been invited to speak at Michigan State University. At the moment, twenty-one writers and thinkers, including Daniel Boorstin and Derek Walcott, are featured. Click on the photo or text and an information page appears with a paragraph about the writer and his or her works, and a bibliography. You can also play an audio clip from the lecture.

Literature (General) 43

The Mysterious Home Page
http://www.db.dk/dbaa/jbs/homepage.html
Jan B. Steffensen
- Indexes and Resource Lists, Literature, Writing
- All

This page will fascinate anyone interested in watching, reading, or writing mysteries. One set of links takes visitors to specific authors, characters, or themes in mystery fiction; another set links to conferences, conventions, mystery organizations, and awards. You can find news groups, mailing lists, publishers, book dealers, mystery reviews, mystery magazines, film and TV mysteries, pulps, mystery games, and interactive fiction. From this site one can also link to Sherlockiana, electronic texts, and other miscellaneous sites.

✔ *Blue Planet Cool Site of the Day, Hotspot Official Gamespot, WebCrawler Outstanding Web Site, Luckman 4-Star Site.*

The Objectivism Resource Guide
http://www.oms.com/org/
Mark J. Gardner
- Literature, Philosophy
- 11, 12, AP

This site is devoted to the philosophy of "Objectivism" as espoused in the works of Ayn Rand and others. The category "What Is Objectivism" contains information from several areas—Metaphysics, Epistemology, Ethics, Politics, and Esthetics. There is a list of resources including events and conferences, publications and campus clubs. Of most interest to students would be the Special Features area, which includes an article "Objectivism in the Media," a list of Objectivist texts on-line, and a link to the Objectivism Bookstore.

✔*Magellan 4 Star Site.*

Project Bartleby
http://www.columbia.edu/acis/bartleby/index.html
Columbia University
- Literature
- AP

Project Bartleby provides the full text of more than twenty-five classics (ranging from Chapman's translation of the *Odyssey* to W. E. B. Du Bois's *The Souls of Black Folks*. What makes this site unusual is that all are recreated to the highest standards of scholarly fidelity to the original editions using professional editorial standards in the scanning, data entry, spell-checking, proofreading, and markup protocols. The site also includes several reference works such as the *Inaugural Addresses of U.S. Presidents*, *Bartlett's Quotations* (1901 edition), and William Strunk's original *Elements of Style* (1918). Poets are particularly well represented by the works of John Keats, Percy Bysshe Shelley, William Wordsworth, Walt Whitman, William Butler Yeats, Robert Frost, Edna St. Vincent Millay, and Oscar Wilde.

The Pulp Page
http://www.columbia.edu/~mfs10/pulp.html
Internet Fans of Bronze
- English, Literature
- All

This site is dedicated to the pulp magazines of the 1920s, 1930s, and 1940s. Categories on the page include Introduction, History, Fantasy and Science Fiction, Hero Pulps, and Hard-Boiled. Each heading includes a bibliography and links to other resources pertaining to that type of pulp literature.

The Quarterly Black Review
http://www.bookwire.com/qbr/qbr.html
Bookwire
- English, Literature
- AP

This site presents the latest views and reviews from the journal, synopses of articles from back issues, a statement from the publisher, and a note from the editor. Typically, each issue has fiction, nonfiction, poetry, something for children, and features. This information may lead to a research paper topic or an essay of your own. This is a good place to find writers who are writing about today's issues.

Romance Novels and Women's Fiction
http://www.writepage.com/romance.htm
The Write Page
- English, Literature, Writing
- All

Besides a listing of over one hundred authors in this genre, this Web site offers links to related topics such as Lilley's Mail Order and Book Search Service; an article on the fashion, dance, and literature of the Regency era; an article on how to tell if you might be a romance writer; and A Reader's Guide to Romance and Women's Fiction. In addition, the last section contains links to women's writings done by suffragettes, temperance workers, and women writers included in the *Encyclopedia Britannica* of 1911.

✔ *Angel Award for Excellence in Promoting Romance on the WWW.*

Romantic Circles
http://www.inform.umd.edu/RC/rc.html
Neil Fraistat, Steven Jones, Donald Reiman, and Carl Stahmer, University of Maryland
- Literature
- All

This is a relatively new site that promises to widen its offerings in the future. The page is devoted to Byron, the Shelleys, Keats, and their contemporaries. In mid-1997 the following categories were available: Publications, Features, Scholarly Resources, Critical Exchange, Conferences, and Electronic Editions. Features will be a rotating page on topics of interest to Romanticists; at the time of this review, the feature was on Hungarian Romanticism.

Speak Out!
http://vida.com/speakout/home.html
Speak Out!
- Current Events, English, Indexes and Resource Lists, Literature
- 11, 12, AP

This is a resource page sponsored by the country's only not-for-profit speakers' and artists' agency. It lists contemporary writers, where they will appear (including on college campuses), and titles of their works. A biography page for each person on the list, which is accessible by topic, is brief but carries pertinent information.

The Victorian Web
http://www.stg.brown.edu/projects/hypertext/landow/victorian/victov.html
George P. Landow, Brown University
- Art History, Indexes and Resource Lists, Literature, Religion, U.S. History, World History
- 11, 12, AP

Designed by a professor for use in connection with literature classes at Brown University, the Victorian Web covers all aspects of society in the Victorian era from religion and philosophy to the arts, sciences, and even gender matters. The Victorian Web includes a sizable amount of first-rate original content. Organized by subject and fully searchable, the site is clearly laid out, making its scholarly articles and richly detailed graphics and pictures easy to navigate. The site includes biographies of famous Victorians, timelines, bibliographies, a dozen links to other sites, and numerous embedded hypertext links.

✔ POINTCommunications Top 5% Web Site, Education World Education Site, Mèdaille d'Or, Top 50 the WEB Award.

Victorian Women Writers Project
http://www.indiana.edu/~letrs/vwwp/
The Trustees of Indiana University
- Drama and Theater, English, Indexes and Resource Lists, Literature
- All

The complexity of the Victorian period is evident at this site, devoted to women writers of the period. There is an extensive listing of writers represented along with selections from their works that are available on the Net. These selections are available in downloadable format, including GIF-formatted images of the title page and other significant graphics. There are also links to other electronic texts at Indiana University and related Web resources.

Virtual English
http://tqd.advanced.org/2847/homepage.htm
Academic High School
- Art, English, Literature, Writing
- All

This site is maintained by students from a high school with very high academic standards. Among the offerings are essays on the arts and literature by students from the school. A graphical interface similar to Packard-Bell Navigator greets you. Make a selection of fiction, nonfiction, drama, poetry, or short stories. Or go to the bottom of most of the scenes and choose student essays, authors, art gallery, films, games, or links. The pages on authors lists biographical information and works. The art gallery includes famous works of art inspired by literary works and vice versa.

See Also

DICTIONARIES & REFERENCE chapter (p 21)

INDEXES, SEARCH ENGINES & RESOURCE LISTS chapter (p 1)

256 Shades of Grey http://www.primenet.com/~blkgrnt/index.html (p 135)

American Studies @ The University of Virginia http://xroads.virginia.edu/ (p 67)

Atlantic Unbound *The Atlantic Monthly* http://theatlantic.com/coverj.html (p 126)

Bohemian Ink http://www.levity.com/corduroy/index.htm (p 27)

Children's Literature Web Guide http://www.ucalgary.ca/~dkbrown/ (p 145)

Crack Fiction http://allrise.com/index.html (p 145)

Creative Nexus' Literature Site http://tqd.advanced.org/3089/lit/lit.html (p 135)

English Literature — Voice of the Shuttle http://humanitas.ucsb.edu/shuttle/english.html (p 77)

English & Literature

Favorite Teenage Angst Books
   http://www.echonyc.com/~cafephrk/angstbooks.html (p 145)
First Lines http://pc159.lns.cornell.edu/firsts/ (p 147)
Hard Boiled http://www.voicenet.com/~bmurray/ (p 60)
Literature and Film http://www.mindspring.com/~jamesthomas/ (p 61)
MidLink Magazine http://longwood.cs.ucf.edu:80/~MidLink/index.html (p 136)
New Yorker, The http://www.enews.com/magazines/new_yorker/ (p 127)
Shadow http://metro.net/shadow/ (p 137)
Tales from the Vault http://www.rigroup.com/storyart/tales/message1.html (p 138)
Tree Fiction on the World Wide Web http://www.cl.cam.ac.uk/users/gdr11/tree-fiction.html#Introduction (p 141)
Women's Books Online http://www.cybergrrl.com/review (p 146)

MYTHOLOGY, FAIRY TALES & FOLK TALES

Ancient Chinese Dragon Series
http://www.primenet.com/~eanton/index.htm

Erick Anton
- Literature
- All

	1	2	3	4	5
DEPTH/BREADTH					
QUALITY/ACCURACY					
RELEVANCE					
USEFULNESS					
ENTERTAINMENT					

The Ancient Dragon Series refers to humans, not creatures: the most famous heroes of Eastern cultures were dragons. This site features stories that include such figures. The visitor can read "Within the Dragon," a story about thirteenth-century China (available in English, Spanish, German, and Chinese) or "Heart of the Dragon." Also on the site are other stories by the same author in other series and the text of two of his screenplays.

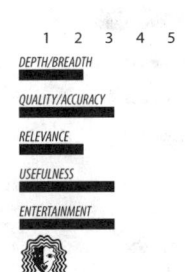

Faeries: Lore and Literature
http://faeryland.etsu.edu/~earendil/faerie/faerie.html

Allen Garvin
- Literature
- All

	1	2	3	4	5
DEPTH/BREADTH					
QUALITY/ACCURACY					
RELEVANCE					
USEFULNESS					
ENTERTAINMENT					

This site, devoted to faeries and their role in literature, begins with its own search engine. The visitor can then sample Faerie Stories or Faerie Poems as examples of the genre. The site also catalogs links to folklore sources, literary sources, a Faerie Art Archive, and related links. This is a substantial site devoted to this topic and would benefit any student who needs to research it.

✔ Orchid Award for Excellence, Webcrawler Select Site, POINTCommunications Top 5% Web Site.

Fairy Tales: Origins and Evolution
http://easyweb.easynet.co.uk/~cdaae/fairy/

Christine Daae
- English, Literature
- All

	1	2	3	4	5
DEPTH/BREADTH					
QUALITY/ACCURACY					
RELEVANCE					
USEFULNESS					
ENTERTAINMENT					

This resource page on fairy tales features an introduction, information on the authors, a section on the evolution of the tales, a bookshelf, and related links. Together these make an attractive and informative package. The bookshelf provides a bibliography and a list of new tales.

✔ CastleNet's BookMarked on the Web, Web Star 10 Lynx of the Week, Cool Site of the Hour, Best of EZ Connect Net Award.

Greek Mythology
http://www.intergate.net/uhtml/.jhunt/greek_myth/greek_myth.html#GreekMythIntro

J. M. Hunt
- English, Indexes and Resource Lists, Literature, Religion, World History,
- All

	1	2	3	4	5
DEPTH/BREADTH					
QUALITY/ACCURACY					
RELEVANCE					
USEFULNESS					
ENTERTAINMENT					

This page offers an introduction to Greek mythology. Although still under construction, it provides a number of links helpful to students studying this topic: Greek versus Roman Mythology, The Gods, Heroes, Creatures, Stories, and Family Trees. There are also links to other Internet sites and a What's New area. The author plans to add cross references to *Bulfinch's Mythology*, the definitive book on the topic, as well as images and links to some of the Greek dramas.

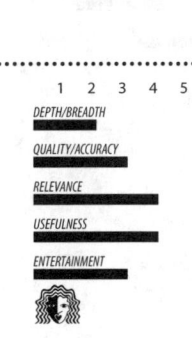

English & Literature

Halloween USA
http://www.emerald-empire.com/holidays/hallowee/hal1.htm

Gold Stag Communications, Inc.

- Literature
- All

This site provides links to the texts of several scary stories, including the novels *Dracula* and *Frankenstein*; background about the Jack O'Lantern; a history of Halloween; and information about Halloween in other cultures.

Japanese Fairy Tales
http://www.io.com/~nishio/japan/fairy.html

Gen-ichi Nishio

- Literature
- All

This site presents four Japanese fairy tales and plans to add several others soon. Visitors will find it interesting to compare the morals of these to those of the more familiar Western fairy tales. The tales are in translation and one must overlook some obvious grammatical errors.

The Literary Gothic
http://www.siue.edu/~jvoller/gothic.html

Jack G. Voller

- English, Indexes and Resource Lists, Literature
- All

This resource site is devoted to literary Gothics, which for the purposes of this page includes ghost stories; classic Gothic fiction (1764-1820); and related Gothic, supernaturalist, and "weird" literature prior to 1960. The page provides links to Authors and Texts, General Resources, the Gothic Community, and Post-1960 Horror.

✔ ZIA Site, Omnivision Winner.

The Perseus Project
http://medusa.perseus.tufts.edu/

Classics Department, Tufts University

- Art History, Literature, Philosophy, World History
- All

The Perseus Project is the classic interactive multimedia database of ancient Greece. This fully searchable, huge database includes ancient Greek texts of mythology, philosophy, and politics and pictures of thousands of vases, coins, and other artifacts from ancient Greece. The Perseus project is probably the most authoritative Internet site on ancient Greece and is constantly evolving and growing.

✔ Magellan 4 Star Site, LookSmart Editor's Choice, NetGuide Gold Site, POINTCommunications Top 5% Web Site, USA Today *Hot Site*.

The Realist Wonder Society
http://www.wondersociety.com/

The Realist Wonder Society

- English, Literature
- All

This site stimulates your imagination through reading and sharing fables. The fables provided at the site include "The Mole and the Owl," "Sailing Through," "The Last Christmas," "Behind the Bookcase," and "Winsor McCay." Visitors are encouraged to share their own ideas; they can also access an archive of fables as well as follow links to film and art adaptations.

✔ Magellan 4 Star Site, POINTCommunications Top 5% Web Site, A Novel Place by Book Stacks, FutureKids Hot Site, Family Jewel Award.

Tales of Wonder: Folk and Fairy Tales from Around the World
http://it.ucdavis.edu/richard/tales/

Tales of Wonder

- Anthropology, English, Geography, Reading, World History
- All

This elegant Web site offers an ample supply of tales from many different cultures and regions from around the world and provides insight into their history and folklore. Arranged alphabetically by country, it is easy to use and easy on the eyes as well, thanks to its use of large font sizes and varied text and background colors.

✔ Education First Blue Web'n Learning Application, Exploratorium Ten Cool Web Sites.

See Also

Irish Literature, Mythology, Folklore, and Drama
   http://www.luminarium.org/mythology/ireland/ (p 78)

POETRY

The Aboriginal Poetry Bibliography
http://www.epas.utoronto.ca:8080/~tfulk/ab_poets/index.html
Aboriginal Poetry Graduate Class, Department of English, University of Toronto
- English, Indexes and Resource Lists, Literature
- 11, 12, AP

This straightforward resource page provides a listing of aboriginal poets and related Web sites. The links to poets offer a biography and bibliography of each author's works, biographical works about the author, video recordings, and places to buy the works. The links to relates sites are comprehensive.

About Poetry — Stuff from Don
http://nthsrv1.jsr.cc.va.us/courses/eng217/lectures.htm
Don Maxwell
- English, Indexes and Resource Lists, Literature, Writing
- 11, 12, AP

This site categorizes links under eleven poetry-related subjects. Some are functional matters such as scansion and writing poetry; others are more subjective, such as how is less more and truth and beauty. Some of these links are short, others more detailed. All are presented with wit, but readers must pick up on the humorous cues. This site is worth a visit if you're writing poetry or need to explain or comment on a poem.

The Academy of American Poets
http://www.poets.org/
The Academy of American Poets
- English, Literature
- 11, 12, AP

This page is a well-conceived and thoughtfully presented site. Click on one of five choices: About the Academy, National Poetry Month, Poetry Exhibits, Calendar of Events, and Membership Benefits. Of these, Poetry Exhibits is the most helpful, with its Listening Booth and Special Events. The Listening Booth features many American poets reading their own works. Current Exhibits provide essays on American poets and their poetry. A future project promises an extensive update to add more poets, essays, biographical information, and photos. Literary Links leads to other related sites.

Asian Poets Page
http://pantheon.cis.yale.edu/~skyjuice/poempg.html
Liu Biming
- English, Literature
- All

This site offers links to poets who have their own Web pages as well as poems found right at the site. The poems are organized into three groupings: Countries, such as the Malay Pantuns and Nepali "Gajal"; Poets on Site, such as Karen Y. Chan, Yeap Yin Woon, and Annabel Tan; and Poets on Other Sites, such as Jennifer Crystal Chen, Rekha Kamath, and Paul Ham. The sponsor of this page hopes to make it the definitive Web site for Asian poetry.

Poetry

Atlantic Monthly Poetry Pages
http://www.theatlantic.com/atlantic/atlweb/poetry/poetpage.htm

Atlantic UnBound

- English, Indexes and Resource Lists, Literature
- 11, 12, AP

This site provides links to poetry published in the *Atlantic Monthly* since 1993, along with in-depth articles on poets and their poetry. There are also links to related sites. While limited to the poetry that has graced the pages of the *Atlantic*, this page provides a wonderful service for anyone studying contemporary poetry. Some of the poems are available in audio.

British Poetry 1780-1910: A Hypertext Archive of Scholarly Editions
http://etext.lib.virginia.edu/britpo.html

Electronic Text Center, Alderman Library, University of Virginia

- English, Indexes and Resource Lists, Literature
- All

This electronic text library provides links to electronic texts of works by many British poets and a few American poets from between 1790 and 1910. You'll find here Coleridge, Tennyson, Rossetti, Hardy, Housman, Keats, Shelley, Wilde, Dickinson, and Whitman. The most important link is to the University of Virginia's Modern English Collection.

Dead Poets Society
http://www.presgroup.com/poets/index.html

Presentation Group

- English, Indexes and Resource Lists, Literature
- 11, 12, AP

While there are only seven sixteenth- or seventeenth-century poets linked to this site in mid-1997, there are many others, as the page labels them, "waiting in the wings." At the date of review, the following were included with links to their lives and work: William Alexander, Robert Devereux, John Donne, Barnabe Googe, Robert Herrick, Ben Jonson, and John Skelton.

Famous Poets
http://tqd.advanced.org/3721/poems/famous/famous.html

Tangerine!

- English, Indexes and Resource Lists, Literature
- All

This resource page has a short list of authors frequently studied in high school English classes, such as Emily Dickinson, Edgar Allen Poe, and William Shakespeare. The links take you to pages with a short introduction to each poet and several of his or her poems. From there, other links take you to related sites on the poet.

HTI American Verse Project
http://www.hti.umich.edu/english/amverse/

University of Michigan Humanities Text Initiative and the University of Michigan Press

- English, Literature
- All

The focus of this project is American poetry prior to 1920. The full text is available for each volume of poetry included. The visitor searches in a number of ways to find material: a Simple Search for a single word or phrase, a Boolean Search for combinations of two or three words, or a Proximity Search to find the co-occurrence of two or three words or phrases. You can also browse the entire project, view the HTI Bibliography, or try the Book-Bagged Amverse link—an easy-to-use interface to select specific works in the collection.

Hyperbibliography to American Poetry
http://www.hti.umich.edu/english/amverse/hyperbib.html

American Verse Project

- English, Indexes and Resource Lists, Literature
- All

This site provides a means to search the Web exclusively for sites dealing with the work of American poets who began publishing before 1921. Type in the poet's name, click on the search button, and the engine goes to work. When it completes the search, you get a page with the results.

The Internet Poetry Archive
http://sunsite.unc.edu/dykki/poetry/

University of North Carolina Press and the North Carolina Arts Council

- English, Literature
- 11, 12, AP

This site is still under construction but promises a wide variety of selections from contemporary poets. Currently featured are Czeslaw Milosz, Seamus Heaney, and Philip Levine. Text from poems is accompanied by a brief biography, photo, and, in some but not all instances, an audio recording of the poets reading their works. Links provide additional information at the site, such as Heaney's Nobel Prize address in its entirety, or quality connections to literary journals such as *The Atlantic*.

The Irish Poetry Page
http://www.spinfo.uni-koeln.de/~dm/eire.html

Dagmar Müller

- English, Indexes and Resource Lists, Literature
- All

Irish poetry and Irish poets are the subject of this site, which opens with an example, "The Dying Synagogue at South Terrace," by Thomas McCarthy. The visitor can then link to major Irish poets—Seamus Heaney, Austin Clarke, and others—additional poetry sites, or the Irish Poetry Index. Other categories are Irish Poems Set to Music, Library of Congress, and Poetry and Ireland, which includes links to relevant news groups on Irish and Celtic culture.

Learning About Poetry
http://tqd.advanced.org/3721/poems/forms/learn.html
Tangerine!
- English, Indexes and Resource Lists, Literature, Writing
- All

This resource page contains a list of the different forms poets use to write their verse. Click on, say, haiku, and you go to a page that explains what haiku is, offers examples of the form, describes how to write one, and lists quality links to related sites. The list of twelve links ends with a link to a dictionary of poetic terms.

Lost Poets of the Great War
http://www.cc.emory.edu/ENGLISH/LostPoets/
Harry Rusche, Emory University
- English, Literature, World History
- All

World War I, called the Great War, produced several great poets. This site offers brief biographies and selections from the works of Rupert Brooke, John McCrae, Wilfred Owen, Isaac Rosenberg, Alan Seeger, and Edward Thomas. Besides the literary information, the visitor also can find facts about the war itself, with a link to a chronology and chart listing the lives lost by each of the combatant nations. There also is included an extensive bibliography related to the topic.

Modern and Contemporary American Poetry
http://www.english.upenn.edu/~afilreis/88/home.html
University of Pennsylvania
- English, Literature
- All

At this extensive site on modern and contemporary American poets, you'll find poetry materials and links to other poetry sites. There is a multitude of links to texts and items related to Allen Ginsberg, Gertrude Stein, William Carlos Williams, and many others. In addition, there are several sound files, such as Robert Frost reciting the first line of "Mending Wall" in pure iambics, summaries of twentieth-century events such as the Spanish Civil War, and miscellaneous references, such as the Kerouac Wore Khakis Gap ad.

Napier University Library: War Poets Collection
http://www.napier.ac.uk/depts/library/poets/introduc.html
Napier University
- English, Literature, World History
- All

This site focuses on Wilfred Owen and Siegfried Sassoon, two British poets hospitalized during World War I for treatment of shell shock. The site offers links to volumes of poetry by these and other war poets, anthologies of poetry and prose, biographies, critical works, and support materials reflecting the time period. The Web page also includes links to photocopies of *Hydra*, the magazine published by the hospital's patients during World War I.

English & Literature

Poet's Park
http://www.soos.com/poetpark

Strong Opinions on Success

- English, Literature
- 12, AP

This site contains works by fifty contemporary poets (unpublished). It is updated periodically with new authors and allows the site visitors to contact the authors via E-mail. Visitors can also sign a guestbook and can view current and past guestbooks.

✔ *"Interesting for creative writing courses."*—Martin Hamburger, Paul D. Schreiber High School, Port Washington, NY.

Poetry Archives, The
http://tqd.advanced.org/3247/

ThinkQuest

- English, Indexes and Resource Lists, Literature, Writing
- All

This site provides links to a substantial list of poems by a broad representation of poets, substantive related sites, and a contest that tests your knowledge of poetry. Also, a wish list provides lots of ideas about where the site is heading. On the list is a promise to help students engaged in writing their own poems.

Poetry Lover's Page
http://www.rit.edu/~exb1874/mine/index.html

Edward Bonver, Rochester Institute of Technology

- English, Indexes and Resource Lists, Literature
- All

Seven poets are represented on this page. The site links to the complete works of Edgar Allan Poe, Robert Louis Stevenson, and Rudyard Kipling. In addition, links are given for the best of Aleksandr Pushkin, Mikhail Lermontov, Aleksandr Blok, and Anna Akhmatova. The visitor who knows only a phrase of a poem can search the site for the complete work; poetry writers can also submit their own work to be posted to this page.

Poets in Person
http://www.wilmington.net/arts/poets/

Modern Poetry Association and the American Library Association

- English, Literature
- All

This resource page affords a basic introduction to thirteen modern American poets. For example, choose Allen Ginsberg and you get a paragraph about him; look further down the page, click the More Information button, and you get loads of information through various links. Choose Sharon Olds and you get the paragraph with some biographical information, a button if you would like to hear her read one of her poems, and an interview. However, choose Karl Shapiro and you get a paragraph with some basic biographical information—that's it.

Poetry 55

Positively Poetry
http://advicom.net/~e-media/kv/poetry1.html

Kellie Vaughn

- English, Literature, Writing
- All

This site brings together poetry written by students from around the world. Many U.S. states are represented as are many countries. Submit your own poems by E-mailing them or use the convenient electronic submission form. A bonus is the list of links to related sites and sites for kids.

✔ *Surfing the Net with Kids, NetGuide Gold Site, World Village Family Site of the Day, Rated A+ by Kids On the Web, National Library of Poetry Top Site.*

The REAL McCoy African American Phat Poetry Book
http://members.aol.com/bonvibre/rmp0a.html

bonVibrè Prosim

- English, Indexes and Resource Lists, Literature
- All

This site provides an anthology of selected works of several African-American writers plus links to sites featuring Maya Angelou, Gwendolyn Brooks, Lucille Clifton, Rita Dove, Jean Toomer, and Paul Laurence Dunbar. Connects to The Other Fat Poetry Book, featuring American writers, and Other Related Links.

Richard's Poetry Library
http://itpubs.ucdavis.edu/richard/library/

Richard Darsie

- English, Indexes and Resource Lists, Literature
- 11, 12, AP

This resource page features two categories, individual poets and links to poetry sites. Choose any one of these links and you go to quality sites. As an option you may click on the hypertext index and get an index by poets with a listing of poems by title. Either way you get to a site where you can read the poems.

✔ *National Library of Poetry Top Site*

The Shiki Internet Haiku Salon
http://mikan.cc.matsuyama-u.ac.jp:80/~shiki

Shiki Team

- Indexes and Resource Lists, Literature
- All

This site celebrates the Japanese literary form known as *haiku*. There is a clear and helpful introduction to haiku plus links to sites devoted to individual haiku poets including Shiki Masaoka, Kametaro Yagi, and others. There is also a link to a haiku mailing list.

✔ *Magellan 3 Star Site, POINTCommunications Top 5% Web Site.*

Spondee

http://www.execpc.com/~jon/

John Faragher

- English, Indexes and Resource Lists, Literature
- AP

This site's goal is to present as many poetry-related URL's as possible. Over 150 links stream from this page. Much of the poetry is contemporary and otherwise unpublished, but not all. For example, one of the links featured on this page is for a little-known female poet of the early twentieth century.

Tangerine: Poetry Site Extraordinaire

http://tqd.advanced.org/3721/

Tangerine Editors: Angeline Tiamson and Alice Vo Edwards

- English, Literature, Writing
- All

This colorful and lively site offers links to four areas: poetry, links, favorites, and discussion forum. Each is linked to others. The poetry page gives you three choices: poetry forms, famous poets, and poems by our poets. Each offers pleasant surprises. The page sponsors encourage you to submit your own poetry.

Twentieth-Century Poetry in English

http://www.lit.kobe-u.ac.jp/~hishika/20c_poet.htm

Eiichi Hishikawa, Kobe University

- English, Indexes and Resource Lists, Literature
- All

Attractive and thoughtful in its presentation, this site features, at the moment, eleven major modern American poets, among them Robert Frost, Marianne Moore, William Carlos Williams, and Wallace Stevens; and links to 140-plus related sites. There also are helpful tips on searches and search engines. Updated and expanded regularly.

✔ LookSmart Editor's Choice.

Voyage to Another Universe: 1994

http://hanksville.phast.umass.edu/title.html

Karen M. Strom

- Anthropology, Art, Astronomy and Space, English, Geography, Indexes and Resource Lists, Literature, Religion, Sociology
- 11, 12, AP

This site contains the journal of a trip through the American Southwest by two writer/astronomers who were raised there and returned partly from nostalgia. More importantly they bring with them their skills as research scientists, which gives the journal focus and depth. The creative use of photography and contemporary Native American poetry and story provide a stimulating, multidimensional perspective. Specifically, the link to the list of poetry alluded to in the journal adds a spiritual/religious dimension to the narrative. A unique contribution.

The Wyoming Companion: Cowboy Poetry and Poets
http://www.wyomingcompanion.com/wccp.html

High Country Communications

- English, Literature
- All

This site is devoted to a uniquely Western literary form: cowboy poetry. Visitors will find a short explanation of the genre, links to cowboy poetry events, and a listing of the contributions of eight poets, such as James Grayford, Stan Paregien, and Elaine Cooke.

	1	2	3	4	5
DEPTH/BREADTH					
QUALITY/ACCURACY					
RELEVANCE					
USEFULNESS					
ENTERTAINMENT					

See Also

PAGES DEVOTED TO SPECIFIC AUTHORS AND WORKS chapter (p 84)

Harlem Renaissance, The http://www.netnoir.com/spotlight/bhm/harlem.html (p 70)

Humanities Scholarship http://www.wam.umd.edu/~mlhall/scholarly.html (p 7)

Literature and Poetry Page, The http://www.netten.net/~bmassey/ (p 42)

Public Domain Modern English Search http://www.hti.umich.edu/english/pd-modeng/ (p 15)

Virtual English http://tqd.advanced.org/2847/homepage.htm (p 45)

Wiretap Electronic Text Archive http://wiretap.area.com/ (p 17)

DRAMA, THEATER & FILM

The 19th Century London Stage: An Exploration
http://artsci.washington.edu/drama-phd/19thhmpg.html
School of Drama, University of Washington
- Drama and Theater, English, Literature
- All

This student-designed page allows visitors to explore four aspects of the London theater of the last century using a graphical representation of intersecting wheels. There are directions on how to navigate the document on the Table of Contents page. The four areas covered are reflections of domestic life; life in and around the City of London Theater; money, commerce, and labor as topics in nineteenth-century drama; and nineteenth-century British playwrights and their work.

American Drama
http://www.uc.edu/www/amdrama/
American Drama Institute
- Drama and Theater, English, Literature
- 12, AP

This site publishes abstracts of scholarly articles from *American Drama* magazine and interviews with living playwrights two months after the most recent issue of the magazine. The articles critically examine trends and discussions of diversity in scripts for stage, film, radio, and television; the careers of dramatists; and various theories of the development of drama from the earliest to the most recent playwrights. Among those featured interviews are such notables as Arthur Miller and August Wilson. Follow hyperlinks to abstracts of the articles listed in the table of contents from the most recent issue or a cumulative index. Also, off-site aids for writers and information about theater are available in a separate link.

American Film Institute
http://www.afionline.org/home.html
American Film Institute
- Drama and Theater, English
- All

The American Film Institute (AFI) Web site, a page that changes monthly, provides information on films and film-making. For example, the June 1997 page offered visitors a list of classes offered, articles on preservation, CineMedia files, a link to the Los Angeles Film Festival, and an AFI tribute to Martin Scorcese. There are links to the purpose and history of the AFI as well.

Asian-American Theatre Revue
http://www.abcflash.com/arts/r_tang/AATR.html
Asian Buying Consortium
- Drama and Theater
- All

This comprehensive site provides information on Asian-American theater. News contains the latest information, Calendar provides a schedule of performances playing around the country, Library has scripts of dramas, Directory has listings of AAS theater groups and artists, and Reviews includes Asian-American events on and off the Web. The final area, Second Stage, includes experimental drama, first drafts, and scripts.

Cinema Sites
http://www.webcom.com/~davidaug/Movie_Sites.html
David Augsburger
- Drama and Theater, English, Indexes and Resource Lists
- All

For the student of cinema, this resource page has links on every conceivable topic. Headings include Databases, Reviews, Previews, Movie Studios, Movie Screenings, Dedicated Fan Pages, Just for Fun, Animation and Visual Effects, Films for Sale on Video, Television, Film and TV Magazines, News on Film and TV Business, Media Contact Listings, Guilds, Associations and Organizations, Festivals, Historical Interest and Film Appreciation, Newsletters and Journals, Academic, Movie Scripts, Production Film Schools, and Other Indexes.

Comedia
http://listserv.arizona.edu/comedia.html
Association for Hispanic Classical Theater, Inc.
- Drama and Theater, Literature, Spanish
- 11, 12, AP

This page is devoted to the Spanish Golden Age *Comedia* and offers links to the Comedia bulletin board as well as an archive of past topics. Of most interest to students would be the access to the collection of Comedia texts in both Spanish and English, which may be downloaded for research purposes. There is also a link to a database containing graphics, text and bibliographic files, and links to other sites pertaining to the Spanish Golden Age.

English Contemporary Theater
http://weber.u.washington.edu/~redmama/barry/tablejm.html
University of Washington
- Drama and Theater, Literature
- All

This site concentrates on English theater in the 1950-1970 period. In Plays and Playwrights, the visitor can find a summary of the life and influences of key authors such as John Osborne, John Arden, and Caryl Churchill as well as synopses of major plays, their social contexts, and main characters. Other links access Significant Theaters, Historical Background, and a bibliography of theater resources.

Guide to Theater Resources on the INTERNET
http://www-old.ircam.fr/divers/theatre-e.html
Institut de Recherche et Coordination Acoustique/Musique
- Drama and Theater, English, Indexes and Resource Lists
- 11, 12, AP

A resource site which will interest serious students of the theater who would like to get more involved in the theater community. Visitors are presented with a very well-organized outline of listservs, electronic newsletters/journals, gophers, Usenet newsgroups, archives, databases, and fee-based communications services. Each entry provides information on how to subscribe, post a message, or contact that group; a short description is included for most items as well. The final category on the site contains Definitions of Terms—Internet terms which have been used in the Guide that may need clarification.

Hard Boiled

http://www.voicenet.com/~bmurray/

Bill Murray

- Literature
- All

This site is devoted to pulp media, from novels to film and TV. For example, there are links to *Mission Impossible*—both the film and the series—*Pulp Fiction*, and *Get Shorty* among others. There is a set of links to other crime and mystery related sites, such as The Case, James Bond 007, and the Mysterious Homepage. Also included is a Hard Boiled chatlink and another to The Maltese Falcon FAQ.

✔ "Catch of the Day," ExciteSeeing Tourstop.

History of Costume

http://www.siue.edu/COSTUMES/history.html

C. Otis Sweezey

Drama and Theater, U.S. History, World History

All

This site provides the text, including pictures, from *The History of Costume* by Braun and Schneider for the years 1861-1880. It is a popular resource for costumes for plays or books on the Victorian era. A graphic index provides links directly to subjects of interest.

Home Page of Theater

http://www.cs.fsu.edu./projects/group4/theatre.html

Florida State University

- Drama and Theater, Indexes and Resource Lists, Literature
- All

This Web site relies heavily on graphics in the links it uses on the Main Page. The site does not try to be a definitive source, but rather to provide some information on major playwrights and links to other sites of interest. The first links include Ray Bradbury's Theater Episode Guide, Images of the Ruins of the Roman Theater, and Images of the Station Theater in Urbana. Additional links in the first section are All the World Is a Stage So Said Shakespeare, The Fire Sign Theater, and information on international drama. The final section contains topics and links such as Computers in Theater, Rights to a Play, and an article on Helping the Visually Impaired View Theater.

Improv Page, The

http://sunee.uwaterloo.ca/~broehl/improv/index.html

Bernie Roehl

- Drama and Theater, English, Literature
- All

This is the homepage for an improvisational theater page—really a clearinghouse for all things that have to do with improvisational theater. Among this page's links that would interest high school students and teachers are those to a history of improvisational theater, games, and terminology.

The Inkwell: In Appreciation of Writers and Writing
http://TheInkwell.com/

The Inkwell

● Drama and Theater, English, Writing

☆ All

This still incomplete Web site focused on screenwriters and screenwriting in mid-1997. There is advice on writing scripts and a step-by-step guide to developing a screenplay. Screenwriter biographies and a glossary of terms provide insight into this writing category. There is a FAQ link planned as are more resources for writers in an area entitled Grab-bag. Additional links also are included.

The Internet Movie Database
http://us.imdb.com/

The Internet Movie Database Ltd.

● Drama and Theater, English

☆ All

This site offers exhaustive information on movies—past, present, and in production. The visitor can search by virtually any category imaginable, even by crew member(s) names. There is a What's New area and a user survey questionnaire. For the visitor who needs up to the minute information there is a Daily Movie News area as well. This site is definitely an important and useful one for cinema research.

Kabuki for Everyone
http://www.fix.co.jp/kabuki/kabuki.html

FiX, Inc.

● Drama and Theater, Literature

☆ All

Kabuki, a traditional form of Japanese theater, is the focus of this site, which relies heavily on the actor Ichimura Manjuro. In On-line Theater, the visitor can download and view video clips of recent plays; Kabuki Sounds links to instruments used in the drama; Make-up shows how a male actor transforms himself into the beautiful woman seen in the play. All about Kabuki links to the drama's history, summaries of major plays, an index of books and movies, and other resources.

✔ *POINTCommunications Top 5% Web Site.*

Literature and Film
http://www.mindspring.com/~jamesthomas/

Mr. Jim Enterprises

● Drama and Theater, Literature

☆ All

This new (June 1997) site plans to study the dynamic involved in transferring a work of literature to the screen. The page has a monthly theme, which may be an author, a director, a particular work, or genre. The first theme is *Hamlet* and includes four cinema adaptations of the play—Laurence Olivier's, Derek Jacobi's, Mel Gibson's, and Kenneth Branagh's. Each month also has links to appropriate teaching resources.

English & Literature

On Broadway WWW Information Page
http://artsnet.heinz.cmu.edu/OnBroadway/

Carnegie Mellon Center for Arts Management and Technology

● Drama and Theater, English, Indexes and Resource Lists, Literature

👑 All

This site is dedicated to the plays and musicals of Broadway, past and present. Under Current Listings, the visitor can access Broadway, Off Broadway, and The Cabaret Hotline. In Broadway History there are links to the Tony Awards and Season Summaries. A third area consists of Theater Links.

✔ Magellan 3 Star Site, Luckman 4-Star Site, Riddlers Choice, recognized by NetGuide.

Playbill On-Line
http://piano.symgrp.com/playbill

***Playbill* On-Line**

● Drama and Theater

👑 All

The *Playbill* On-Line site is the definitive location for theater information. Here you can access theater news, and listings for Broadway, Off-Broadway, Regional Theaters, Tours, London, Brazil, Canada, and Summer Stock. There are features about shows, quizzes, and figures for Broadway grosses. Within the Industry section are casting and jobs, newsletters, and a college database. The section entitled Multimedia offers recordings, art, audio clips, and a bookshop. There is also a reference area for awards and FAQs.

Restoration Drama Homepage
http://ernie.bgsu.edu/~smorgan/publick/resthome.html

Dr. Simon Morgan-Russell

● Drama and Theater, English, Indexes and Resource Lists, Literature

👑 11, 12, AP

This site on the theater of the English Restoration period, 1660-1770, provides links to authors such as Apra Behn, William Congreve, John Dryden, Thomas Otway, Thomas Shadwell, and William Wycherly. There are also links to Background Sites for the student to better understand the topic—Blenheim Palace, Elizabeth Barry, and Restoration Masquerades. In addition, links to The Aphra Behn Page, Restoration Politics, The Rover, and Scenes from Pepys's Diary give even more information.

Screenwriters.com
http://www.screenwriters.com/screennet.html

Internet Entertainment Network

● Drama and Theater, English, Writing

👑 11, 12, AP

This site provides a multitude of links to topics pertaining to film screenwriting. Visitors can link to Hollywood Live to chat with the pros, Screenwriters Lounges, Contests, Agents and Columns, Newsletters, and Special Features. The index includes access to categories such as Crimewriting, Music, Producing, and many others. There is also search capability for the Hollywood Network.

Drama, Theater & Film **63**

Screenwriters/Playwrights Page
http://www.teleport.com/~cdeemer/scrwriter.html

Charles Deemer

- Drama and Theater, English, Writing
- All

At this site, anyone can access information, hints, and tips from experts in the two areas of screenwriting and playwriting. The major categories include Resources for Screenwriters, with nuts and bolts information; Screenwriters FAQs; Film databases; tips; and other links. In Resources for Playwrights are Scripts, FAQs, New York City and London Theater information, tips, and links to theater resources. There is also a large category of General Writing Resources for writers in general.

Set Designs for the *Crucible* by Darwin Payne
http://www.wfu.edu/academic-departments/Theatre/crucible.htm

Darwin Payne

- Drama and Theater, English, Literature
- 11, 12, AP

This page presents a series of preliminary designs by Darwin Payne for the Wake Forest University Theater's production of *The Crucible* in the fall of 1996. Links within the page bring you to designs for the Proctor House, court, and jail.

Silent Movies
http://www.cs.monash.edu.au/~pringle/silent/

Glen Pringle

- Drama and Theater, Indexes and Resource Lists
- All

This silent movie site offers much information on the topic. There is a page of silent film screenings, another listing silent film interest groups, and a listing of films of the silent era. In addition to links to many pages featuring silent film stars, this site focuses on a silent "Star of the Month." There are also headings entitled Music in Silent Films, the Loss and Preservation of Silent Films, and many silent film links.

✓ Magellan 3 Star Site, Classy Site Pick from Duke of URL, Actors Online Pick of the Week.

Snagged Links: On Modern World Drama
http://www.stetson.edu/~csata/snaglnk1.html

Ken McCoy, Stetson University

- Drama and Theater, English, Indexes and Resource Lists, Literature
- All

This resource page was produced by a class of drama students at Stetson University and is quite extensive and well organized. There are links to texts and drama sites, such as Quotes from Playwrights, and a set of links to "-isms" associated with modern drama, such as Existentialism, Expressionism, Postmodernism, and Surrealism. There is also a listing of seventeen playwrights—Chekhov, Ionesco, and Fugard among others—with links for each. The section on Other Stuff includes Theater Guides, Lists and Links, and links to Regional Theaters.

Theater Sites

http://artsnet.heinz.cmu.edu/Artsites/Theater.html

Master of Arts Program in Public Management, Heinz School of Public Policy and Management, Carnegie Mellon University

- Drama and Theater, English, Indexes and Resource Lists, Literature
- All

This resource page contains information about theaters, including production schedules. There are some interesting links for those seeking experience in theater work. The site also provides an overview about what is currently being produced. There is very little information on specific playwrights.

Videomaker's Glossary of Terms

http://www.videomaker.com/edit/other/GLOSSAZ.HTM

Videomaker, Inc.

- Drama and Theater, English, Writing
- All

Students interested in video will find this site with its definitions of video terms quite useful. The visitor can jump to an alphabetical portion of the glossary or go through the terms, beginning with A-B roll and ending with zoom ratio.

Virtual Theater Project

http://www-ksl.stanford.edu/projects/cait/index.html

Stanford University

- Computers, Drama and Theater, English, Literature
- AP

This resource page is the home site for a virtual theater project. There is information about the project and its publications; actual talks and descriptions of productions; and descriptions and images from those productions. This is the brave new world. Welcome to it!

VOID: PERFORMANCE

http://www.voidp.demon.co.uk/index.htm

Peter Ireland and Elizabeth Swift

- Computers, Drama and Theater, English, Literature, Writing
- AP

This site provides a look at the new interactive environment and the interface between technology and performance art. Links take you to background information, past works, and current works. The people in VOID began their work in the late 1980s by combining influences from science fiction, cyberpunk, and technology. Today, they "create information-rich environments for the viewers/audience about creating and receiving art."

Drama, Theater & Film **65**

World Internet Directory: Drama
http://www.tradenet.it:80/links/arsocu/drama.html

Trade-Net

- Drama and Theater, English, Indexes and Resource Lists, Literature
- All

This resource page contains a long list of drama-related sites. At last count, there were 237 links. Many are to theaters and provide information about productions. However, other links provide information about theater groups, improvisational theater, and playwrights.

	1	2	3	4	5
DEPTH/BREADTH					
QUALITY/ACCURACY					
RELEVANCE					
USEFULNESS					
ENTERTAINMENT					

The World of London Theatre: 1660-1800
http://www.ucet.ufl.edu/~craddock/lonthe1.html

University of Florida

- Drama and Theater, English, Literature
- 11, 12, AP

This site—maintained by literature students at the University of Florida—is based on the belief that to understand a play, or any piece of literature, you must also understand the other aspects of society during the period. Very much a work in progress, the site contains links to the following categories pertaining to the topic: people in the British theater during the period, a chronology of the period, a map of London, a bibliography, and relevant images and comments from contemporaries on London life of the day. There are also additional links to Hogarth's engravings, a History of Costumes, Women in the Theater after the Restoration, The Age of Style 1660-1800, and Regency Fashions.

	1	2	3	4	5
DEPTH/BREADTH					
QUALITY/ACCURACY					
RELEVANCE					
USEFULNESS					
ENTERTAINMENT					

See Also

American Scenes: Lorraine Hansberry
http://www.en.utexas.edu/~daniel/amlit/scenes.html (p 99)

Books in Chains http://www.uc.edu/~RETTBESR/Links.html (p 2)

CyberSchool Magazine http://www.cyberschoolmag.com/ (p 39)

David Mamet http://www.levity.com/corduroy/mamet.htm (p 106)

Essays on the Craft of Dramatic Writing
http://www.teleport.com/~bjscript/index.htm (p 130)

Glass Menagerie, The
http://www.susqu.edu/ac_depts/arts_sci/english/lharris/class/WILLIAMS/titlepag.htm (p 124)

HUMBUL Gateway, The http://info.ox.ac.uk/oucs/humanities/international.html (p 8)

Inter-Play http://www.portals.org/interplay/ (p 8)

Irish Literature, Mythology, Folklore, and Drama
http://www.luminarium.org/mythology/ireland/ (p 78)

Julius Caesar Web Guide
http://www.bell.k12.ca.us/BellHS/Departments/English/SCORE/caesarwebguide.html (p 115)

Mr. William Shakespeare and the Internet
http://www.palomar.edu/Library/shake.htm (p 115)

NM's Creative Impulse http://www.evansville.net/~nbmautz/index.html (p 14)

Oz Project Home Page
http://www.cs.cmu.edu/afs/cs.cmu.edu/project/oz/web/oz.html (p 140)

Romeo and Juliet Web Guide
http://www.bell.k12.ca.us/BellHS/Departments/English/SCORE/webguide.html (p 116)

Science Fiction Resource Guide http://sflovers.rutgers.edu/Web/SFRG/ (p 15)

SIRS: The Knowledge Source: Arts and Humanities
http://www.sirs.com/tree/artshum.htm pxxx (p 15)

English & Literature

Sixties Project and Viet Nam Generation, Inc.
http://jefferson.village.virginia.edu/sixties/ (p 74)

Virtual English http://tqd.advanced.org/2847/homepage.htm (p 45)

Webspeare http://idt.net/~kcn/shakes~1.htm (p 115)

World Internet Directory: Drama
http://www.tradenet.it:80/links/arsocu/drama.html (p 65)

Yellow Wallpaper, The http://www.media.mit.edu/people/davet/yp/ (p 97)

AMERICAN & CANADIAN LITERATURE

African American Literature
http://www.usc.edu/Library/Ref/Ethnic/black_lit_main.html
Department of Ethnic Studies, University of Southern California
- English, Indexes and Resource Lists, Literature, Reading, U.S. History
- All

This site is the gateway to loads of information about African American literature. But do not count out trips to the library just yet. The trick is to figure out how to get your hands on the works referenced here—the speeches, reference books, books of criticism, and actual works by many writers linked here. A good site to start researching the books you need for your report or reading assignment on African American literature.

✔ *Up-Set Approved.*

The Algonquin Round Table
http://www.buffalo.edu/~raines/algtab.html
Steve Raines
- English, Literature
- All

The Algonquin Round Table met at the Algonquin Hotel during the 1920s and 1930s and included some of the best-known writers, journalists, and artists in New York City of the day. This Web site contains biographies of the generally recognized members, how the group received its name, and the years the group met. There are also links to *The New Yorker* magazine; The Algonquin Hotel; a bibliography; a summary of "Mrs. Parker and the Vicious Circle," a USA movie; and a USA documentary, "The Ten Year Lunch."

American Literature Survey Site
http://www.cwrl.utexas.edu/~natasha/316/index.html
Natasha Sinutko
- English, Indexes and Resource Lists, Literature, Writing
- 11, 12, AP

This is not just another college-level course on the Web. Here you will find links to resources and typical assignments. The resources are divided between electronic texts available on-line and excellent links to sites on American literature or leading authors. Check out the assignments. These are worth reviewing simply for the instructions; follow them and you will do well on your own research assignments. But that's not all; the link to student projects is outstanding. Click on this link and choose a project. You will be excited—and challenged.

American Studies @ The University of Virginia
http://xroads.virginia.edu/
The University of Virginia
- Literature, U.S. History
- All

This resource page offers an excellent collection of Web pages on America's early history and media driven future. Cultural Maps is a Web page that uses various types of maps to follow America's development. Virgin Land is an electronic text that looks into the American West as both symbol and myth. Another linked page consists of a collection of classic American books put into hypertext, including the works of Mark Twain and the Uncle Remus books. Finally there is The Capital Project, which explores the National Capital as icon.

✔ *Lycos Top 5% Web Site, Starting Point Hot Site.*

English & Literature

Black Classic Press
http://www.blackclassic.com/

Black Classic Press
- English, Indexes and Resource Lists, Literature
- All

This is the home site of Black Classic Press. It is promotional in nature, but also informative on classic literature written about and by authors of African American descent. Each of the fifty or so books on the BPC list are found here with a brief description. In addition, an entire page is dedicated to mystery writer Walter Mosley. Linked to his page is the introduction and first chapter of his latest book, and the dates of Mosley's appearances for 1997. There are a few links to related sites but not many, and none of them deal directly with African American literature.

A Black Cultural Studies Website
http://www.tiac.net/users/thaslett

Tim Haslett
- Drama and Theater, English, Indexes and Resource Lists, Literature
- All

This site contains resources on black literary criticism, black popular culture, critical race theory, and film theory. In mid-1997, the site listed seventeen "cultural workers," each with a brief bibliographical entry. The site is strictly an alphabetical listing, one to which information is constantly being added. There is also a set of links to similar sites.

Documenting the American South
http://sunsite.unc.edu/docsouth/

Academic Affairs Library, University of North Carolina
- English, Indexes and Resource Lists, Literature, U.S. History
- All

Part of a multifaceted project at the University of North Carolina, this site contains resources on the southern experience in nineteenth-century America. The student can find narratives on slavery, diaries and memoirs, exhibits, autobiographies, and indexes. There are also links to other resources on southern Americana and the University of North Carolina at Chapel Hill Libraries Home Page. New and planned additions include a digitized library of Southern Literature: Beginnings to 1920 and First-Person Narratives of the American South, 1860-1920.

✔ Winner of the Library of Congress/Ameritech National Digital Library Competition.

Electronic Archives for the Teaching of American Literatures
http://www.georgetown.edu/tamlit/tamlit-home.html

Department of English, Georgetown University
- English, Literature
- AP

This site is more for teachers than students. It contains essays, syllabi, bibliographies, and related resources for the teaching of the "multiple literatures" of the United States.

English 102: Multicultural English Web Page
http://parallel.park.uga.edu/~dfelty/eng102m.html
Darren Felty
- English, Grammar and Style, Indexes and Resource Lists, Literature, Writing
- 11, 12, AP

This resource page provides instruction and materials from an introductory college-level English course that focuses on multiculturalism. Included are sample materials, sample essays, and links to related sources on the Web. Because the course deals with multiculturalism, there are links to historical, African-American, and Native-American sites as well as the more obvious links to writing-related sites.

Epistrophy: The Jazz Literature Archive
http://ie.uwindsor.ca/jazz/welcome.html
Michael Borshuk, University of Alberta
- Literature, Music and Dance
- All

This site is devoted to the relationship between jazz and literature. The student will find here links to *A Journal of Jazz and Literature*, sites on a number of relevant poets (such as Langston Hughes), and Notable Prose links. There are essays on the connection between the two genres as well as a jazz glossary and Carl Con's Slanguage of Swing. Links are also provided to strictly musical sites, such as The Jazz Net, Jazz Online, and The BioJazz Network.

✔ *Magellan 3 Star Site.*

Gender Issues in American Literature
http://www.cwrl.utexas.edu/~gsiesing/316/collaborative/gender/
John Mackovic, Chris Roberts, and Elizabeth Curtice, students in Gina Siesing's class at the University of Texas at Austin
- English, Indexes and Resource Lists, Literature
- 11, 12, AP

This resource page focuses on four female American writers: Elizabeth Cady Stanton, Harriet Jacobs, Charlotte Perkins Gilman, and Audre Lorde. Each link has biographical information, a discussion about gender issues, and class-related material. An added feature is a timeline with links to many more sites where you'll find additional insight into gender issues.

Godey's Lady's Book Online Home Page
http://www.rochester.edu/godeys/
Electronic Historical Publications
- Literature, U.S. History
- All

Godey's Lady's Book was one of the most popular women's periodicals of the nineteenth century with each volume containing poetry, engravings, and articles by well-known authors and artists of the day. The student who visits this site will find links for the volumes January-April and November 1850. Each link contains the Table of Contents and the articles that appeared, allowing the visitor to get an excellent idea of what women in the mid-nineteenth century were reading and talking about.

✔ *Librarian's Site du Jour.*

English & Literature

DEPTH/BREADTH 1 2 3 4 5
QUALITY/ACCURACY
RELEVANCE
USEFULNESS
ENTERTAINMENT

The Harlem Renaissance
http://www.netnoir.com/spotlight/bhm/harlem.html
NetNoir
- English, Literature, U.S. History
- All

This resource page celebrates black history and would be a good resource for Black History Month. Listed here under Literature, Music, Performance Arts, Poetry, and Social are the names of important people from the Harlem Renaissance. What follows is an overview of the era and brief biographies of the people. Click on the impressive graphics and a selection of historical essays appear.

DEPTH/BREADTH 1 2 3 4 5
QUALITY/ACCURACY
RELEVANCE
USEFULNESS
ENTERTAINMENT

Harlem Renaissance, 1919-1937
http://www.csustan.edu/english/reuben/pal/chap9/CHAP9.HTML
Paul P. Reuben
- English, Indexes and Resource Lists, Literature
- 11, 12, AP

This resource page is one in a series of chapters in an ongoing project from PAL—Perspectives in American Literature: A Research and Reference Guide. This site offers links to a number of pages dedicated to different writers and musicians of prominence during the time of the Harlem Renaissance. Behind the names, find biographical information, a bibliography of works, influences, and a general assessment of each author's works and his or her place in American letters.

DEPTH/BREADTH 1 2 3 4 5
QUALITY/ACCURACY
RELEVANCE
USEFULNESS
ENTERTAINMENT

Hemingway and Fitzgerald
http://www.cas.usf.edu/english/sipiora/public_html/hemfitz.html
Phillip Sipiora
- English, Indexes and Resource Lists, Literature
- 11, 12, AP

This resource page links you to several college-level discussions of the literary legacy of Ernest Hemingway and F. Scott Fitzgerald. There are also a few links to other related sites.

DEPTH/BREADTH 1 2 3 4 5
QUALITY/ACCURACY
RELEVANCE
USEFULNESS
ENTERTAINMENT

Indigenous People's Literature
http://www.indians.org/welker/natlit02.htm
Glenn Welker
- Anthropology, Indexes and Resource Lists, Literature
- All

This expansive site is devoted largely to the literature of Native Americans, but it also includes literature from other indigenous peoples from Latin America, Europe, and the Pacific. Pages can be found for specific groups and tribes as well as general topics such as Columbus, eagles, leaders and chiefs, origin stories, and poetry. Writings abound from the leaders of indigenous North and South American Nations, such as Cochise, Crazy Horse, Dan George, and many others. There are links to other sites devoted to indigenous peoples in North and South America, as well as Europe, Asia, Africa, and Oceania. This is an important bookmark for anyone interested in Native American culture.

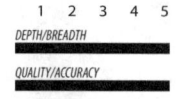

American & Canadian Literature

Literary Kicks
http://www.charm.net/~brooklyn/LitKicks.html
Levi Asher
- English, Literature
- All

Devoted to the Beat Writers of the 1950s and 1960s, this site is an "unofficial" effort to provide information on their literary accomplishments and their influence. Visitors can find information on specific writers such as Jack Kerouac, Allen Ginsberg, Neal Cassady, William S. Burroughs, Gary Snyder, Lawrence Ferlinghetti, Gregory Corso, or Michael McClure. There are also links to related topics such as The Beat Generation, Beat Connections in Rock Music, Films about the Beats, and the origin of the term "Beat."

Lost Generation
http://www.hawken.edu/class/e3losf/
Hawken School
- English, Indexes and Resource Lists, Literature
- All

This resource site featuring links to 1920s culture and the "Lost Generation" writers was put together by a high school class. The writers linked to this page are Hemingway, Cummings, Fitzgerald, Hart, Crane, and Faulkner. Under the category Mentors/Older Writers, there are links for James Joyce, Ezra Pound, T. S. Eliot, Sylvia Beach, and Gertrude Stein. The related fields section includes links to Jazz music, Cubism, Fauvism, and Dada.

Many Voices: American Indian Students Journal
http://thecity.sfsu.edu/users/BANN/journal/cover.html
San Francisco State University
- Literature, Writing
- All

This Web site contains an edition of the *American Indian Students Journal*. The articles exemplify the ability and interests of that group of young people and include both fiction and nonfiction; the listing includes President Clinton's Proclamation of American Indian Heritage Month. This would be an excellent site to visit for students interested in the writing and ideas of their peers.

Minority Literatures — Voices of the Shuttle
http://humanitas.ucsb.edu/shuttle/eng-min.html
Voices of the Shuttle and Alan Liu, English Department, University of California, Santa Barbara
- English, Indexes and Resource Lists, Literature
- 11, 12, AP

Among the many resources linked to this page are those relating to African American, Chicano/Latino, Jewish, and Pacific literatures. Click on any one of the links and go to original works in their entirety, criticism, and journals. For teachers, there is a special link to syllabi and other teaching resources.

The Mississippi Writers Page

http://www.olemiss.edu/depts/english/ms-writers/

English Department, University of Mississippi

- English, Indexes and Resource Lists, Literature
- 11, 12, AP

This multifaceted resource page is centered around the listing of Mississippi writers. Click on a name from the list of writers from, living in, or associated with Mississippi and you get an information page with biographical data, bibliographies, honors, and awards. Also, from the homepage you may access the information by genre (poetry, fiction, drama, or nonfiction). You'll find a timeline, literary landmarks, and news and events as well.

National Library of Canada

http://www.nlc-bnc.ca/

National Library of Canada

- English, French, Indexes and Resource Lists, Literature
- 11, 12, AP

This site is available in English and French. Among its many features, only a few that can be utilized on-line. Most features allow you to look up a book title or author or find out basic information about literature in general and Canadian literature in particular. More friendly are the links to various sites that provide information on-line.

Native American Authors

http://www.ipl.org/ref/native/

Internet Public Library

- English, Indexes and Resource Lists, Literature
- All

This resource page provides texts, bibliographies, biographies, and related links to interviews, on-line texts, and Native American Web sites. From the homepage, search by author, title, or tribe. The information about the authors and their works is brief, but the combination of resources available is substantial.

Native American Indian Resources

http://indy4.fdl.cc.mn.us/~isk/mainmenu.html#mainmenutop

Not Listed

- Anthropology, Art, English, Geography, Indexes and Resource Lists, Literature, U.S. History, World History
- All

This resource page has more than 300 hotlinks. Many of them have to do with geography and history, but others deal with literature, books, children's stories, and art. Under the stories menu there are links to learning and teaching materials, traditional stories, E-texts, authors, and a fiction bookshelf.

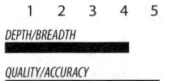

Native American Literature Online
http://www.maxwell.syr.edu/nativeweb/natlit/NAlit.html
Native Web
- Anthropology, English, Indexes and Resource Lists, Literature, U.S. History
- All

This resource site includes Native North American authors and their works from the late-nineteenth century to the present. General links are provided to the Internet Public Library and Trophies of Honor; the Books and Articles section includes links to the University of Virginia Electronic Text Center and articles from *The Atlantic Monthly*, *Harper's*, and others from 1880-1905. In addition, there are links to Native American Short Stories Online, Writing by Contemporary Native Writers (such as Sherman Alexie, Russell Banks, and Leslie Marmon Silko), and Speeches and Interviews.

Native Lit-L: A Mailing List for Native Literature
http://www.uwm.edu/~mwilson/lit.htm
Michael Wilson
- English, Indexes and Resource Lists, Literature
- 12, AP

This resource page is the door to a listserv for Native American literature and many sites related to Native American literature. Book reviews, biographical information about Native American authors, lists of their books and where to buy them, and searchable archives are all here. For teachers, there are course materials; for students, some actual texts.

Nick Evans' Survey of American Literature
http://wwwvms.utexas.edu/~NICKE/index.html
Nick Evans, University of Texas
- English, Indexes and Resource Lists, Literature
- 11, 12, AP

This resource site is based on a college-level class. As with many comparable sites, the links are limited but useful. You will be surprised how many of the writers cited here are discussed in your own class. You might want to join the on-line discussion area where students meet to exchange ideas. This site also has a couple of handouts that you might find useful: (1) Why Read Literature and (2) A Method of Interpreting Literature.

North American Native Authors Catalog
http://nativeauthors.com/search/home.html
Greenfield Review Press
- Anthropology, Current Events, English, Indexes and Resource Lists, Literature, Music and Dance, U.S. History
- All

Click on a button and view a list of books/audios, their cost, a blurb about the work, and something about the author/creator. Search by title, tribe, author, or any combination. Order a book. Yet, this is more than just a catalog of books and audio tapes. You'll find special links to take you to a featured book and author and award winners, too. Current events are also important at this site. The appropriate button takes you to a page about someone or something of interest in the news. The immensity of the project becomes readily apparent after exploring the offerings. The mission of the site is to help people learn about the Native American.

✔ *Wolfsong Award of Excellence.*

Researching American Literature on the Internet
http://www.sccd.ctc.edu/~sbeasley/mais/amlittoc.html

Seattle Community College District

- English, Literature
- All

This is a resource site for materials primarily devoted to American literature. Links on this page are organized under the following headings: Reference, Academic Sites, Electronic Texts and Journals, Listservs and News groups, Genre and Media, Standard Directories, Writers, Personal Collections, Book Information, and Libraries. This is an excellent place to start your Internet search on any American literature topic.

Resources for American Literature
http://www.en.utexas.edu/~daniel/amlit/amlit.html

Daniel Anderson, University of Texas at Austin

- Drama and Theater, English, Indexes and Resource Lists, Literature
- All

This site, developed by students at the University of Texas, provides analysis and criticism of American authors in two general categories—The American Literature Survey and An American Reader. The writers included are Lorraine Hansberry, Frank Norris, Charlotte Perkins Gilman, Herman Melville, Washington Irving, and Sarah Orne Jewett. Links to each author's work provide access to a number of essays and critical analysis of their work.

Romancing the Indian
http://xroads.virginia.edu/~HYPER/HNS/Indians/main.html

Adriana Rissetto, University of Virginia

- English, Literature
- All

This small site is devoted to a comparison of how James Fenimore Cooper and Mark Twain treated Native Americans in their works. There are quotes and interpretations given for Cooper's *Last of the Mohicans* and *Notions of the Americans*. Several of Twain's works are included—*The Nobel Red Man* and the depiction of Injun Joe in *Tom Sawyer* are two. The site would be an excellent stop for the student reading these works to get the authors' views on Native Americans.

The Sixties Project and Viet Nam Generation, Inc.
http://jefferson.village.virginia.edu/sixties/

Institute of Advanced Technology in the Humanities, University of Virginia, and Viet Nam Generation, Inc.

- English, Literature, U.S. History
- All

This humanities site is devoted to collecting information about the 1960s and particularly the impact of the Vietnam War on that period. The Sixties Personal Narrative Project, which includes personal stories submitted by those who lived through the turbulent decade, will be of particular interest to students. There are also links to book, film, music, and multimedia reviews; an index to texts by author or title; a book catalog; and *Viet Nam Generation: A Journal of Recent History and Contemporary Culture*.

South Asian American Literature
http://alumni.EECS.Berkeley.EDU:80/~manish/index.html
Manish Vij
- English, Indexes and Resource Lists, Literature
- 11, 12, AP

This resource page has five pages: the study, chat room, garden, launch pad, and mailroom. The study provides reviews of South Asian American books; the chat room, discussion of authors and information about the authors; the garden, information about writing contests and calls for papers; the launch pad, information about new authors, the mailroom, and E-mail. Most valuable is the launch pad, with its lists of South Asian American Web sites, but don't discount the study and chat room—they provide good, fairly informal introductions to this literature.

✔ Free Speech Online Blue Ribbon Campaign.

Women in Canadian Literature
http://www.nlc-bnc.ca/digiproj/women/ewomen3.htm
National Library of Canada
- English, French, Literature
- All

This page offers short biographies and analyses of the writings of eight Canadian women authors. The authors are Félicité Angers (Laure Conan), Robertine Barry, Harriet Vaughan Cheney, Eliza Lanesford Cushing, Eleanor Lay, Rosanna Leprohon, Agnes Maule Machar, and Isabella Valancy Crawford. Each segment includes a list of selected works, some of which are in French.

See Also
LITERATURE(General) chapter (p 38)
PAGES DEVOTED TO SPECIFIC AUTHORS AND WORKS chapter (p 84)
Cool School Tools — Literature and Rhetoric
http://www.walker.public.lib.ga.us/cst/literatu.htm (p 4)
Crack Fiction http://allrise.com/index.html (p 145)
English Literature — Voice of the Shuttle http://humanitas.ucsb.edu/shuttle/english.html (p 77)
High School English Resource Page
http://www.bham.wednet.edu/ENGLISH2.HTM (p 7)
Writing Black http://www.keele.ac.uk/depts/as/Literature/amlit.black.html (p 18)

BRITISH & IRISH LITERATURE

British Women's Novels: A Reading List, 1777-1818
http://locutus.ucr.edu/~cathy/womw.html

Catherine Decker, University of California at Riverside

- English, Literature
- All

This reading list includes British women's novels from the period 1777-1818. The list is organized by decade and in many cases includes a brief abstract of the novel, its date of publication, and publisher. Examples of authors and novels included are Frances Burney's *Evelina,* Charlotte Smith's *Emmeline,* Ann Radcliffe's *The Italian,* and various works by Mary Wollstonecraft and Jane Austen. When available, links connect you to other sites that have information on the authors.

The Camelot Project
http://rodent.lib.rochester.edu/camelot/cphome.htm

University of Rochester and Alan Lupack

- Literature, World History
- All

This site makes available a database of Arthurian texts, images, bibliographies, and basic information in an electronic format. Organized by subject, author, and even artist, the Camelot Project includes detailed descriptions of many of the characters involved in the Arthurian legends. These descriptions are complimented with several images and numerous hypertext links to both bibliographies and electronic texts that involve each character.

✔ *LookSmart Editors Choice, Mèdaille d'Or, POINTCommunications Top 5% Web Site.*

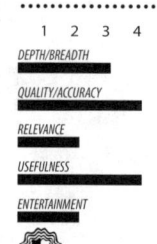

A Collector's Guide to Regency Romances
http://locutus.ucr.edu/~cathy/regcoll.html

Catherine Decker, University of California at Riverside

- English, Indexes and Resource Lists, Literature
- All

This site is a resource page of information on authors and works in the Regency Romance genre. There are hypertext guides to Barbara Cartland's works divided into five categories based on time period. The bulk of the site provides links to other pages, such as the Society of London Ladies, the Reader's Corner, the Romance Novel Database, and the Romance Reader; each of these will help Regency fans track down information. There are also links to British Women's Novels: A Reading List and several individual authors' homepages.

British & Irish Literature

The Electronic Beowulf
http://www.uky.edu/~kiernan/BL/kportico.html

The British Library Board

- English, Literature
- All

The digitization of the eleventh-century *Beowulf* manuscript, the first great English literary masterpiece, has enabled more scholars to view the document and has also provided new insights. This Web site allows the student to view the eighteenth-century transcripts of the manuscript, selections from nineteenth-century collations, fiber optic readings of hidden letters, and ultraviolet readings of text erased in the early eleventh-century manuscript. The site plans to add images of contemporary manuscript illuminations as well.

✔ 1994-1995 Library Association Mecklermedia Award for Innovation Through Information Technology.

English Literature — Voice of the Shuttle
http://humanitas.ucsb.edu/shuttle/english.html

Voices of the Shuttle and Alan Liu, English Department, University of California, Santa Barbara

- English, Indexes and Resource Lists, Literature
- 11, 12, AP

This resource page contains links to a spectrum of sources for many English Literature topics. Each literary era, from the Middle Ages to the Restoration to Victorian times, has its own set of links. Also, there are links to sources organized under categories such as literary genres, creative writing, theory, criticism, and analysis.

Fabulists Home Page
http://homepages.iol.ie/~phcasey/

Philip Casey

- English, Literature
- All

This site (still a work-in-progress) includes a biographical dictionary of contemporary Irish writers. The main impetus for the page is the sponsor's own novel, *The Fabulists*, but the biographical dictionary, the links provided, and the Encyclopedia Hibernica Online, have useful information on Irish literature.

Gaelic and Gaelic Culture
http://sunsite.unc.edu/gaelic/gaelic.html

University of North Carolina

- Literature, Music and Dance
- All

Devoted to the language and culture of the Gaels, this resource page will help students who need information on Gaelic languages, the Celts and Celtic languages, Gaelic language books and tapes, Gaelic music, and general information on the Celts. There is also a link to the *Irish Times* newspaper. The more adventurous visitor can explore several links in Gaelic.

English & Literature

Gothic Literature 1764-1820

http://members.aol.com/iamudolpho/basic.html

Franz Potter

- English, Indexes and Resource Lists, Literature
- All

This site contains a variety of links to topics related to the Gothic novel. The links are presented in a grid format and include the following: The Gothic Novel, Papers on the Gothic, Ann Radcliffe, Gothic Plot Summaries, a Gothic Bibliography, a Bibliography of Critical Sources, Gothic Texts, Gothic Resources and Writings, and Links.

Initiatives for Access: Beowulf Project

http://portico.bl.uk/access/beowulf/electronic-beowulf.html

The British Library Board

- Literature
- All

This first great English literary masterpiece was transcribed from a late-eighteenth century manuscript, which was badly damaged in a fire. The transcript shows that over the years, many hundreds of words have crumbled away. Therefore, in an effort to save this most fundamental of literary treasures, the British Library digitized the entire manuscript, which provided a solution to the problem, as well as providing new insights. Assembling a huge database of digitized images, the Electronic Beowulf Project already includes fiber-optic readings of hidden letters and ultraviolet readings of erased text dating from the early-eleventh century manuscript.

✔ *The Electronic Beowulf Project won the 1994-1995 Library Association/Mecklermedia Award for Innovation Through Information Technology.*

Irish Literature, Mythology, Folklore, and Drama

http://www.luminarium.org/mythology/ireland/

Anniina Jokinen

- Art History, Current Events, Drama and Theater, Indexes and Resource Lists, Journalism, Literature, Music and Dance, World History, Writing
- All

This resource site should be visited by anyone interested in Ireland. Links are organized under major areas such as history, language, periodicals, literature, mythology, theater, folklore, fine arts, food, and marketplaces. Each of the headings includes numerous links —some to sites in Gaelic, some to Irish authors, and some to Celtic topics.

✔ *Lycos Top 5% Web Site, Telecom 4-Dora Site.*

King Arthur: History and Legend

http://britannia.com/history/h12.html

Geoffrey Ashe

- Indexes and Resource Lists, Literature, World History
- All

Geoffrey Ashe, an historian and leading Arthurian scholar, uses this Web page to explore the legend of King Arthur and its factual roots based on evaluation of existing historical material. This fascinating site includes an interview with Ashe, a series of articles, the "Magical History Tour"—a virtual tour with over one hundred photographs and maps—a bibliography of Arthurian literature for young people, and a vast number of links to additional resources.

The Middle English Collection at the Electronic Text Center, University of Virginia
http://etext.lib.virginia.edu/mideng.browse.html

Electronic Text Center, University of Virginia
- English, Literature
- All

This site provides access to key documents in Middle English. There are a number of works in the Anonymous category as well as works by Chaucer, Dunbar, Gower, Henryson, Langland, Layamon, and the Pastor family. A portion of the site is set aside for University of Virginia (UVA) users only, but there are two search capabilities of all publicly accessible texts and those at UVA to enable visitors to access more information.

Scottish Literature at the University of South Carolina
http://www.sc.edu/library/scotlit/scotlit.html

Studies in Scottish Literature, University of South Carolina
- English, Indexes and Resource Lists, Literature
- All

The University of South Carolina is a major center for the study of Scottish literature, and this page contains links to much of its information resources. The most valuable section on the page is "Other Sources of Information," which includes links to general resources, such as the National Library of Scotland, sites on authors and language (with many resources on Gaelic), academic links, and other related links

See Also

LITERATURE (General) chapter (p 38)
PAGES DEVOTED TO SPECIFIC AUTHORS AND WORKS chapter (p 84)
Cool School Tools — Literature and Rhetoric
   http://www.walker.public.lib.ga.us/cst/literatu.htm (p 4)
High School English Resource Page
   http://www.bham.wednet.edu/ENGLISH2.HTM (p 7)
Indigenous People's Literature http://www.indians.org/welker/natlit02.htm (p 70)
Lost Generation http://www.hawken.edu/class/e3losf/ (p 71)

WORLD LITERATURE

African Writers: Voices of Change
http://www.uflib.ufl.edu/hss/africana/voices.html
George Smathers Libraries, University of Florida
- Literature
- All

This Web site provides short biographies and lists of published works for major African writers. Information is included on authors such as Chinua Achebe, Nadine Gordimer, Bessie Head, Alan Paton, Kenule B. Saro-Wiwa, and Amos Tutuola. There are also links to other sites related to the topic, such as H-Africa, a bibliography of Francophone African Woman Writers, and Heinemann's Studies in African Literature.

Books of South Asian Writers Writing in English
http://www.ntu.edu.sg/home/mdamodaran/sabooks.html
Murali Damodaran, Nanyang Technological University
- English, Indexes and Resource Lists, Literature
- All

A valuable site for the visitor interested in locating literature written by South Asian authors. The main content consists of links to the following areas: Voices of South Asian Writers (English), Voices of South Asian Writers (Translated), General Books from South Asia, Literature with Themes on South Asia, Voices of South Asian Women, and Children's Books with Themes on South Asia. There are related links to SASIALIT, a forum for discussion of South Asian Literature; *The South Asian Graduate Research Journal*; *South Asian American Literature*; and NAVRANG, a book shop dealing with South Asian books and literature.

Emory University Postcolonial Studies
http://www.emory.edu/ENGLISH/Bahri/
English Department, Emory University
- Indexes and Resource Lists, Literature
- All

This site offers an introduction to major topics and issues in postcolonial studies. The page is not exhaustive but is meant to offer a framework for study in the area. It includes an introduction plus pages on authors, theorists, terms, and issues. This site would be a good starting point for a study of the topic.

Introduction to Chicana/o Literature
http://www.en.utexas.edu/~sheilac/chicana.html
Sheila Contreras
- English, Literature, Spanish
- AP

This site is for and by college-level students. Under the direction of the instructor, it lists assignments, reading lists, links to related sites, and other information you would expect if you were taking a college-level course. However, a requirement of the course is that each student create and maintain a Web page. The pages are all here. So this is a beginning point in your research about Chicano literature, and it will require planning and perseverance on your part to glean information pertinent to your project. Of particular interest is the class interchanges button.

Italian Literature
http://www.italy1.com/literature/
Italy1
- Literature
- All

This is an excellent starting place to find information on Italian literature. The information is organized by centuries. The visitor can access any of the time periods to find a list of major authors and their works; in some cases commentary and/or analysis is included. The main page also includes a search feature if the time period is unknown.

The Lansdowne Local — Review of Southern African Literature
http://www.uct.ac.za/projects/poetry/reviews/reviews.htm
Lansdowne Review
- English, Literature
- All

As its name implies, this site reviews literature from southern Africa. In mid-1997, there were twenty reviews, some of specific books, such as Sarah Ruden's *Other Places*. Others addressed broader literary themes, such as "Ethics and Aesthetics in Nadine Gordimer's Fiction." There is no mention of archives of past reviews or how often the contents of this page are updated.

Latino Literature Web Page
http://www.ollusa.edu/alumni/alumni/latino/latinoh1.htm
Blanco-Cerda Communications
- Anthropology, Geography, Literature, Religion, Spanish
- 11, 12, AP

This page offers links to a variety of literature topics for all ages. The different subject areas covered include religion, mythology, Aztecs, and Mayans. The types of literature are also broken down into regions (Mexico, Central, and South America). The works are accessible via time period and author. Of special interest is a link to Mexican American folklore. This site is in English. Most links are in Spanish with a very few appearing in English.

✓ Planet Earth "Top 100 Sites on the Planet," Infoseek Select Site.

Literature in India: An Overview
http://www.stg.brown.edu/projects/hypertext/landow/post/india/indlitov.html
Scholarly Technology Group, Brown University
- Indexes and Resource Lists, Literature
- All

Literature of postcolonial India is the focus of this small resource page. There is a link to an alphabetical list of authors of the Indian subcontinent with works in English. There is also a link to literatures in indigenous languages, such as Tamil, and the Urdu Poetry Page.

Literature from Many Countries

http://www.xs4all.nl/~pwessel/country.html

Piet Wesselman

- English, Indexes and Resource Lists, Literature
- All

This page provides links to sites that offer information on literature from a specific country or region. Some of the countries represented are Afghanistan, Austria, Bulgaria, Finland, India, Japan, Nepal, the Philippines, and Venezuela. The sites offered, however, do not always provide the literature in an English translation.

Other Literatures Written in English—Voice of the Shuttle

http://humanitas.ucsb.edu/shuttle/english3.html

Voices of the Shuttle and Alan Liu, University of California, Santa Barbara

- English, Indexes and Resource Lists, Literature
- 11, 12, AP

This resource page links you to literature written in English by authors who are not American or British. There are links to Canadian, Caribbean, African, Scot, Welsh, and Irish sites among others. As with all Voices of the Shuttle sites, there are many historical and criticism sites.

OzLit@Vicnet — Australian Books, Australian Literature

http://yarra.vicnet.net.au/~ozlit/index.html

Mareya and Peter Schmidt

- English, Indexes and Resource Lists, Literature
- All

The goal of this site is to make Australian writers and literature better known throughout the world. The site is organized like a book: the Introduction has general information; Chapters 1 and 2 are links to Australian literature sites; Chapter 3 is OzLit Bookmarks; Chapter 4 contains links to literary sites; Chapter 5 provides research tools; and Chapter 6 is a poetry collection. The remaining Appendices contain items like an editorial, a searchable books and writers database, an authors' contact list, and links to Australian newspapers.

Russian Literature

http://www.bucknell.edu/departments/russian/ruslit.html

Robert Beard, Bucknell University

- Indexes and Resource Lists, Literature
- All

Russian literature is the focus of this Web site. There are links to General Literary Resources (such as the Bakhtin Center), the Public Electronic Library, and Russian Literature on the Net. The remainder of the site consists of a listing of seventeen major Russian writers. The works of each that are available on the Net—many only in Russian—and related links are given for each author. Some of the authors are Anna Akhmatova, Anton Chekhov, Fyodor Dostoevsky, Vladimir Nabokov, Boris Pasternak, Leo Tolstoy, and Ivan Turgenev.

West Indian Literature
http://members.home.net/westindiesbooks/
Patrick Jamieson
- English, Indexes and Resource Lists, Literature
- All

This page is a resource list on literature by West Indian authors, arranged alphabetically by author's last name. The first section on the page is a listing of books published in recent months that have not yet been added to the author listings. The rest of the site is best accessed by using the alphabet at the top of the page to view a list of authors and their publications.

See Also
PAGES DEVOTED TO SPECIFIC AUTHORS AND WORKS chapter (p 84)
Gaelic and Gaelic Culture http://sunsite.unc.edu/gaelic/gaelic.html (p 77)
Indigenous People's Literature http://www.indians.org/welker/natlit02.htm (p 70)
Internet Classics Archive http://classics.mit.edu/ (p 9)

PAGES DEVOTED TO SPECIFIC AUTHORS AND WORKS

Chinua Achebe: An Overview
http://www.stg.brown.edu/projects/hypertext/landow/post/achebe/achebeov.html

George Landow

- English, Indexes and Resource Lists, Literature
- AP

This resource page provides links to sophisticated criticism and analysis of the African author Chinua Achebe's works. Categories included in the discussion are history, politics, religion, setting, characterization, image and symbol, and narrative structure. (Caution: some sites are still under construction.) The entire enterprise is under the aegis of a larger program on postcolonial literature in English.

Deborah Adams
http://members.aol.com/dkadams/index.htm

Deborah Adams

- English, Literature
- All

This resource page promotes the author Deborah Adams and her series of Jesus Creek mysteries. Click on the cover of one of her books and you go to the first chapter. At the end of the chapter, there is a link to a biography page, which features an interview with the author and a photo.

Louisa May Alcott (1832-1888)
http://www.tetranet.net/users/stolbert/alcott/lma_main.html

Susan Lank Tolbert

- English, Literature
- All

This is a small page focusing on Louisa May Alcott. The visitor will find biographical and bibliographical information. The latter includes a list of books by her and an annotated bibliography of books about her. There is also a Photo Album that provides visual information and another on Alcott in the News.

Hans Christian Andersen: Fairy Tales and Stories
http://www.math.technion.ac.il/~rl/Andersen/

Zvi Har'El

- English, Literature
- All

At this useful site, you'll find a complete list of Andersen's 168 stories. Visitors may scroll the chronological list or search by cross-reference. The information on Andersen consists of an explanation of the list's notations, translations, and dates of publication. Of all his stories listed here, 128 are in hypertext, making this an excellent resource site on his work. The remaining are only listed.

The Sherwood Anderson Page
http://www.nwohio.com/clydeoh/sherwood.htm

Robert L. Liebold

- English, Literature
- All

Although attractive, there is not much to this page. It offers a brief biography, a photo, and information about the writer's hometown, including a directory. Most of the links are to current books about Anderson and his work.

✔ *Starting Point Hot Site.*

Maya Angelou Home Page
http://www.cwrl.utexas.edu/~mmaynard/Maya/maya5.html

University of Texas

- English, Literature
- All

The poetry and books of Maya Angelou can be accessed at this site. You will also find a biography, criticisms, an audio recording of her reading a poem, and a video of her speaking at the Million Man March. Among the eleven poems available are "The Black Family Pledge," "Insomniac," and "Still I Rise." The twelve books written by Angelou are not available on-line but are listed here for reference.

Maya Angelou Pages
http://members.aol.com/bonvibre/mangelou.html

Circle Association

- English, Indexes and Resource Lists, Literature
- 9, 10

This resource page provides links to biographical and bibliographical information, some of Maya Angelou's poems, and other resources on the Web. It may be fun to see pictures of the poet and read some of her poems, but working on a research paper you will need more substance. Luckily, this page links to Worldfests's More Links to Maya Angelou Page.

✔ *Fledge Approved by McGraw-Hill Home Interactive.*

Margaret Atwood Information
http://www.cariboo.bc.ca/ae/engml/FRIEDMAN/atwood.htm

Thomas B. Friedman

- English, Indexes and Resource Lists, Literature
- 12, AP

This resource page offers bibliographies, guides to the Canadian author's most popular books, background information, and links to quality sites. There are videos and speeches. Atwood's favorite charities and pet projects are here, too.

✔ *Selected by Women Celebrities.*

W. H. Auden (1907-1973)
http://www.lit.kobe-u.ac.jp/~hishika/auden.htm

Eiichi Hishikawa

- English, Indexes and Resource Lists, Literature
- All

This site offers a brief biography and critical treatment of Auden, links to his poetry, and an extensive bibliography. A treat is Auden's poem "Musée des Beaux Arts" linked to a picture of Breughel's painting "Fall of Icarus," which inspired it. But keep in mind that many textbooks offer the same combination. The bibliography is particularly helpful.

James Dawe's Jane Austen Page
http://www.ee.ualberta.ca/~dawe/austen.html

James Dawe

- English, Indexes and Resource Lists, Literature
- 11, 12, AP

This resource page holds biographical information and links to some esoteric Jane Austen trivia, such as a recipe for white soup. Also, it contains information about recent films, photos from the films, and links to the actors in the films. Hyperlinks take you to many other Austen sights, including university archives and electronic texts.

Jane Austen Campfire Chat
http://killdevilhill.com/janeaustenchat/wwwboard.html

Raft, Knottingham & McGucken

- English, Indexes and Resource Lists, Literature
- All

This resource page posts messages from Austen fans and readers who have questions or information about the great British author or her works. It's an informal site that tries to recreate the campfire experience by allowing everyone a chance to speak.

Jane Austen Info Page
http://uts.cc.utexas.edu/~churchh/janeinfo.html

University of Texas

- Literature
- All

A must bookmark for all Austen fans, this well-designed site lists the author's novels with links to E-texts. There are also brief discussions of each work, lists of Austen Web resources, links to other Jane Austen homepages, a selective bibliography, and even a "Jane Austen Top Ten Song List." Students will discover everything they ever wanted to know regarding the genealogy of the Bennets, the Bingleys, Mr. Collins, Mr. Darcy, and more.

Simone de Beauvoir
http://userzweb.lightspeed.net/~tameri/debeauv.html
Christopher Scott Wyatt
- English, French, Literature
- 11, 12, AP

	1	2	3	4	5
DEPTH/BREADTH			3		
QUALITY/ACCURACY				4	
RELEVANCE			3		
USEFULNESS					5
ENTERTAINMENT			3		

3   4   3   5   3   3

page. There is a short biography and commentary focusing on one of her works (*The Blood of Others*), a brief chronology, a listing of her works, quotes, and resources. The page also contains links to information on Jean-Paul Sartre, her colleague, friend, and lover.

Samuel Beckett
http://www.levity.com/corduroy/beckett.htm
Bohemian Ink
- Drama and Theater, English, Indexes and Resource Lists, Literature
- 11, 12, AP

This page provides an overview of the life and works of the writer. Further down the page there is a list of biographical and bibliographical information from which to research the Nobel Prize-winning author of the absurd. There are also essays and articles about Beckett and his works, links to other related sites, and a linked list of all of his works still in print available through Amazon.com.

Elizabeth Bishop
http://iberia.vassar.edu/bishop/
Barbara Page
- English, Indexes and Resource Lists, Literature
- 11, 12, AP

This site is under construction, but promises good things to come. It offers links to a biography of the American poet, a bibliography of works by her and about her, two Elizabeth Bishop societies, selected papers, and announcements. The biography and the bibliography present two valuable resources for students simply because they may have difficulty locating any of Bishop's works outside of anthologies.

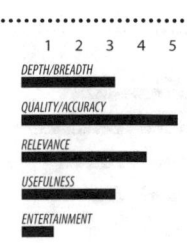

Blake Multimedia Project, The
http://www.multimedia.calpoly.edu/libarts/smarx/Blake/blakeproject.html
Steven Marx, English Professor
- English, Literature
- 11, 12, AP

Although as it is, this site only peeks the interest of surfers, it holds great promise. The Blake Multimedia project aims to study and teach Blake using computer technology. A sample page from the project appears here. Several others are linked to the page. You can also to see some of Blake's art. That's it for now. As yet, there are no links to a biography or bibliographies.

The William Blake Archive

http://www.iath.virginia.edu/blake/

Library of Congress, University of Virginia, and Sun Microsystems

- English, Literature
- All

This site was still under construction in mid-1997 but does have significant information for the visitor on the British poet William Blake. One can search the archive, view works in the archive by Blake and his circle, link to a selected bibliography, view the plan of the archive, and read an archive update. There is also a related sites link and a user comments area.

Judy Blume's Home Base

http://www.judyblume.com/home-menu.html

Judy Blume

- English, Literature, Writing
- 9, 10

For high schoolers, this page may be a turnoff because it is directed to a younger audience. But the information offered is valuable for anyone reading the author's young adult books and especially for anyone who has ever thought about writing. The author provides candid information through encouraging and brief essays and thoughtful answers to questions posed by young writers. Special links to a subject close to the author are included—you guessed it, to sites about censorship.

Gwendolyn Brooks Page

http://members.aol.com/bonvibre/gbrooks.html

The Circle Association

- English, Indexes and Resource Lists, Literature
- All

This site contains a photo of Gwendolyn Brooks, selections from her poems, a brief biography, a selected bibliography of her works, and links to other Circle Association sites featuring African American writers.

Elizabeth Barrett Browning: An Overview

http://www.stg.brown.edu/projects/hypertext/landow/victorian/ebb/browning2ov.html

George Landow, Brown University

- English, Indexes and Resource Lists, Literature
- All

This is an excellent resource site for the study of Elizabeth Barrett Browning and her work. Links are organized under Biographical Materials, Other Works, Literary Relations, The Cultural Context of Victorianism, Religion and Philosophy, Social and Political Contexts, and Science and Technology. Under Theme and Technique can be found links to Themes, Imagery, Symbolism and Motifs, and Genre and Mode.

Burns—The National Bard
http://www.glen.co.uk/culture/burns.html
Glen Internet
- English, Literature
- All

Robert Burns, the national bard of Scotland, has several of his more well-known works showcased on this Web site. After a short overview of his life, five works are listed: "Green Grow the Rashes, O," "To a Mouse," "Scots Wha Hae," "Auld Lang Syne," and "My Heart's in the Highlands." The text of each is provided with a brief description, which emphasizes the lasting impact of Burns's work.

Edgar Rice Burroughs: From Africa to Mars
http://www.wowdesign.com/erb/main.htm
Robert Greer, Northwestern State University
- English, Literature
- 4 4 3 3 3 3

This page puts the work of Edgar Rice Burroughs in the context of his time—the early 20th century—and shows how he reflected the concerns of the day. The site includes a biography, sections on Tarzan and Barsoom, a conclusion, and links to related sites. Especially in the coverage of the Tarzan and Mars serials, this page provides insight into Burroughs's own personal perspective and his criteria for exemplary moral citizenship.

William S. Burroughs
http://studwww.rug.ac.be/~fvcauwel/burrough.html
Flo at Ghent University
- English, Literature
- AP

This page represents the enthusiastic contribution of an erudite Burroughs fan. Here you'll find an introduction to the writer and his work, some pictures, a snippet of a letter to Allen Ginsberg, the glossary from Burroughs's "Junky," an appreciation by Timothy Leary, and links to sites on the Beat poets and Jack Kerouac.

The William S. Burroughs Files
http://www.hyperreal.com/wsb
Malcolm Humes
- English, Literature
- 11, 12, AP

This page is a reference guide to works of William S. Burroughs, his literary works, recordings, film/video appearances, and other publications. There are links to personal information, a bibliography of his works, and sites of related interest.

Selected Poetry of George Gordon, Lord Byron
http://library.utoronto.ca/www/utel/rp/authors/byron.html
University of Toronto
- English, Literature
- All

Part of the Representative Poetry On-line Project, this site contains twenty-five links to Lord Byron's Poems. His most famous, "Don Juan," is represented by Cantos 1, 2, 4, 8, 11, and 12. There are also only excerpts from *English Bards and Scotch Reviewers*, "Lara," "Childe Harold's Pilgrimage" (Cantos 3 and 4), and "The Vision of Judgment." Other poems, including "Prometheus," "Epistle to Augusta," and "Darkness," are available in full text.

Albert Camus
http://members.aol.com/KatharenaE/private/Philo/Camus/camus.html
Katharena Eiermann
- English, French, Literature
- 11, 12, AP

This site provides information on the French novelist, essayist, and Nobel Prize winner Albert Camus. There is biographical information; a Camus Sampler, including *The Absurd Man* and *The Minotaur*; links to movies based on his works; and essays, reviews, and study guides. The visitor can also follow links to other Camus pages and further information on Existentialism.

Thomas Carlyle
http://www.stg.brown.edu/projects/hypertext/landow/victorian/carlyle/carlyleov.html
George Landow, Brown University
- English, Literature
- All

This site puts the writer and historian Thomas Carlyle in the context of his time. The visitor can access a biography and a list of his works as well as information on Victorianism and Science, Literary Relations, Visual Arts, and Religion and Philosophy. For the visitor who needs specific information on his style, there are links to Themes, Symbolism, Characterization, Narration, and Genre. This site is a comprehensive one for the student doing research on Carlyle or his period.

Lewis Carroll Home Page
http://www.lewiscarroll.org/carroll.html
Joel M. Birenbaum
- English, Indexes and Resource Lists, Literature
- All

This Web site offers four areas for the student of Lewis Carroll and his works. Under Carroll's Genius one can access on-line texts, photos, games, and riddles. In Carroll Studies there are links to academic information, publications, and references. The Communication Area accesses Carroll Societies, a bulletin board, a discussion board, and contacts. Students will find The Fun Stuff area particularly interesting; here they can find information on Carroll in the popular culture, graphics, places, and things to buy.

✔ *Magellan 4 Star Site, Iway 500 Site, WebScout Way Cool Site, POINTCommunications Top 5% Web Site.*

The Rachel Carson Issues Forum
http://www.dep.state.pa.us/dep/Rachel_Carson/Rachel_Carson.htm
Department of Environmental Protection, Harrisburg, PA
- Environmental Studies, Literature
- All

While primarily a site dedicated to environmental issues, this page shows the impact a piece of literature can have on society. The publication of *Silent Spring* in 1962 brought environmental threats to public attention. At this site, the student of literature can link to a biography of Rachel Carson and the Rachel Carson Homestead Association. The student interested in environmental issues can find more information on Carson's Innovative Ideas, Issues/Programs, Observations and Remarks, and Speeches.

Willa Cather Page
http://icg.harvard.edu/~cather/
Instructional Computing Group, Harvard University
- English, Literature
- All

This site provides information on Willa Cather's life and works, with many hyperlinks to places she lived and people she knew. The visitor to this page can link to Events, Publications, Locations, Quotations, Biography, and Other. Each category provides you with additional areas to explore to find more information about this famous Nebraska author.

Baragona's Chaucer Page
http://www.vmi.edu/~english/chaucer.html
Alan Baragona, Department of English and Fine Arts, Virginia Military Institute
- English, Indexes and Resource Lists, Literature
- 11, 12, AP

This resource page is a guide to Internet resources for the study of Chaucer. A variety of bibliographies, including Baragona's Unsystematic Bibliography, and texts of Chaucer's tales, are available. Click enough buttons and, if you have the appropriate plug-ins, there are audios of the music of the Chaucerian era. This is a good resource if you get stuck with too little resource material and you aren't afraid of using interlibrary loan to get some of the more obscure publications.

G. K. Chesterton
http://www.dur.ac.uk/~dcs0mpw/gkc/
Martin Ward, University of Durham
- English, Literature
- All

This is a page of resources and information on Gilbert Keith Chesterton, the versatile British writer. The visitor will find a biography and links to other resources including a listing of Chesterton's works on the Web, a picture archive, and works about him by Hilaire Belloc and John C. Tibbets. Of special interest is the related links area that reflects Chesterton's varied interests and influences; it includes, for example, links to The Hilaire Belloc Page as well as Christian Resources on the Net.

The Noam Chomsky Archive
http://www.worldmedia.com/archive/index.html

New World Media

- Current Events, English, Literature, Political Science, U.S. History
- 11, 12, AP

Chomsky may not write as well as George Orwell but he is certainly as tireless a commentator on doublespeak and double standards. This resource page provides links to audios of Chomsky's speeches and most recent articles. If you like what you read, you can purchase his books. Categories on the page are for audio, on-line books, 'zine articles, and Lies of Our Times letters. A special feature is an interview of Chomsky by the rap-metal band Rage Against the Machine.

The Kate Chopin Project
http://www.lacollege.edu/chopin/chopin.html

Honors English Program, Louisiana College

- English, Indexes and Resource Lists, Literature
- All

This resource page connects anyone interested in Kate Chopin and her works to four areas of the Kate Chopin Project: a biography of the writer, Chopin's short stories, a bibliography, and a list of contributors to the project. Most helpful are the biography and the short stories, which are hyperlinked to annotations and critical analyses. The project is supposed to be ongoing, but there is no evidence of recent updates to the page.

"Forever Pedaling the Road to Realism"—Robert Cormier's World in the High School Literature Classroom
http://www.uiowa.edu/~english/litcult2097/tlucht/lit-teachingcormier.html

Thorven Lucht

- English, Indexes and Resource Lists, Literature
- 9, 10

This page contains several essays about Cormier and his works, with tips for lessons. The page focuses on three realistic novels by Cormier: *After the First Death*, *I Am the Cheese*, and *The Chocolate War*. Another essay discusses the autobiographical elements in *Fade*. The page can make your research fun and help you make some good points in a report. Also, the page lists a bibliography and related links.

Stephen Crane: Man, Myth, and Legend
http://www.en.utexas.edu/~mmaynard/Crane/crane.html

Michele Maynard, University of Texas at Austin

- English, Literature
- All

If you're reading or researching Stephen Crane you will find much useful information at this site. There's a brief biography, links to related sites, common themes and issues, literary techniques, a list of his most famous works, and a bibliography. For additional interest, there are also links to images of Crane and sound clips of the opening passages of several of his works.

e. e. cummings
http://www.imsa.edu/~junkee/cummings.html

Moe Chaddha

- English, Literature
- All

This e. e. cummings page offers a short biography, a selection from his over nine hundred poems, and a listing of other links. The fifty-two poems available at this site reflect cummings's innovative punctuation, capitalization, and word order. For example, "anyone lived in a pretty how town" or "Me up at does" are two representative of his style.

An Unofficial E. E. Cummings Starting Point
http://www.voicenet.com/~dougw/cummings.html

Douglas M. Wipf

- English, Indexes and Resource Lists, Literature
- All

The author of this resource page does not lie when he says this is a starting point. (cummings, ever the opponent of dishonesty—or is it nontruthfulness?—would appreciate the truth of the page title but perhaps not so much the capitalization of his name, e. e. cummings.) What you get is a short bibliography, a chronology of the life of cummings, and links to related sites.

Roald Dahl Home Page, The
http://www.nd.edu/~khoward1/Roald.html

Kristine Howard

- English, Indexes and Resource Lists, Literature
- All

At this resource page devoted to Roald Dahl, visitors can find a biography, a bibliography, The Dahl Catalogue, a list of Dahl booksellers, a timeline, photo archives, and related links. Anyone seeking more information on this popular children's author should check out this site.

Dante Alighieri on the Web
http://www.geocities.com/Athens/9039/main.htm

Carlo Alberto Furia

- Literature
- All

The Italian poet Dante Alighieri is the focus of this Web site. There is a Why Dante page as well as pages on His Time, His Work, His Life, and a glossary. Several of his works are available for downloading from this site, including *The Ecologues* and *Detto d'Amore*. Recently, audioclips have been added. There are also links to related sites.

Charles Dickens

http://www.bibliomania.com/Fiction/dickens/DickensIntro.html

Bob Heaman

- English, Indexes and Resource Lists, Literature
- 11, 12, AP

This site contains a long essay about Charles Dickens and his works. At the bottom of the page is the Bibliomania search engine, WebGlimpse. Use it to find references or links to information about Dickens, his writing, characters from his books, or anything else; search the essay for this information or search the Bibliomania archive—and go directly to the line of the work where the information you request is found.

Charles Dickens, The *Great Expectations* Index

http://www.vanderbilt.edu/AnS/english/English104W-15/greatexpectations[index].htm

Gregg A. Hecimovich

- English, Literature
- All

This resource site is part of a larger package offered by a university professor. You'll find a digitized version of *Great Expectations*, notes on the novel, student commentary, and links to related sites. The notes section includes information on the composition of the novel, its plot, its publication and reception, criticism, and a separate index for *Oliver Twist*.

The Dickens Page

http://lang.nagoya-u.ac.jp/~matsuoka/Dickens.html

Mitsharu Matsuoka, Nagoya University

- English, Indexes and Resource Lists, Literature
- All

This exhaustive site is dedicated to Charles Dickens and his contemporaries. Links are provided to the Dickens Fellowship, the Dickens Society, the Dickens Project, and mailing lists, as well as to the Victorian Web, homepages, a chronology, a bibliography, works and E-texts, and academic and recreational resources. The What's New category contains an extensive listing of Dickens-related information and sites, some commercial, which have been added in 1997.

Emily Dickinson

http://lal.cs.byu.edu/people/black/dickinson.html

Paul Black, Brigham Young University

- English, Literature
- All

The entire body of Dickinson's works is available to download at or through links from this site. There are also biographical links, a timeline, critical essays, an E-mail discussion list, links to audio recordings, and even Dickinson poems translated into Russian and Polish.

✔ LookSmart Editor's Choice. "This is an asset for the casual student of Dickinson as well as the more studious researcher."—*Rose E. Cerny, Maple Valley Schools, Vermontville, MI.*

Emily Dickinson
http://www.geocities.com/Paris/LeftBank/3607/emily.htm

Erin Marie

- English, Literature
- All

This site is managed by a seventeen-year-old high school student who's an Emily Dickinson fan. It is straightforward in its presentation. You get a photo of the poet and selections for biography written by the student, favorite poems, and links to other sites with Dickinson for a subject. These links to other sites are helpful. If you are beginning your research on Dickinson, this site is a good introduction and a fine jumping off point for more involved research. All visitors are invited to sign Erin Marie's guestbook.

A Guide to the Works of John Donne
http://www.total.net/~impulsar/donne.html

Ross O'Connell

- English, Literature
- All

This resource site links visitors to pages containing information on the life and works of the English poet John Donne. The page links to five sites, the most significant being that of Anniina Jokinen on Donne; another link takes the visitor to the University of Missouri Press where books about Donne may be ordered. The page also contains the text of several of Donne's works—"The Bait," "The Flea," and "Meditation 17" from *Devotions upon Emergent Occasions*.

Fyodor Dostoevsky
http://grove.ufl.edu/~flask/Dostoevsky.html

University of Florida

- Indexes and Resource Lists, Literature
- All

This well-rounded site starts with a biographical sketch, a chronology, and a bibliography. It also has nine images of the author and family members in GIF format. There are links to his major works in English translation, such as *The Brothers Karamazov* and *Crime and Punishment*. There are additional links to information on Russian literature, film adaptations of his works, St. Petersburg, the Russian Orthodox Church, and other Dostoevsky pages.

Rita Dove Page
http://members.aol.com/bonvibre/rdove.html

The Circle Association

- English, Indexes and Resource Lists, Literature
- All

This site contains a photo of Rita Dove, selections of her work, a brief biography (under construction), a selected bibliography of her works (under construction), and links to an interview with the poet and other sites featuring African-American writers. Several selections of the poetry on the page are accompanied by the artwork mentioned in the poetry.

221B Baker Street: Sherlock Holmes

http://www.cs.cmu.edu/afs/andrew.cmu.edu/usr18/mset/www/holmes.html

Michael Sherman

- English, Literature
- All

This site provides access to forty-eight of the sixty Sherlock Holmes stories written by Sir Arthur Conan Doyle. For the visitor who needs specific references, there is a word search that searches the stories for a specific word or phrase. There is also an area of illustrations from several of the stories and an extensive listing of related links to help researchers.

✔ *Magellan 4 Star Site, Star Five of the Web, Mèdaille d'Or.*

Sherlockian Holmepage

http://watserv1.uwaterloo.ca/~credmond/sh.html

Chris Redmond, University of Waterloo

- Drama and Theater, English, Indexes and Resource Lists, Literature
- All

A page that not only contains listings of the original Sherlock Holmes stories and a biography of Arthur Conan Doyle but virtually any item related to the fictional character. Here the visitor can find lists of Sherlockian resources on the Web; stage, screen, and television adaptations; Sherlock Holmes Societies, with homepages of individual members; Sherlockian things for sale; companies called Sherlock; and other notes. There are also links to libraries with Holmes collections. From this page one can also link to a number of sites in the following categories: mysteries in general, England and the Victorian era, and science fiction, horror, and kindred fields.

The T. S. Eliot Page

http://virtual.park.uga.edu/~232/eliot.taken.html

Bruce Bong

- English, Literature
- All

A helpful site on T. S. Eliot offering texts of his works as well as criticisms, parodies, and allusions to his work. The Eliot Cluster contains useful background works on Eliot; there are links to a mailing list and discussion groups as well as other sites and biographies. The bulk of the site consists of a listing of his major works. Some listings, such as "The Love Song of J. Alfred Prufrock," "The Wasteland," and "The Hollow Men," include allusions and sources, criticism, parodies, and mentions in other works besides the text. Other works listed have only the text available: "Preludes," "The Journey of the Magi," "Ash Wednesday," "Four Quartets," and "Macavity: The Mystery Cat."

Invisible Man

http://www.randomhouse.com/knopf/read/invisible/invisible.html

Reading Group Center, Vintage Books

- English, Literature
- All

This page exists to stimulate thinking about Ralph Ellison's book. It features a link to biographical information, which is helpful, but further down the page there are discussion questions, suggestions for further reading, and other books by Ellison available from Vintage.

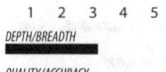

Erasmus Text Project
http://smith2.sewanee.edu/Erasmus/etp.html
The University of the South
- Literature, Philosophy, World History
- 11, 12, AP

The works of Desiderius Erasmus are the focus of this site. The visitor can view graphics by Albrecht Dürer and download several of Erasmus's works in the original Latin or in translation. Works at the site in mid-1997 included *Colloquia*, *Moriae Encomium*, and *The Praise of Folly*. The goal of the project is to get more of Erasmus's works on-line as soon as possible.

William Faulkner on the Web
http://www.mcsr.olemiss.edu/~egjbp/faulkner/faulkner.html
John B. Padgett
- English, Indexes and Resource Lists, Literature
- 11, 12, AP

An exhaustive treatment of America's premiere writer—meaning there's lots of stuff here that can be used for papers and, if you are reading one of Faulkner's books, that will help you understand what's happening in it. Characters and places from the stories get linked to a Faulkner Glossary with links to more explanations. You can have some fun here, too: A Faulkner Playroom connects to trivia and quotes. Down one side of the homepage is a column for announcements of events that have to do with Faulkner and/or his writing.

✔ Magellan 3 Star Site, LookSmart Editor's Choice, POINTCommunications Top 5% Web Site.

F. Scott Fitzgerald Centenary
http://www.sc.edu/fitzgerald/index.html
University of South Carolina
- English, Indexes and Resource Lists, Literature
- All

This site provides links to pages having to do with F. Scott Fitzgerald's writings and life. Its outstanding feature is the archive of audio and film clips featuring the celebrated author reading selections from Keats and Shakespeare. Photos of the author are included with separate listings. There is also a chronology of his life, essays and writings, a bibliography, a brief biography, and information about his publisher. Updated regularly but not frequently.

Yellow Wallpaper, The
http://www.media.mit.edu/people/davet/yp/
David Tames
- Drama and Theater, English, Literature, Writing
- 9, 10

This site provides information about the David Tames film based on the Charlotte Perkins Gilman short story, "The Yellow Wallpaper." The film is not found at the site. However, you can read the script from the film and the text of the short story to compare them. There also are a few still photos from the film. If you're thinking about writing a movie script of your own, here's a good working model.

English & Literature

Johann Wolfgang von Goethe
http://members.aol.com/KatharenaE/private/Pweek/Goethe/goethe.html
Katharena Eiermann
- English, Indexes and Resource Lists, Literature
- 11, 12, AP

Goethe's life, works, and current place in history all get their own treatment on this thoughtful and well-organized page, which even provides background music from the era in which Goethe lived. Also, a good sampling of his works are linked to the page, as are other informative sites, including study guides and literary criticism.

✔ Great Books 5-Star Site.

Lord of the Flies
http://www.pernet.net/~chadly1/lord_of_the_flies/index.html
Chad Johnson and Emily Hicks
- English, Literature
- All

This very colorful page is devoted to William Golding's novel *Lord of the Flies*. The visitor will find helpful information organized under the headings Golding, Plot, Character Sketches, and the Island. There are also links to Criticism and Commentary, Themes, and Other Resources. This page will help students assigned to read this novel.

Nadine Gordimer: An Overview
http://www.stg.brown.edu/projects/hypertext/landow/post/gordimer/gordimerov.html
Scholarly Technology Group, Brown University
- English, Literature
- All

At this uniquely organized Web site on Nadine Gordimer, the visitor is presented with a grid of fifteen topics. Choosing any topic will bring up information culled from Gordimer's works and/or times that are related to the topic. The topics are Works, Post-Colonial Overview, Literary Relations, History, Politics, Religion, Science and Technology, Visual Arts, Theme and Subject, Genre, Characterization, Setting, Image and Symbol, Narrative Structure, and Bibliography.

The Robert Graves Society Information Centre
http://www.nene.ac.uk/graves/graves.html/
Ian Firla
- English, Indexes and Resource Lists, Literature
- 11, 12, AP

A wide variety of information, especially bibliographies of Robert Graves's poetry, drama, fiction, nonfiction, and editorships and translations, appears here. You'll also find information about and the contents of *Gravesiana*, the journal of the society. Aside from the bibliographies, a brief biography gives a good overview of the work and the life of this twentieth-century writer.

Graham Greene
http://www.umsl.edu/~s1006642/
Anne Sherry
- English, Literature
- 11, 12, AP

Although still under construction, this resource page promises good things about the British author some people consider one of the greatest English writers of the twentieth century. Links include "Fiction to Film," "About Graham Greene," "A List of Greene's Writings," "An Excerpt from *The Heart of the Matter*," "A Note from the Author [of this page]," "The Reader Reaction Form," "Slightly Relevant Sites," and "Guestbook."

American Scenes: Lorraine Hansberry
http://www.en.utexas.edu/~daniel/amlit/scenes.html
Daniel Anderson, University of Texas at Austin
- Drama and Theater, English, Literature
- All

This is an excellent resource page on Hansberry's *Raisin in the Sun*, covering both the play and the 1961 film version. The visitor can access a transcript of an electronic discussion about the play as well as eleven other critical essays concerning aspects of the work. For example, there is a discussion of African culture, heritage, assimilation, and tradition; an analysis of pride in the Younger family; and a discussion of the generation gaps shown in the work.

Nathaniel Hawthorne
http://www.tiac.net/users/eldred/nh/hawthorne.html
Eric Eldred, eldred@tiac.net
- Literature
- All

Everything you could possibly want to know about the author of *The Scarlet Letter*—and probably a good deal more—can be found at this site or by its links to related Web sites. Created by a Hawthorne fanatic, this site includes an extensive timeline of dates and events, a biographical summary, E-texts for most of his novels, sketches, and magazine pieces—even a description of a dinner with Henry Thoreau. Also found here are bibliographies of Hawthorne's writings and criticism, favorite quotes by the master, memoirs of him by contemporaries, and much more. Do you know the relation between Hawthorne and Mount Everest, Neil Simon, Lionel Trilling, Rube Goldberg, MGM, Cal Coolidge, Meyer Lansky, and Henrietta Leavitt (the Cepheid variables astronomer)? See if more people celebrate on Hawthorne's birthday than celebrate on John Lennon's.

Seamus Heaney
http://sunsite.unc.edu/dykki/poetry/heaney/heaney-cov.html
University of North Carolina
- English, Literature
- All

This site is devoted to Seamus Heaney, the Irish Nobel Laureate poet. The student can link to nine of his major poems: "Personal Helicon," "Bogland," "Tollund Man," "Casualty," "Song," "Harvest Bow," "From Clearances-3," "From Clearances-5," and "From Lightenings." In addition, there is a bibliography, a biography, the texts of his Nobel Citation, his Nobel Lecture, and his commencement address at the University of North Carolina, Chapel Hill, on 12 May 1996.

English & Literature

1 2 3 4 5
DEPTH/BREADTH
QUALITY/ACCURACY
RELEVANCE
USEFULNESS
ENTERTAINMENT

Ernest Hemingway Campfire Chat
http://killdevilhill.com/hemingwaychat/wwwboard.html

Raft, Knottingham & McGucken

- English, Indexes and Resource Lists, Literature
- All

This resource page posts messages from Hemingway aficionados and readers who have questions or information about the great American author or his works. It's an informal site that tries to recreate the campfire experience by allowing everyone a chance to speak.

---

1 2 3 4 5
DEPTH/BREADTH
QUALITY/ACCURACY
RELEVANCE
USEFULNESS
ENTERTAINMENT

Ernest M. Hemingway's Home Page
http://rio.atlantic.net/~gagne/hem/hem.html

English Department, University of Florida

- Indexes and Resource Lists, Literature
- All

Discover the genius of Ernest Hemingway. Explore themes of love and warfare, courage and death—all captured by Hemingway's concise narrative style. Of all the Hemingway links on the Internet, this one is the most thorough. There is a growing collection of essays and papers written by and about the author, links to a timeline of Hemingway's life, a large picture album on the Papa Page, and lots of quotes and quips—all just a click away.

---

1 2 3 4 5
DEPTH/BREADTH
QUALITY/ACCURACY
RELEVANCE
USEFULNESS
ENTERTAINMENT

The Papa Page
http://www.ee.mcgill.ca/~nverever/hem/cover.html

Marcel Mitran

- English, Indexes and Resource Lists, Literature
- 11, 12, AP

This resource site has everything you ever wanted to know about Hemingway. Click on Hemingway and enter a page filled with links to biographical, bibliographical, anecdotal, and pictorial gems. A favorite is the link to the stories Hemingway wrote as a cub reporter at the *Kansas City Star*. Not only are the stories interesting and models of good journalism—they are linked to the story behind the story, anecdotes about the young Hemingway and his exploits.

✔ POINTCommunications Top 5% Web Site, GNN Map Site, Magellan 3 Star Site. "The ultimate Hemingway page! Pictures, bibliographies, quotes and a wonderful biography." —Infoseek Guide.

---

1 2 3 4 5
DEPTH/BREADTH
QUALITY/ACCURACY
RELEVANCE
USEFULNESS
ENTERTAINMENT

Zora Neale Hurston
http://pages.prodigy.com/zora/index.htm

Kip Hinton

- English, Indexes and Resource Lists, Literature
- All

4   5   5   5   5   5

This lively and colorful resource page offers stories, photographs, information, and links to related sites; all with a fondness and appreciation for the African-American writer Zora Neale Hurston. Get a flavor for her work by clicking on the story button; see what she looked like by clicking on the photographs button; find out what others think of her work by clicking on the information button; and locate bibliographical information by clicking on the links button. There is even a video for you to download.

✔ POINTCommunications Top 5% Web Site.

Zora Neale Hurston (1901-1960)
http://www.cwrl.utexas.edu/~gsiesing/316/collaborative/hurston/

Colin, Kristin, and Jason, students at the University of Texas

- English, Indexes and Resource Lists, Literature
- 11, 12, AP

This resource page is a project put together by college students. It has links to a biography and bibliography of Hurston's works. Several essays interpret and analyze her work. Photos are a bonus.

Eugène Ionesco (1912-1994)
http://www.levity.com/corduroy/ionesco.htm

Dan Levy

- Drama and Theater, English, Literature
- 11, 12, AP

This limited site is devoted to the Romanian playwright Eugène Ionesco. There is a brief biography taken from the *Grolier Encyclopedia* and several links to material by Ionesco: *The Bald Soprano*, *Exit the King*, and *Fire*. There is general information on Romanians and their contributions to the world, an essay on "The Meaning of Life" in *Rhinoceros*, information on the *Evergreen Review Reader*, and other interpretations of his work. There is also a link to Amazon.com with a list of his works available for purchase.

A Very Unofficial John Irving Page
http://members.aol.com/forestben/irving.htm

Ben, an Irving Aficionado

- English, Indexes and Resource Lists, Literature
- All

This unofficial page contains some official bibliographies. Also, there are links to Web sites with more information about Irving. But the charm of this site is in its enthusiasm for Irving and his works; as a result, you get informal polls about Irving's best work and which one of his novels should be made into a film. Also, there is lots of feedback from people who've visited the page and have E-mailed comments. These get "published."

Henry James Scholar's Guide to Web Sites
http://www.newpaltz.edu/~hathaway/

Richard Hathaway, State University of New York (SUNY) New Paltz

- English, Indexes and Resource Lists, Literature
- All

This resource page offers an exhaustive list of sites pertaining to Henry James, including the Henry James E-journal and links to the several Henry James E-texts at New Paltz. There are also links to texts at other sites, Jamesf-1 (a bulletin board), Henry James conferences, homepages of authors, academic links, library and college homepages, teaching ideas, and materials and general information about using the Web.

Samuel Johnson

http://www.english.upenn.edu/~jlynch/Johnson/index.html

Jack Lynch

- English, Indexes and Resource Lists, Literature
- 11, 12, AP

If you want to know something about Johnson, his life, or his work, this page has it. The page is well-planned and everything on it is relevant to the subject. The page begins with a guide to Johnson followed by links to electronic texts by Johnson and others on Johnson, to scholarship and books on Johnson, to quotes from *Bartlett's*, and to other search engines. Johnson would be proud.

James Joyce Web Page

http://www.ozemail.com.au/~caveman/Joyce/

Charles Cave

- English, Indexes and Resource Lists, Literature
- 11, 12, AP

The Irish writer James Joyce is the focus of this Web site. The items linked on this site are heavily Australian-oriented, such as brochures from "Bloomsday" in Sydney, but the site does offer material for the student researcher. There is, for example, a Joyce bibliography, information on David Norris' *Joyce for Beginners*, an essay, and quotations from *Ulysses*. This is an idiosyncratic personal page that details the sponsor's growing interest in Joyce; much of the content, including the numerous listing of Web pages, reflects his tastes.

Ulysses for Dummies

http://www.bway.net/~hunger/ulysses.html

From Hunger

- English, Literature
- All

James Joyce, whose *Ulysses* is being presented for "dummies," had a sense of humor and so does this site. *Ulysses* can seem a tangled mess for the beginner. At the same time that this site parodies Joyce's style, it offers a crib of the plot. This is a valuable aid for anyone encountering the novel for the first, second, or third time. In so many words, this site offers a comic book version of *Ulysses* in the best sense of the word "comic."

Work in Progress: A James Joyce Website

http://www.2street.com/joyce/

R. L. Callahan, Temple University

- Indexes and Resource Lists, Literature
- 11, 12, AP

Everything you want to know about Irish novelist James Joyce can be found at this site. A timeline from the life and works of Joyce, audio files of Joyce reading his own works, links to the court cases about his works, discussion groups (both E-mail and real-time), links to off-site resources, and electronic texts are all here. (U.S. users are warned that accessing some of the electronic texts may violate copyright laws.) Associates of Joyce and characters from his books as well as keywords from his works are hyperlinked to a variety of sources such as maps, audio files, timelines, and a photo gallery.

The Castle: Joseph K.'s Franz Kafka Homepage
http://www.fairhavenuhs.k12.vt.us/TheCastle/

C. M. Wisniewski

- English, Indexes and Resource Lists, Literature
- 11, 12, AP

This resource page offers links to biographical and bibliographical information on Franz Kafka. Also featured are a chronology of the Czech author's life, some creative writing by the page sponsor, a search for information link, a master's degree-level exam, Kafka's texts, and related sites.

✔ *Gamespot HotSpot, POINTCommunications Top 5% Web Site.*

Jack Kerouac (1922-1964)
http://www.levity.com/corduroy/kerouac.htm

Bohemian Ink

- English, Indexes and Resource Lists, Literature
- 11, 12, AP

This resource page offers a brief biography, an excerpt from *On the Road*, and many links to sites featuring Kerouac's writing or information about Kerouac. Several links provide audios of Kerouac reading from his works. Categories include Homepages, Biographies, Bibliographies; Works Online; Articles, Essays, Reviews; Mailing List; Newsgroup; Kerouac Recordings; Jack Kerouac at Amazon.com; and Other Links.

Omar Khayyam
http://www-leland.stanford.edu/~yuri/Omar/omar.html

Yuri Takhteyev

- Geography, Literature, Math, Religion, World History
- All

Omar Khayyam, the author of the *Rubayyat*, was also a mathematician. This site will not only give you an overview of Khayyam's life and works, but also a view of the culture and geography of Iran at his time.

Stephen King WebSite
http://www.pobox.com/~jepace/king.html

James Pace

- English, Literature
- All

The depth of material related to Stephen King found at this site attests to the popularity of horror fiction. This site has links to a number of sites; a FAQ; King's mailing address; lists of his works, movies, and works on audiocassette; and *Phantasmagoria*, the Stephen King newsletter. The visitor will also find here a link to the Stephen King Newsgroup, the Betts Bookstore, various publishers of horror fiction, as well as personal pages in English, German, and French.

English & Literature

Complete Collection of Poems by Rudyard Kipling
http://www.rit.edu/~exb1874/mine/kipling/kipling_ind.html

Edward Bonver

- English, Literature
- All

The title of this site accurately describes its contents: all of Kipling's poems will be found here in an alphabetical list. The visitor may use the letter index to go to a listing of titles beginning with that letter or may use the search engine designed for the site's poetry pages.

The "White Man's Burden" and Its Critics
http://www.rochester.ican.net/~fjzwick/kipling

Jim Zwick

- English, Journalism, Literature, U.S. History, World History
- All

When published in *McClure's Magazine* in February 1899, Rudyard Kipling's poem "The White Man's Burden" reflected the then current debate on the benefits and costs of imperialism. The site offers the original of the poem in *McClure's* as well as a racial cartoon interpreting its meaning in the Philippines, which appeared in the *Detroit Journal* in February 1899. The majority of the site, however, is devoted to discussion of the topic in the press of the day; links included range from Senator Benjamin Tillman's speech in the U.S. Senate on 7 February 1899 to a poem by C. E. D. Phelps, published on 12 December 1903, entitled "The Burden of Profit."

Horagai: Abe Kobo
http://www.win.or.jp/~horagai/abe/xabe000.html

Kato Koiti, Horagai

- Literature
- All

This Japanese-based site has a few areas that are only in Japanese. However, students who want to know more about Abe Kobo, a prominent Japanese author, can find the basic information here in English. The site contains a brief biography, a bibliography, how his contemporaries read him, E-mail correspondence on him, and other Abe Kobo sources on the Web. There is also an interesting image of his manuscript of *The Face of Another* in the original Japanese.

Mothers Who Think: Word by Word—Annie Lamott's On-line Diary
http://www.salonmagazine.com/july97/mothers/lamott.html

Salon Magazine

- English, Literature, Writing
- 11, 12, AP

This page contains the latest essay by Annie Lamott, a living American writer who writes everyday. Turn to this page if you need some inspiration for your essay assignment. Also, find here links to previous essays that make up Lamott's on-line diary, plus connections to the *Salon Magazine* homepage, its archives, and other related links.

D. H. Lawrence
http://home.clara.net/rananim/lawrence/
The Rananim Society
- English, Indexes and Resource Lists, Literature
- All

This site, sponsored by a D. H. Lawrence E-mail discussion group, offers biographical information about the British author and plenty of other anecdotal information from members of the sponsoring organization, including lively essays. Aside from the repartee, there are bibliographies and links to other Lawrence sites on the Web. Several links connect you with Lawrence's fiction and poems. In a special treat, the Shakespearean actor Kenneth Branagh reads one of the poems to you.

Doris Lessing: A Retrospective
http://tile.net/lessing/
Jan Hanford
- English, Indexes and Resource Lists, Literature
- 11, 12, AP

There are many lists linked off of this page: to Lessing's fiction, drama, and poetry—searchable by publisher or by title and cross-referenced with other publications. Occasionally a link will present an excerpt or a Real Audio snippet to whet the appetite. Most valuable are the selections under her life and bibliography: what follows is a detailed biography, an extensive bibliography, photos, and awards. Several interviews are featured in a separate section that provide insight into the writer and her works.

The Jack London Collection
http://sunsite.Berkeley.Edu/London/
Berkeley Digital Library SunSITE
- English, Literature
- All

The Jack London Collection page offers a biography, essays about the writer and his works, photographs of London and his family members, and recently available information. The latest addition is a section featuring two newspaper articles. This site will be useful for teachers, students, and scholars.

A Naguib Mahfouz Page
http://kmi.open.ac.uk/peterm/mahfouz.htm
Peter Murray
- English, Literature
- 11, 12, AP

This plain page provides biographical information, a list of the Egyptian writer's books with publication dates, and a short list of books about the Nobel Prize-winning author and his writings.

David Mamet
http://www.levity.com/corduroy/mamet.htm
Bohemian Ink

- Drama and Theater, English, Indexes and Resource Lists, Literature
- 11, 12, AP

A basic introduction to the contemporary American playwright, this site has a brief biography and links to related sites including some that offer interviews, more biographical information, reviews of his work, and more generic works about American theater and films.

Katherine Mansfield, Short Story Writer
http://www.buffnet.net/~starmist/kmansfld/kmansfld.htm
Starmist

- English, Literature
- All

This site may be the only one dedicated to Katherine Mansfield, the extraordinary writer of short fiction who had a great influence on the short story. There is biographical information, a chronology, and pictures. The site sponsor has typed in many stories and poems, and they become available with a click of the mouse. The pictures are fun.

Christopher Marlowe (1564-1593)
http://www.luminarium.org/renlit/marlowe.htm
Anniina Jokinen

- Drama and Theater, English, Indexes and Resource Lists, Literature
- 11, 12, AP

Everything you want to know about Christopher Marlowe with background music, and if you are willing to click on a few buttons, you get artwork from the period in which Marlowe lived. The site's other features include links to favorite quotes, which are hyperlinked to works referred to in the quotes; a life of Marlowe, with links to the several delightful sites from Virtual English; the works of Marlowe; essays and articles about Marlowe and his works; additional sources; and books in print with a brief review.

✔ Digital Library Award, Kaplan Student Choice, Yahoo's Cool Pick of the Day, Visit CityScapes Cool Site of the Week.

Gabriel Garcia Marquez
http://www.fedepatin.org.co/colombia/garcia.htm
Cafe de Colombia

- English, Indexes and Resources Lists, Literature
- 11, 12, AP

Offered in Spanish and English, this resource page has bibliographies, timelines, biography, and criticism of the masterful Colombian writer and his works. This is more than a page for beginners, yet beginners would profit from the more basic information. The criticism, however, is especially sophisticated. But what would you expect from someone who is commenting on Marquez's forte—magical realism? A note at the bottom of the page states that the page is updated regularly, but clicking on a couple of the links did result in Not Found messages.

Gabríel José García Márquez-Macondo
http://www.microserve.net/~thequail/libyrinth/garcia.marquez.html

Allen Ruch

- Literature
- 11, 12, AP

This site devoted to Gabríel Márquez, the Colombian-born, Nobel Prize-winning author, is more than a listing of his works. Here the visitor can find a biographical timeline, a short essay on magical realism (a style of literature Márquez pioneered), and a comprehensive bibliography with synopses of his major works. One can go to another link and find critical analysis, a listing of nonprint media featuring Márquez, a gallery of photos and book covers, and links to other sites pertaining to Márquez.

Hunger
http://expo.nua.ie/wordsmith/MaighreadMedbh/index.html

Nua Ltd.

- Literature, World History
- All

This site uses hyperlinks to unite literature and historical facts. There are twenty poems, of a planned twenty-six, by the Irish poet Mághréad Medbh. The poems follow a poor rural family through the Great Irish Famine of 1845-1849 and contain extensive links to historical information as well as giving explanations of Irish words and phrases. The page also has links to Famine Pages and other poetry sites.

✔ LookSmart Editor's Choice.

The Life and Works of Herman Melville
http://www.melville.org/

Multiverse

- English, Indexes and Resource Lists, Literature
- All

This site has everything you want to know about Herman Melville's life and works, including such minutiae as his lifetime literary earnings. Without leaving this resource page, there is breaking news, biographical information, the works, a postscript, and credits. Links from these categories provide information—from criticism to letters to Nathaniel Hawthorne—and electronic texts of his more popular works.

✔ NetGuide 3-Star Site, Magellan 4 Star Site, Kaleidoscope Cool Site of the Month, Adora's Literary Research Award.

Thomas Middleton (1580-1627)
http://www.med.virginia.edu/~ecc4g/middhome.html

Chris Cleary

- Drama and Theater, English, Literature
- 11, 12, AP

This ambitious site was still under construction in mid-1997 but promises to be a comprehensive source of information for the visitor. The page makes heavy use of graphics as each of Thomas Middleton's plays is identified by an image. The plays are organized into three categories: those for which Middleton was the sole author, those on which he collaborated, and those of questionable attribution. There are also images of some collaborators and rivals, which link to additional information. Finally, there are hypertext links to other secondary sources.

✔ Kaplan Student Choice Award, NetSchool Award, Walking the World Wide Web Premiere Site, Literary Research Award, and several other awards.

The Milton-L Home Page

http://www.richmond.edu/~creamer/milton.html

University of Richmond

- English, Literature
- All

This site is devoted to the life, times, and literature of John Milton. Students will find a wealth of information in the following categories: What's New, About Milton-L, Milton Events, Milton Texts on the Internet, Milton on the Web, Milton Review, the Milton Transcription Project, and Other Resources of Interest. In the Milton on the Web category, for example, are not only links to articles and reviews but graphics that could be used by the visitor.

Morrison, Toni: 1931-

http://educeth.ethz.ch/english/ReadingList/EducETH-Morrison,Toni.html

Hans G. Fischer of EducETH

- English, Indexes and Resource Lists, Literature
- All

Created with students and teachers in mind, this site incorporates questions and answers from students and teachers about Morrison's work. Also, there are links to biographical and bibliographical information, synopses of her works, and speeches delivered upon her acceptance of the Nobel Prize for Literature and other awards. A link to The English Page Web site is very helpful.

Zembla: The Nabokov Butterfly Net

http://www.libraries.psu.edu/iasweb/nabokov/nsintro.htm

University Libraries of The Pennsylvania State University

- Literature
- All

A noted lepidopterist as well as an author and translator, Vladimir Nabokov's interests are all reflected on this page. The visitor can find a chronology of his life, current events and special features, criticism, scholarly resources and bibliographies, and indexes. There are also sections entitled The Lolita Effect and Nabokov Sights.

✔ Net Site of the Month, Luckman 4-Star Site.

Life of Pablo Neruda

http://www.uchile.cl/actividades_culturales/premios_nobel/neruda/Vida_Nerudaing.html

Universidad de Chile

- English, Literature, Spanish
- All

This reference page provides biographical information about the Chilean poet and Nobel Prize winner. Photos, hyperlinks to photos of the poet at different times of his life, and summaries in Spanish of hyperlinked titles of the poet's works are the highlights of this page. Also available are links to geographical information about Chile.

Celestial Timepiece: A Joyce Carol Oates Home Page
http://storm.usfca.edu/~southerr/jco.html

Randy Souther

- English, Literature
- All

The contemporary author Joyce Carol Oates is the subject of this very artistic homepage. There are links to an Oates Discussion List and Archive, her Latest Publications, Forthcoming Publications, Lectures, Appearances and Events, a Bibliography, Film Adaptations, and Theater Productions of her works. Her work is broken down into seven categories: novels and novellas, short story collections, poetry, nonfiction, drama, edited works, and selected stories and essays. One can also find here a biography; a link to her awards, prizes, and honors; and various reviews.

Flannery O'Connor Collection
http://library.gac.peachnet.edu/~sc/foc.html

Georgia College & State University

- English, Indexes and Resource Lists, Literature
- 11, 12, AP

The most useful entry on this resource page is the link to writers' resources, covering other writers who either influenced Flannery O'Connor or were influenced by her. A second link is to frequently asked questions about the author. Most of the site deals with accessing information on site at the Ina Dillard Russell Library on the campus of Georgia College and University.

Ben Okri Page
http://humanitas.ucsb.edu/users/rbennett/okri/okritext.html

Robert Bennett, University of California at Santa Barbara

- English, Literature
- All

This small Web site is devoted to the works of the African author Ben Okri. Here one can access biographical information, primary texts, secondary criticism, quotes, multimedia images, and links to other Ben Okri information on the Web. If specific information is desired, there is also a link to an AFRLIT Internet discussion of his work *The Famished Road*.

Animal Farm
http://www.ruf.rice.edu/~jchance/animal_f.html

Jane Chance

- English, Literature
- All

This site uses many graphics to help readers of George Orwell's novel *Animal Farm*. There is a Farm Map that shows the layout of the area, a page containing morphs of the major characters, and a set of links to associated topics. The Info link contains all the material on plot, characters, main idea, and differences between the book and the movie. Finally, one can join a Java chatgroup on topics related to the novel or the author.

The Walker Percy Project
http://sunsite.unc.edu/wpercy/frames.html

The Walker Percy Educational Project, Inc.

- English, Indexes and Resource Lists, Literature
- 11, 12, AP

Walker Percy was a novelist, scientist, and philosopher. This resource page is dedicated to making him and his work better known. For students and teachers alike, there is plenty of information linked to this page to help achieve these goals. Scholarly essays and research are offered alongside educational activities for the advanced student. Casual photos of the author and stories from people who knew him provide a personal look at the author, who only died recently.

Marge Piercy Homepage
http://www.capecod.net/~tmpiercy/

Jackie Rosenfeld

- English, Indexes and Resource Lists, Literature
- All

Anytime the work of a modern, living, American literary writer who hasn't won a Nobel Prize becomes accessible, it's good news. Piercy is one such writer. Marge Piercy has won plenty of awards, as evidenced by her resume found at this site. This resource page is only a beginning, but it does include her picture, new projects, criticism, a bibliography, reference pieces, a book list, brief reviews, a schedule of readings and workshops, several poems, and links to related sites.

The Lost Minds' Christopher Pike Page
http://web.arcos.org/stinger/pike/index.htm

Jen and Ankur

- English, Literature
- 9, 10

This lively resource covers Christopher Pike's popular books. There is a list of the books, ratings, reviews, and comments from readers. A special treat is a review, by Jen, written for her English class.

✔ Top 1000 World Sites.

Sylvia Plath
http://www.informatik.uni-leipzig.de/privat2/beckmann/public_html/plath.html

Anja Beckmann

- English, Indexes and Resource Lists, Literature
- All

This site provides insight into Sylvia Plath's poetry and life. There is an English-American bibliography, a link to books on Sylvia Plath, articles and dissertations on her, a German bibliography, and a bibliography of translations into other languages. In addition, there are poems by Sylvia Plath and a list of other Net resources including French and Spanish homepages devoted to her life and work.

The Complete Works of Edgar Allan Poe
http://www.visi.com/~talon/bizarre/poe2.html

Nevermore

- English, Literature
- All

A comprehensive site providing access to all of Poe's works by an alphabetical listing. There are also links to biographical works, including "Did Edgar Allan Poe Die of Rabies?" Other links take you to films based on his works or ideas, and FTP sites honoring Poe, including museums, National Historic Sites, and the Poe Cottage.

The House of Usher: Edgar Allan Poe (1809-1849)
http://www.comnet.ca/~forrest/index.html

Peter Forrest

- English, Literature
- All

This site relies heavily on graphics to provide visitors with an introduction to Edgar Allan Poe and his work. The first links take the visitor to a number of Poe's "favorites"—Art Gallery, Felines, Flies, Haunts, Songs, and his Pet Raven. There is also a link to Poe's Incomplete Works. You can visit Poe's Virtual Library and Who Was Poe? There is a French version of this site.

✔ POINTCommunications Top 5% Web Site, WebCrawler Select Site, Fledge Approved by McGraw-Hill Home Interactive.

The Rape of the Lock Home Page
http://www-unix.oit.umass.edu/~sconstan/

S. Constantine, University of Massachusetts

- English, Indexes and Resource Lists, Literature
- 11, 12, AP

Alexander Pope's poem "The Rape of the Lock" is the focus of this small resource page. There are links to a brief biography of Pope, the story behind the poem, a chronology of early editions, and a chronology of his published work. Versions of the poem at this site include an annotated edition and translations in German and French. There are a number of illustrations, including one of Pope, and related material links. Of particular interest to students would be "A Key to the Lock" where Pope explains his poem. The site is rounded out by links to related resources, journal articles, and trivia questions.

Ezra Pound (1885-1972)
http://www.lit.kobe-u.ac.jp/~hishika/pound.htm

Eiichi Hishikawa

- English, Indexes and Resource Lists, Literature
- All

This is an extremely valuable resource site on the poet Ezra Pound (1885-1972). The visitor will find biographical information (still under construction) and a bibliography that contains sixty-five works about Pound. There are listings for a discography, a filmography, library collections, Pound pages, a mailing list, the *Pound Journal*, related links, and the Ezra Pound Poetry Award.

English & Literature

The Pushkin Page
http://falcon.jmu.edu/~gouldsl/Pushkin/
Stephany Gould
- Literature
- All

This site is devoted to Alexander Pushkin, the Russian author. There are links here to Pushkin's Life, Texts, Pushkin and Culture, and Humor. Each of the last two categories give quotes and examples from his works to show his impact on Russian culture.

Thomas Pynchon Home Page
http://pete.pomona.edu/pynchon/
San Narcisco Community College
- English, Literature
- All

This site is a graphic-heavy depiction of the works of Thomas Pynchon; each of his works is accessed by clicking on an icon representing the cover of the book. There are also links to a bibliography, a biography and FAQs. Finally, you can visit an area devoted to his theme of entropy and another to various sound files and QuickTime video clips.

Isaac Rosenberg's "Break of Day in the Trenches"
http://info.ox.ac.uk/departments/humanities/rose/
Dr. Stuart Lee, Humanities Computing Unit, Oxford University
- English, Literature
- All

This site comprises a WWW tutorial on Isaac Rosenberg and his poem, "Break of Day in the Trenches." It is part of the Virtual Seminars for Teaching Literature Project based at Oxford University. The Hypermedia Edition of the poem links significant passages to explanations, which enables you to better understand the author's intent. After reading the poem, you can record and submit your own ideas and have them held in an archive at the site.

Christina Rossetti
http://www.stg.brown.edu/projects/hypertext/landow/victorian/crossetti/crov2.html
George P. Landow
- English, Indexes and Resource Lists, Literature
- 11, 12, AP

This resource page has links to quality essays about Christina Rossetti and her works. Begin with an overview of the Victorian period, including technological, philosophical, and religious commentary, and continue to themes and techniques, with subcategories such as imagery, symbolism, and motifs.

Salman Rushdie
http://www.crl.com/~subir/rushdie.html

Subir Grewal

- Current Events, Literature, Religion
- 11, 12, AP

Salman Rushdie has been living incognito since the publication of his novel *Satanic Verses* in 1989 led to assassination threats by the Iranian government for Rushdie's alleged insults toward Islam. This site not only provides information on all his published works but also includes interviews, articles, quotes, a bibliography of published works on-line, and a glossary of colloquialisms he has used in his works. In addition, there is a substantial list of related material, many in other languages, about Rushdie, his work, and the general issues of free speech and terrorism. Finally, there is a listing of other Rushdie sites, including one for French readers.

Catcher in the Rye
http://members.aol.com/nellansd/english/index.html

David Nellans

- English, Literature
- All

This site is a reader's guide to J. D. Salinger's novel *Catcher in the Rye* and an exploration of its main character, Holden Caulfield. Links are organized under headings such as Summary and Analysis, Critical Reviews, and Biographical Information. The first stop should be the Essay, which lays out the main ideas of which the reader should be aware. An interesting last page, Assessment, allows the student visitor to respond to essay questions and have them critiqued by the sponsor of the site.

The Catcher in the Rye Campfire
http://killdevilhill.com/salingerchat/wwwboard.html

Raft, Knottingham & McGucken

- English, Indexes and Resource Lists, Literature
- All

This resource page posts messages from J. D. Salinger's readers who have questions or information about Salinger or his works. It's an informal site that tries to recreate the campfire experience by allowing everyone a chance to speak.

Page Index for *The Catcher in the Rye*
http://www.nyx.net/~smorine/catch.htm

smorine@nyx.net

- English, Literature
- All

For a simple page, this site offers a valuable learning tool: it indexes the appearances of characters, favorite scenes, and memorable phrases from J. D. Salinger's *Catcher in the Rye* for easy access.

Ken Saro-Wiwa
http://www.derechos.org/nigeria/sarowiwa/saro.html
Derechos Human Rights
- Current Events, Indexes and Resource Lists, Literature
- All

Writer Ken Saro-Wiwa and other Nigerians executed by the Nigerian government are featured at this site. There are four links to other homepages on Saro-Wiwa or the topic of human rights in Nigeria. In the "Information and News" category there is a list of writings by Saro-Wiwa, a newspaper advertisement about Saro-Wiwa's culpability, and several news reports on the killing of the dissident. The page also contains links to other human rights pages.

Original Home Page of Robert W. Service, The
http://www.top.monad.net/~artude/service.html
Art Ude
- English, Indexes and Resource Lists, Literature
- All

This resource page contains a brief biography, poems, and a picture or two. But you can also launch an effective search for all pages relating to Robert Service from this page. The links take you to quality sites. For example, if you want more of Service's poetry, there is a link to Project Gutenberg where you can download E-text files of entire collections.

Collected Works of Shakespeare/The Works of the Bard
http.www://gh.cs.su.oz.au/~matty/Shakespeare/Shakespeare.html
University of Sydney
- Drama and Theater, Literature
- All

This site includes the complete text of all of Shakespeare's works, drama and poetry, all of which can be downloaded in their entirety. In addition, a search engine can be used to find key words, phrases, etc. There is also a list of links to other Shakespeare-related sites.

✔ Magellan 4 Star Site, Top 5% from POINTCommunications. "A wonderful source of Shakespeare's texts including histories, comedies, tragedies, and poetry. All of these texts are linked to an on-line glossary.... Definitely a valuable site for Shakespeare students and teachers."—*Jeffery D. Conn, Homestead High School, Mequon, WI.*

The Complete Works of William Shakespeare
http://the-tech.mit.edu/Shakespeare/works.html
Jeremy Hylton
- English, Indexes and Resource Lists, Literature
- All

Not only does this site provide electronic texts of the complete works of William Shakespeare, it also provides a discussion area, a search engine, links to other related resources on the Web, chronological and alphabetical listings, frequently asked questions, and familiar quotations.

✔ GNN Best of the Net Nominee 1995, WebCrawler Select Best of the Web, POINTCommunications Top 5% Web Site, PC Magazine *Top 100 Websites*, Magellan 4 Star Site, IWAY 500 Site, Lycos 250 Literature.

Shakespeare's Globe Theatre
http://www.delphi.co.uk/delphi/interactive/16.Globe/walk_intro.html
Camden Lock
- Drama and Theater, English, Literature
- All

The rebuilding of the Globe Theatre in London is to be completed in 1999. In the meantime, take a tour of the building that saw the first performances of Shakespeare's Othello, MacBeth, Lear, and Hamlet. Links to different shots of the building are the main feature, but there are also links to related Shakespeare sites and information about the building project.

Julius Caesar Web Guide
http://www.bell.k12.ca.us/BellHS/Departments/English/SCORE/caesarwebguide.html
Bell High School
- Drama and Theater, English, Literature
- 9, 10, 11

A site designed as a guide to the teaching of Shakespeare's *Julius Caesar* in tenth grade, this page offers students ideas and strategies in several areas. Research strategies for the Web are provided as well as information on analyzing character and describing plot in a compare/contrast essay. Character and plot information are tied to specific lines of the play to enable the student to better understand the characters and their motivations.

✔ PacBell Education First Learning Application Award.

Mr. William Shakespeare and the Internet
http://www.palomar.edu/Library/shake.htm
Terry Gray
- Drama and Theater, English, Indexes and Resource Lists, Literature
- All

This page provides extensive links to Shakespeare-related information. The Introduction includes annotated links to scholarly sites. Other categories include The Man, The Works, Criticism, Shakespeare in Education, Aspects of Elizabethan Performance, Literary Journals and Renaissance Journals, and Primary and Secondary Sources. The page also links to Five Diamond sites pertaining to Shakespeare as well as nonscholarly sites available on the Web.

Webspeare
http://idt.net/~kcn/shakes~1.htm
Brick Tree Designs
- Art, Drama and Theater, English, Indexes and Resource Lists, Literature
- All

5   5   5   5   5   9

This Shakespeare site links to five major areas: complete works, a program allowing you to search the plays for specific references, art inspired by Shakespeare's works, discussion groups organized by topic, and questions. Each section is informative and easy to use. The search program requires basic information, such as the name of the play where the reference is to be found. Discussion groups may require some browsing before settling on a topic. Asking a question? If you can't find a pre-existing question, it will take a little patience while awaiting a reply. There are also links for learning how to speak with a Shakespearean accent, for films, and for study guides. Teachers will find the discussion area filled with suggestions for teaching the Bard.

English & Literature

Romeo and Juliet Web Guide

http://www.bell.k12.ca.us/BellHS/Departments/English/SCORE/webguide.html

Bell High School

- Drama and Theater, English, Literature
- 9, 10

Primarily a teaching guide to Shakespeare's *Romeo and Juliet*, this site offers ideas and strategies for plot and character analysis and for producing a unified composition about the play. Links to Student WWW Resources provide access to other sites relevant to the topic as well as a Dictionary of Literary Terms, a site helpful to an understanding of drama. The Student Resources area also includes brief essays and QuickTime movies on some of the characters.

Elizabethan Times

http://www.romeoandjuliet.com/author/times.html

Twentieth Century Fox

- Drama and Theater, English, Literature
- 9, 10

This graphic site is in the form of the front page of a tabloid-type newspaper. The half-dozen articles headlined on the cover provide information on the drama of the star-crossed lovers, Romeo and Juliet, in a format sure to attract the attention of modern-day students. For example, "You Make the Call" tells how the play originally had two endings, which played on alternating nights at the Globe Theater. Clicking on the graphic on the front page will bring up information relevant to the play; other links provide information on the author, the setting, and the players. The references on the site are to the recent Twentieth Century Fox remake of the drama.

Falcon Education Link

http://www.falconedlink.com/falcon/home.html

Roger Burnich

- Drama and Theater, English, Literature
- All

This site provides chatty, contemporary translations of Shakespeare's *Hamlet* and *Macbeth*, two of the most commonly assigned plays for high school students. The translations, accessible by act, may be helpful to new readers of the plays, but they contain a significant number of typos and are a bit simplistic. The *Macbeth* site is complete, but the *Hamlet* page is still under construction as of mid-1997; the site also offers links to other courses the sponsor has developed, such as Creative Writing and a Survey of British Literature.

✔ Education World *Education Site Award*, Classroom Connect Editor's Choice, Education First Blue Web'n Learning Application.

Shakespeare Classroom, The

http://www.jetlink.net/~massij/shakes/

J.M. Massi Ph.D.

- English, Indexes and Resource Lists, Literature
- All

This resource site has a lot of information and looks good too. You'll find links to materials for teaching Shakespeare, other Shakespearean resources, and non-Shakespearean resources. Links with hypertext take you to further links with explanatory information.

✔ *Magellan 3 Star Site and Excite 3 Star Site.*

MacBeth Plugged
http://tqd.advanced.org/2888/
ThinkQuest
- Drama and Theater, English, Literature
- 11, 12, AP

This site contains an annotated, on-line version of Shakespeare's play MacBeth. There is an introduction, a list and description of characters, a discussion of themes, a glossary, and summaries. Each is hyperlinked to the on-line text. This arrangement really lets the student see just how much Shakespeare gets into his scenes. Related sites include other resources, reviews, a plain-text version of the play, the Interactive Zone, Multimedia, and a search engine. With the correct plug-ins, you can listen to and see scenes from various renditions of MacBeth.

Frankenstein: Mary W. Shelley
http://www.emerald-empire.com/holidays/hallowee/frankenstein.html
Gold Stag Communications, Inc.
- English, Literature
- All

This page holds the complete novel *Frankenstein* by Mary Shelley.

Mary Shelley and Frankenstein
http://www.netaxs.com/~kwbridge/maryshel.html
KW
- English, Indexes and Resource Lists, Literature
- 11, 12, AP

This resource page links to people, places, and writing associated with Mary Shelley and her book *Frankenstein*. There are links to her mother and father, husband, and friends. The information on each contains hyperlinked words to further information and definitions, which really gives this site its substance. The page sponsor provides a list of sources from which the site was constructed and depends upon for its scholarship.

Percy Bysshe Shelley Home Page
http://www.geocities.com/Athens/Acropolis/8916/shelly.html
John W. Leys
- English, Indexes and Resource Lists, Literature
- All

This small Web page focuses on the poet Percy Bysshe Shelley and his works. There is a list of sites that have a selection of his poetry on-line and a link to a Shelley Chronology, which is still under construction. There is also a short Shelley bibliography but the entries are not linked to other sites.

Upton Sinclair
http://venus.twu.edu/~S_2stone/upton.html
Seth Stone
- English, Literature, U.S. History
- All

Visitors to this site are greeted by a large outline map of the United States. There are then links to a chronology, a critical biography, an annotated bibliography, and additional links pertaining to Upton Sinclair, the muckraking journalist and novelist. The material in the biography area has three areas of focus: his candidacy for governor of California, his sex life, and his artistic limitations.

English & Literature

The Edmund Spenser Home Page
http://darkwing.uoregon.edu/~rbear/
University of Oregon Library
- English, Indexes and Resource Lists, Literature
- 11, 12, AP

The goal of this site is to collect and provide links to all Edmund Spenser material on the net. To that end, the page links to his major works, *The Faerie Queene* being the most important for student visitors. There are also links to Spenser material on other sites, including resources such as the Spenser Society and the Spenser-L Discussion list. Finally, there is a very useful set of links to libraries and sites that pertain to English literature.

✔ *Magellan 4 Star Site, Telecom Internet 3-Dora Site, Best of Campus (University of Oregon).*

John Steinbeck
http://www.luhsd.k12.ca.us/library/stein.html
Lemoore, CA, High School
- English, Literature
- All

This small site is devoted to the author John Steinbeck and his works. You can visit the Steinbeck Research Center, see contemporary reviews of his works, or read *Steinbeck Country*, an autobiography. The site focuses on *Of Mice and Men* and *The Grapes of Wrath*, the two Steinbeck works most frequently found in high school curriculums. Visitors can also access a listing of the various locations he used in his novels and take a tour of his home.

John Steinbeck
http://www.steinbeck.org/bio/index.html
National Steinbeck Center
- English, Indexes and Resource Lists, Literature
- All

This site offers information about Nobel Prize-winning American author John Steinbeck. The information is divided into four categories: Steinbeck, Works, Facts, and Links. In the Steinbeck category, there is a brief biography, several photos, and an excerpt from his Nobel Prize acceptance speech. Under Works, there is a list with a brief description of his published works—his more famous works are linked to detailed descriptions including historical background. Facts provides basic autobiographical information, e.g., birth date, etc.; information about Steinbeck's family; a list of awards and honors; and Steinbeck and Salinas. Links connects you to other Web sites about Steinbeck.

Treasure Island
http://www.ukoln.ac.uk/treasure/
UK Office for Library and Information Networking
- Literature
- All

This Web site offers virtually everything a student would want to know about *Treasure Island*. One link accesses information on the author, Robert Louis Stevenson; a second takes the visitor to an on-line version of the book and a discussion of plot and characters. The links category provides information on ships, pirates, treasure, and tropical islands. The Things to Do section lists activities and resources to make the book come alive.

✔ *Blue Web'n Site of the Week, Youth Compass Ultimate Destination Site, WebCrawler Select Outstanding Site.*

Bram Stoker Home Page
http://userwww.sfsu.edu/~arf/
San Francisco State University
- English, Literature
- All

Any fan of *Dracula* or vampires in general will find a lot to study on this Web page. Besides an introduction, you'll find a biography of Bram Stoker, links to "Possible Influences," The Vampire in Literature, The Lure of Dracula, a comparison chart of vampire characteristics, and a bibliography. There is also a section on how superstitious hysteria has prolonged the vampire myth. You can access the entire text of *Dracula*, look at seventy-three years worth of Dracula films, learn more about "Vlad the Impaler," and link to the Transylvania Society of Dracula.

Gulliver's Travels by Jonathan Swift
http://www.jaffebros.com/lee/gulliver/index.html
Jaffe Bros.
- English, Literature
- All

This *Gulliver's Travels* Web site offers a comprehensive look at the novel and related topics. You can access the on-line version of the text, memorable quotes, notes and sources with a bibliography and background, and images and illustrations. Links to related on-line sources and a link to timelines of Swift's life, work, and times provide added information to enable the student to understand the topic.

Anniina's Amy Tan Page
http://www.luminarium.org/contemporary/amytan/
Anniina Jokinen
- English, Indexes and Resource Lists, Literature
- All

One of the last items on this page is a note, signed by Amy Tan. Without saying it directly, the note gives an official air to the page. It might well be called Amy Tan's Official Homepage. Tan is frank about her writing, its origin, and her aspirations as a writer. Featured are interviews, biographical information, photos, book reviews, and a bibliography. The site provides plenty of—mostly anecdotal—information. Not everything one could ask for, but enough. Added bonuses include audios of Tan reading from her works and an illustrated short story.

Dylan Thomas
http://pcug.org.au/~wwhatman/dylan_thomas.html
Warrick Whatman
- English, Literature
- All

This Dylan Thomas (1914-1953) Web site contains a brief biography of the Welsh poet and links to other areas of interest: a video, "Dylan Thomas: Return Journey"; a bibliography; "A Letter to My Aunt," discussing his approach to poetry; "A Tribute"; Swansea; The Dylan Thomas Suite; and Dylan Thomas Poems. There is also information on the Dylan Thomas Society of Australia, only the second to be formed in the world.

The Great Thompson Hunt
http://www.geocities.com/Athens/Acropolis/3203/hstmp.htm

Christine Othitis

- English, Indexes and Resource Lists, Journalism, Literature
- 11, 12, AP

Here you'll find everything you want to know about the king of Gonzo Journalism and Gonzo Journalism as a style and genre. This resource page includes links for information about Hunter S. Thompson and his associates, articles and essays about him, pictures, awards, and related sites.

CyberSaunter—Henry David Thoreau
http://umsa.umd.edu/thoreau/

Sean Mahoney and Joe Smith

- English, Literature
- All

Although still under construction in mid-1997, this page will be useful to the student visitor who needs to find out more about Thoreau. The following links are provided at this point: Introduction to Thoreau, Background Behind Walden, Family, Friends and Love Interests, Formal Education, and Employment. The Image Library includes pictures and drawings to be added as the site is expanded.

The Writings of Henry D. Thoreau
http://www.library.ucsb.edu/depts/thoreau/

University of California at Santa Barbara

- English, Literature
- 11, 12, AP

This site provides information about a project to collect Henry David Thoreau's writing, all of it. When finished the work will comprise thirty volumes. What does this page do for the student or teacher? It provides several informative essays, including "Introduction to the Life and Times of Henry D. Thoreau" and "Walden after 150 Years." Also, the description of the project has good information about the plight of Thoreau's work, which apparently had fallen into the hands of "well-intentioned" amateurs whose contributions are "inaccurate and incomplete."

The Tolkien Guild
http://www.miworld.net/~gdonaldsonjr/tolkien.html

Gregg C. Donaldson, Jr.

- English, Indexes and Resource Lists, Literature
- All

4   5   4   5   5   9

This resource page provides links to the Tolkien Forum with 110 questions and 160 answers, a picture archive, Tolkien games, Tolkien movies, alphabets, and related sites—with background music. The questions and answers are provocative, the pictures glorious, the other stuff fun as well as illuminating. Don't be misled, however, there is a good deal of scholarly information here.

✔ *Elven Award for Excellence, NightWriter's Genesis Award, A Dragon Myer Award Winning Site, Hey You Sir's Royal Site Award.*

Mark Twain from the Mining Company
http://marktwain.miningco.com/
The Mining Company
- English, Indexes and Resource Lists, Literature, Writing
- 11, 12, AP

A tour guide welcomes you to this site with its links to up-to-date articles on current events stimulated by Twain's writings and scholarship on selected works. The guide, someone who has been studying Twain and his works, gets to share some thoughts in essays linked to the page. Offers links to additional Mining Company sites that feature connections to other writers, such as Anne Rice, or genres, such as mystery.

Mark Twain's Huckleberry Finn
http://etext.lib.virginia.edu/twain/huckfinn.html
Virginia H. Cope, University of Virginia
- English, Indexes and Resource Lists, Literature
- All

This site offers a complete early edition of Huckleberry Finn, the 174 illustrations from the first edition, and the obscene illustration that appeared in the sales prospectus. There are also links to early reviews and ads, three F. W. Kimble illustrations, and an article written in 1930 by Kimble describing his experiences illustrating the novel. Links to on-line texts of *Tom Sawyer*, *A Connecticut Yankee in King Arthur's Court*, and other Mark Twain resources on the Web round out the site.

The Centaurian: John Updike Home Page
http://www.users.fast.net/~joyerkes/
James Yerkes
- English, Literature
- All

This site, devoted to the writer John Updike, is more than a resource page of links to his writings; it is meant to provide a location for those interested to engage in an on-line dialogue on the man and his works. For example, every month the page proposes a question and visitors are urged to send in comments to the area entitled "Grazing among the Centaurs." More traditional information presented includes What's New in Updikiana, A Brief Biographical and Literary Chronology, Selected Bibliography, Latest and Forthcoming Publications, Lecture and Appearance Schedule, Genre List of Trade Publications, Video and Feature Film Adaptations, and Awards, Prizes, and Honors.

The Life and Works of Jules Verne
http://avery.med.virginia.edu/~mtp0f/flips/jules.html
Prasad Phillips
- English, Literature
- All

This site focuses on the nineteenth-century French science fiction writer Jules Verne. The visitor can first link to Verne's Life History, a short biography and chronology of his work. Links follow for his three major books: *20,000 Leagues under the Sea*, *A Journey to the Center of the Earth*, and *Around the World in Eighty Days*. The site also provides access to a commentary, a bibliography of sources, and a picture gallery.

English & Literature

Kurt Vonnegut Corner
http://www.geocities.com/Hollywood/4953/vonn.html

Marek Vit

- English, Literature
- All

This site provides the visitor with basic information on Kurt Vonnegut and his works. There are links to an Essay Collection, Vonnegut's Works, a Quote Collection, *Kilgore Trout*, and other Useful Links. There is also a What's New area to keep the visitor up-to-date on the topic.

Alice Walker—Womanist Writer
http://wwwvms.utexas.edu/~melindaj/alice.html

University of Texas

- English, Literature
- All

Alice Walker's work is celebrated at this site. There is a list of her twenty-two books, a biography, and a list of books about her. A category entitled "Other Web Information" includes links to various media articles concerning Walker. For example, here the visitor could link to several other Web pages, read Alice Walker's letter to President Clinton, and access a list of journal and magazine articles written by her.

Evelyn Arthur St. John Waugh
http://e2.empirenet.com/~jahvah/waugh/menu.html

Sir Roderick Spode

- English, Literature
- All

This site attempts to provide a basic introduction to the life and times of British writer Evelyn Waugh. The visitor can access a hypertext biography, a bibliography, "Bibliophilia," "World Wide Waugh," and the Waugh Newsletter. This page is an excellent starting point for research on Waugh, the author of *Brideshead Revisited* and numerous comic novels.

Study Guide for H. G. Wells: *War of the Worlds*
http://www.wsu.edu:8080/~brians/science_fiction/warofworlds.html

Paul Brians, Washington State University

- English, Literature
- All

This site was established by the Discovery Channel as a resource for its program on *War of the Worlds*, which aired in 1996. The visitor to the site will find a chapter-by-chapter guide to both parts of the novel. In some cases the guide includes additional insights, in others there are questions for the reader to consider. The introduction puts Wells's work in context and also contains links to other study guides and the Science Fiction Research Bibliography.

Edith Wharton
http://history.hanover.edu/20th/wharton.htm
Hanover College
- English, Literature
- All

A simple resource Web site for students needing access to Edith Wharton's (1862-1937) major works. At this site one can find fifty works by the author that can be read on-line or printed for future use. The site is in alphabetical order, making it easy to find a particular item.

The Walt Whitman Collection
http://lcweb2.loc.gov/ammem/wwhome.html
Library of Congress
- English, Indexes and Resource Lists, Literature
- All

This homepage links to images of four notebooks and a cardboard butterfly of Whitman's. The items were stolen in 1942 from the Thomas Biggs Harned Walt Whitman Collection housed in the Library of Congress, and returned in 1995. For those thrilled with seeing the unadorned pages of an author's private musings, the links are worth a visit. The notebooks will be of interest to students seeking primary sources for papers on Whitman or teachers seeking interesting anecdotes for classroom instruction. Note: a valuable link on the page is the Learning Page of the Library of Congress.

Laura Ingalls Wilder, Frontier Girl
http://webpages.marshall.edu/~irby1/laura.htmlx
Rebecca Irby and Phil Greetham
- English, Literature
- All

Laura Ingalls Wilder, best known for *Little House on the Prairie* and its sequels, is the focus of this Web page. You can discover more about her life, her houses, her books, her friends and family, her letters, and her Bible by visiting this site. The menu also offers a photo album, announcements, useful addresses, teachers' links, and background articles. This is a very comprehensive site for a student doing research on Laura Wilder or related topics.

Thornton Wilder (1897-1975)
http://www.sky.net/~emily/thornton.html
Emily M. Parris
- Drama and Theater, English, Indexes and Resource Lists, Literature
- 11, 12, AP

A labor of love, this resource page has links to many sources of information about Thornton Wilder and his works. However, some links take you only to bibliographical information or one or two lines of biography when you might expect a more thorough treatment. Aside from the traditional links, there are links to newsgroups.

The Glass Menagerie

http://www.susqu.edu/ac_depts/arts_sci/english/lharris/class/WILLIAMS/titlepag.htm

Susquehanna University

- Drama and Theater, Literature
- All

Tennessee Williams's well-known play *The Glass Menagerie* is studied on this page. Here the visitor can access a biography of Williams, a complete list of his works, and a bibliography. The aspects of *The Glass Menagerie* covered are Plot Summary, Character Sketches, Literary Criticism, Scene VII, Pictures, Sound, and Video. This is a very thorough Web site.

Thomas Wolfe (1900-1938)

http://www.cms.uncwil.edu/~connelly/wolfe.html

Sharon Connelly

- English, Literature
- All

This site devoted to Thomas Wolfe (1900-1938) offers links to the Thomas Wolfe Memorial with a Photo Tour, a Photo Gallery, the Thomas Wolfe Society, and Wolfe News. In addition, there is a biography, a chronology of his life, a link to the 1996 Thomas Wolfe Festival, a bibliography, writings about him and his work, and letters from Wolfe fans.

✔ *Magellan 3 Star Site, POINTCommunications Top 5% Web Site.*

Mary Wollstonecraft

http://www.ehche.ac.uk/college/schools/human/english/mw.htm

Harriet Devine Jump, Edge Hill University

- English, Indexes and Resource Lists, Literature
- All

This resource site contains links to other sites with information on Mary Wollstonecraft, the British writer of the Romantic period. Especially useful to the student visitor are links to a complete list of her writings, a chronology, and a bibliography. For more in-depth research there are reviews of her work from eighteenth-century journals and links to women Romantic era writers and related sites.

Virginia Woolf

http://www.rocky.edu/~dejones/virginia.html

Danell Jones

- English, Literature
- All

This site devoted to Virginia Woolf (1882-1941) was still under construction in mid-1997. So far, it consists of four of her works, "Haworth, November 1904," "Wilcoxiana," "Mrs. Gaskell," and "George Eliot," as well as an overview and articles about her work such as Grace Radin's "Virginia Woolf's the Years: The Evolution of a Novel."

Richard Wright—Black Boy
http://www.itvs.org/programs/RW/
Independent TV Service
- English, Literature
- All

This site is a companion to a PBS program on Richard Wright, which aired in September 1995. Visitors can find more information in the form of a short biography and a list of people interviewed for the program, including classmates from Jackson, Mississippi; critics; authors; and friends. There is also a chronology of his life and a selected bibliography.

William Butler Yeats (1865-1939)
http://www.lit.kobe-u.ac.jp/~hishika/yeats.htm
Eiichi Hishikawa
- English, Indexes and Resource Lists, Literature
- All

Although this Web site contains a biography and short bibliography, these are taken from the 1995 Grolier Multimedia Encyclopedia. Following this material there is a short list of links to Yeats pages including the Bartleby Project at Columbia, another link to a collection of over 310 poems, Notes on Yeats, The Yeats Society Sligo Home Page and Bibliography, and another to the Yeats Links Page.

See Also

Athena: Authors & Texts http://un2sg1.unige.ch/www/athena/html/authors.html (p.1)

Books in Chains http://www.uc.edu/~RETTBESR/Links.html (p. 2)

CM http://www.mbnet.mb.ca/cm/home/about.html (p. 4)

Great Writers http://www.xs4all.nl/~pwessel/writers.html (p. 7)

Hemingway and Fitzgerald http://www.cas.usf.edu/english/sipiora/public_html/hemfitz.html (p. 70)

Hola! (Hello) Oh What a Book! Science and More!! http://tqd.advanced.org/3240/ (p. 41)

Literary Menagerie, The http://sunset.backbone.olemiss.edu/~egcash/ (p. 11)

Literature and Poetry Page, The http://www.netten.net/~bmassey/ (p. 42)

LSU Libraries Author Webliography http://www.lib.lsu.edu/hum/authors.html (p. 12)

Luminarium http://www.luminarium.org/lumina.htm (p. 42)

MacBeth Plugged http://tqd.advanced.org/2888/ (p. 117)

Michigan State University Celebrity Lecture Series http://hs1.hst.msu.edu/~cal/celeb/index.html (p. 42)

Public Domain Modern English Search http://www.hti.umich.edu/english/pd-modeng/ (p. 15)

Virtual English http://tqd.advanced.org/2847/homepage.htm (p. 45)

Voices from the Gaps: Women Writers of Color http://www-engl.cla.umn.edu/lkd/vfg/VFGHome (p. 16)

WebCrawler Guide:Arts:Literature http://www.webcrawler.com/select/art.histlit.html (p. 17)

Yahoo! Arts: Humanities: Literature: Authors http://www.yahoo.com/Arts/Humanities/Literature/Authors/ (p. 18)

JOURNALISM

Atlantic Unbound—*The Atlantic Monthly*
http://theatlantic.com/coverj.html

The Atlantic Monthly Company

- English, Literature
- All

The on-line home of the prestigious *Atlantic Monthly*, this site offers the current features of the magazine on a monthly basis. The site also provides a search feature that allows the visitor to access past editions. In addition, the on-line version offers a Reader Forum area where readers can post comments and an Atlantic Unbound Roundtable on changing controversial issues.

The Bosnian Virtual Fieldtrip
http://geog.gmu.edu/gess/jwc/bosnia/bosnia.html

Jeremy Crampton and Beth Rundstrom

- Current Events, Geography, Journalism, Writing
- All

This site takes a viewer on a fieldtrip to Bosnia. It contains hypertext links to places and people, regions and history. A part of the trip involves writing skills. A question-and-answer piece pops up on each leg of the trip. Answering the questions requires some thought, journalistic enterprise, and writing ability.

✔ *POINTCommunications Top 5% Web Site.*

Crayon—CReAte Your Own Newspaper
http://crayon.net/

NETPressence, Inc.

- Current Events, English, Indexes and Resource Lists, Journalism, Writing
- All

This site allows you to create your own free newspaper. Follow the instructions. By the time you finish, you have access to loads of news in the order you asked for it. Includes links to many news forums, including print, radio, television, and cable services.

✔ *NetGuide Platinum Site, Cool Link of the Week, Hot Learning Site of the Week, Magellan Featured Site, POINTCommunications Top 5% Web Site, and many other awards.*

eZines: Ultimate Magazine Database
http://www.dominis.com/Zines/

Otis Gospodnetic and COIS

- Indexes and Resource Lists, Journalism, Literature
- All

This resource page lists more than forty magazine categories, enabling the visitor to access a multitude of on-line sources. A sampling of the categorizes includes Alternative Lifestyles, Cooking, Environment, Hobbies, Literary, Military, Recreation, Reviews, and Travel. One may also search the site by the eZine Search Engine.

✔ *Starting Point Hot Site.*

Freedom of Information Center
http://www.missouri.edu/~foiwww/
University of Missouri School of Journalism
- Current Events, Journalism, Political Science, Writing
- All

This Web page will be useful to students interested in journalism and related topics or to anyone who needs to ferret out government information. The page provides access to a variety of journalism and communications organizations as well as government Web sites. One can also link to Guides to Freedom of Information (FoI) Center Resources, Federal and State FoI Records and Sunshine Acts (including sample request letters), Other Resources on Control of Information Issues, Links to Government Information Available Online, and International FoI Topics.

The New Yorker
http://www.enews.com/magazines/new_yorker/
The Electronic Newsstand
- English, Journalism, Literature
- 11, 12, AP

This Web site allows visitors to access selected articles from current issues of *The New Yorker* magazine. In addition, you can find past articles in *The New Yorker* archives, read about the magazine, talk to *The New Yorker*, and subscribe on-line.

Newseum
http://www.newseum.org/
The Freedom Forum
- Current Events, English, Indexes and Resource Lists, Journalism, U.S. History
- All

This site claims to be "the world's only interactive museum of the news." The building that houses the Newseum is in Arlington, VA. The information therein lies only a few clicks of the mouse away. Here you get information about special programs that the Newseum sponsors—if you are in the area—but you also get reports, transcripts, and pictures from each one. You get links to The Freedom Forum, First Amendment Center, and Media Studies Center, which are linked to many more information sites, from the big news stories of the day to anniversaries and background about history-making events such as Watergate. The site offers opportunities to ask questions and share your wit and wisdom with other visitors.

Newspaper Archives on the Web
http://sunsite.unc.edu/slanews/internet/archives.html
Special Libraries Association
- Current Events, English, Journalism, Literature
- All

This resource page provides a chart that lists state, city, publication, the Web site host, and cost, if any, of access. Click on the newspaper's name, etc., and go to its homepage. Find out before accessing it whether there will be a cost by clicking on the appropriate link.

English & Literature

Newsport
http://newsport.sfsu.edu/

Journalism Department, San Francisco State University

- English, Grammar and Style, Journalism, Literature, Writing
- 11, 12, AP

This site calls itself the "first university journalism site in a true multimedia environment." The journalists at work here stick to the good old-fashioned rules of news-gathering, yet make a conscious effort to avoid becoming an on-line newspaper or TV news station. They experiment with the old forms and try to imagine what the future will bring. Click on a button and go to past stories, or entire back issues of the "journalism of the future."

The Reporters Network
http://www.reporters.net/

Bob Sablatura

- English, Journalism, Writing
- 11, 12, AP

This resource page may provide a young reporter with some information and contacts for any class project, but it is meant for professionals. It features bulletin boards, journalism resources, lists of organizations, a media directory, and a newsletter—and it's free.

virtually react
http://www.react.com/

Advance Magazine Publications and ParadeNet Inc.

- Current Events, English, Journalism, Literature
- All

This is the home site of an on-line magazine for teens that features lively graphics and catchy phrases. Click on any button at the top of the new page and a factoid appears—for example, "The human skull contains 28 bones." Many surveys ask about the habits, likes and dislikes of young people. Articles are current, and there is plenty of opportunity to offer comments and opinions. To find out about movies, click on "Field and Screen." If you're thinking about buying something, click on "The Mall." There are also links to many newspapers, jokes, and more interesting factoids.

✔ InfiNet Cool Site of the Day, POINTCommunications Top 5% of Web Site, Internet Newsroom's CyberTypewriter, NetGuide 4 Star Site.

See Also

Algonquin Round Table http://www.buffalo.edu/~raines/algtab.html (p. 67)

Books in Chains http://www.uc.edu/~RETTBESR/Links.html (p. 2)

Canadiana—The Canadian Resource Page
http://www.cs.cmu.edu/Unofficial/Canadiana/README.html (p. 3)

Curmudgeon's Stylebook: Contents and Index http://www.theslot.com/contents.html (p. 130)

Electric Library http://www.elibrary.com/search.cgi (p. 5)

English Server, The http://english-server.hss.cmu.edu (p. 5)

John Hewitt's Writer's Resource Center
http://www.azstarnet.com/~poewar/writer/writer.html (p. 131)

Irish Literature, Mythology, Folklore, and Drama
http://www.luminarium.org/mythology/ireland/ (p. 78)

Journalists' Resource List http://www.mediasource.com/links.html (p. 10)

SIRS: The Knowledge Source: Arts and Humanities
   http://www.sirs.com/tree/artshum.htm (p. 15)
Writing Resources http://www.missouri.edu/~wleric/writehelp.html (p. 133)
Young Canadian Voices: An Independent Literary Journal for Young Writers
   http://www.ugalumni.uoguelph.ca/~ttsuchid/ycv.html (p. 138)

TIPS & RESOURCES FOR WRITERS

1 2 3 4 5
DEPTH/BREADTH
QUALITY/ACCURACY
RELEVANCE
USEFULNESS
ENTERTAINMENT

The Curmudgeon's Stylebook: Contents and Index
http://www.theslot.com/contents.html

Bill Walsh

- English, Grammar and Style, Journalism, Writing
- All

Although designed for professionals, this Web site has interesting and useful information for student writers. Visitors may use a comprehensive index or choose a category from among the following: Word Choice, Capitalization, Compounds, Spelling and Style, Punctuation, Reader-friendliness, Quotations, Matters of Sensitivity, Headlines, Captions, Newspaper Issues, and Walshisms.

---

1 2 3 4 5
DEPTH/BREADTH
QUALITY/ACCURACY
RELEVANCE
USEFULNESS
ENTERTAINMENT

Division of Rhetoric and Composition
http://www.dla.utexas.edu/depts/drc/drc.html

University of Texas

- Computers, English, Indexes and Resource Lists, Literature, Writing
- 11, 12, AP

Three topics covered at this site are useful to high school students and teachers: Computer Writing and Research Lab (CWRL), Other Resources on Writing, and Undergraduate Writing Center. The first provides information on using the computer in the classroom and on using a Web page design language such as HTML. Also, and more importantly, CWRL offers course information and handouts for literary research. Other Resources on Writing provides links to on-line writing centers. The Undergraduate Writing Center provides help for students with writing assignments.

---

1 2 3 4 5
DEPTH/BREADTH
QUALITY/ACCURACY
RELEVANCE
USEFULNESS
ENTERTAINMENT

Eclectic Writer, The
http://www.eclectics.com/writing/writing.html

Eclectic Authors

- English, Grammar and Style, Literature, Writing
- 11, 12, AP

This resource page offers links to a variety of sites for writers. Students with an interest in writing will find good advice, support for their efforts, and plenty of challenges. The well-chosen links are categorized by genre. The site also provides access to reference material, specialized articles, and Usenet newsgroups.

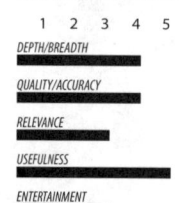

---

1 2 3 4 5
DEPTH/BREADTH
QUALITY/ACCURACY
RELEVANCE
USEFULNESS
ENTERTAINMENT

Essays on the Craft of Dramatic Writing
http://www.teleport.com/~bjscript/index.htm

Bill Johnson

- Drama and Theater, English, Writing
- All

This is a useful Web site for aspiring writers of screenplays, books, or plays. In each area there are links to one or more essays that develop an aspect of character or plot. In Movie Reviews there are links to *Groundhog Day* and *The Usual Suspects*; in the section on writing for the stage, you can explore how great plays were constructed by reviewing *Romeo and Juliet*, *'Night Mother*, and *The Iceman Cometh*. In the novel-writing section you'll find an exploration of how the plot of *The Hunt for Red October* was constructed and several links to aspects of the dramatic structure of *The Exorcist*.

✔ POINTCommunications Top 5% Web Site.

Indispensable Writing Resources
http://www.stetson.edu/~rhansen/writing.html

Randall S. Hansen, author of *Write Your Way to a Higher GPA*

- English, Grammar and Style, Indexes and Resource Lists, Literature, Writing
- AP

This resource page provides information in six categories: reference material, writing style guides, search engines, Internet reference resources, writing-related sites, and writing reference sites on the Web. These links take you to bibliographical listings or sometimes to sites where you get the information immediately. To purchase the most current books, you can connect with an on-line bookseller.

Inkspot: Resources for Writers
http://www.inkspot.com/

Debbie Ridpath Ohi

- English, Writing
- All

This very helpful site for the would-be writer offers information and comprehensive links to other writer-related pages. Topics include Networking, Market Info, Craft, Genres, Reference, Authors, and others. There are also links to discussion forums, classifieds, articles, FAQs, young writers, and a writers' poll. Additional links take the visitor to related sites in the WWW Virtual Library: Electronic Journals, Humanities, Journalism, Libraries, and Literature. There is the capability to search the Inkspot site or *Inklings*, the biweekly electronic newsletter for writers.

✔ USA Today *Hot Site*, GNN Select Site, Magellan 4 Star Site, POINTCommunications Top 5% Web Site, and nearly forty others!

John Hewitt's Writer's Resource Center
http://www.azstarnet.com/~poewar/writer/writer.html

John Hewitt, a professional technical writer

- English, Indexes and Resource Lists, Journalism, Literature, Writing
- 11, 12, AP

This resource page is directed at professional and would-be professional technical writers, but the information found here will certainly be useful to students and high school teachers. For example, the link to the site on journalism has tips for the writing the timed essay. There is also information about coping with the isolation writers face and advice on software.

✔ Awards: Top 1% Award and Luckman Interactive 5-Star Site.

Readers' and Writers' Resource Page
http://www.diane.com/readers/

WebFeats

- English, Indexes and Resource Lists, Writing
- All

This page is an invaluable resource for students interested in writing. There are three categories of links provided: Writers' Resources includes links to books useful for writers; Readers' Resources are links to on-line books, on-line bookstores, and A Reader's Resource; Reference includes links to daily news and quotation sources. The visitor is also invited to contribute to the Ten All-Time, Not-to-Be-Missed, Favorite Book List.

✔ Books A to Z Site of the Week.

English & Literature

1 2 3 4 5
DEPTH/BREADTH
QUALITY/ACCURACY
RELEVANCE
USEFULNESS
ENTERTAINMENT

Rhetoric and Electronic Arts Site
http://uts.cc.utexas.edu/~susanw/
Susan Warshauer
- Computers, English, Grammar and Style, Writing
- 11, 12, AP

This site is produced for and by a college class. The course deals with rhetoric, how to say or write things just the right way to elicit a particular response from a particular audience. On this page you find the classroom assignments in hypertext. Click on an assignment and you get details. Back on the home page, below the assignments, you find a section where there are samples of completed assignments. To learn something about rhetoric and the electronic arts, check out this site.

1 2 3 4 5
DEPTH/BREADTH
QUALITY/ACCURACY
RELEVANCE
USEFULNESS
ENTERTAINMENT

Speech Writing
http://speeches.com/index.shtm
David Slack Communications
- Political Science, Speech, U.S. History, World History
- All

This site offers free advice on your personal speeches, speech-writing tutorials, a large collection of historic and contemporary speeches on a wide variety of subjects (organized by category), links to other rhetoric sites, and even automatic speech writing for business or weddings. It also contains a speech search engine and very impressive links to writers' resources and communications sites.

✔ Magellan 4 Star Site. "Wonderful place to find good speech materials, copies of speeches to peruse ... from Martin Luther King to F. D. R. to Churchill to Mark Twain."—Steven J. Klass, G. C. Marshall High School, Falls Church, VA.

1 2 3 4 5
DEPTH/BREADTH
QUALITY/ACCURACY
RELEVANCE
USEFULNESS
ENTERTAINMENT

Virtual Presentation Assistant
http://www.ukans.edu/cwis/units/coms2/vpa/vpa.htm
Department of Communications, University of Kansas
- Debate, English, Grammar and Style, Speech
- All

This page offers an on-line tutorial to improve public-speaking skills. The site covers topics such as Determining Your Purpose, Selecting Your Topic, Researching Your Topic, Analyzing Your Audience, Supporting Your Points, Outlining Your Points, Using Visual Aids, and Presenting Your Speech. The visitor can follow the entire list or link to one area that needs improvement.

1 2 3 4 5
DEPTH/BREADTH
QUALITY/ACCURACY
RELEVANCE
USEFULNESS
ENTERTAINMENT

Writer's ToolBox
http://www.geocities.com/Athens/6346/
Brian Pomeroy
- English, Grammar and Style, Indexes and Resource Lists, Literature, Writing
- 11, 12, AP

This resource site caters to beginners as well as established writers. There are 10 neatly organized categories for easy access to information. Among the featured links are reference, research, fiction, drama, business, and software. The page is frequently updated.

✔ Awards: Suite 101 Top 5 Web Site, WebCrawler Select, and Winner NBNSoft Content Awards.

Writers Free Reference Desk
http://www.writers-free-reference.com/
World Wide Writer
- English, Grammar and Style, Indexes and Resource Lists, Reference (General), Writing
- All

This resource page lists links for anyone interested in writing or anyone who has been assigned a writing task. The links range from general reference resources to those that assist with the preparation of a term paper. Professionals and students alike will benefit from bookmarking this page. The page sponsor holds a monthly writing contest for as yet unpublished authors. Contest rules, submission guides, and winning entries can be found at this site

The Writers' Workshop: Online Resources for Writers
http://www.english.uiuc.edu/cws/wworkshop/writer.html
University of Illinois at Urbana-Champaign
- English, Grammar and Style, Indexes and Resource Lists, Writing
- All

This "write"-to-the-point site has thoughtful advice for students and teachers plus links to The Writers' Workshop Online Writing Guide, the Best Web Sites for Writers, and Reference Texts and Directories. A further breakdown of subjects gives you the following: Web-based help for writers, resources for teachers of writing, and the Writing Process Handbook. If you are having a tough time with "the writing process," a stop here is in order. It won't be easy, but it will give you a perspective on what is expected of you. You might even pick up a few good ideas for questions to stimulate your teacher.

Writing Resources
http://www.missouri.edu/~wleric/writehelp.html
University of Missouri
- English, Grammar and Style, Indexes and Resource Lists, Journalism, Literature, Writing
- All

This is a resource page for students and writers who want help with their writing. Links take the visitor to General Resources (such as Writer's Resources on the Web), Pulitzer Prizes, and The Playwright's Project. There are also links to authors and to such sites as the Seamus Heaney Cover Page and the InterNovel Home Page. There are also links to on-line writing labs, publishers, and to the Children's Writing Resource Center.

Young Writers Clubhouse
http://www.realkids.com/club.htm
Deborah Morris
- English, Writing
- All

Ever thought about writing but didn't know where to turn for advice and encouragement? Here's an oasis, a spot of refreshment for your weary writer's bones. On this lively page, young authors ages eight to eighteen find an encouraging message from author Deborah Morris. This page features advice from real authors, answers to frequently asked questions, a section on how to get started, a chatroom, and critiques of your writing by peers. Also there are monthly writing contests.

See Also

WRITING STYLE & COMPOSITION TIPS chapter (p. 33)

BookZone http://www.bookzone.com/ (p. 144)

Bosnian Virtual Fieldtrip, The http://geog.gmu.edu/gess/jwc/bosnia/bosnia.html (p. 126)

For Young Writers http://www.inkspot.com/young/ (p. 135)

Inkwell, The: In Appreciation of Writers and Writing http://TheInkwell.com/(p. 61)

Judy Blume's Home Base http://www.judyblume.com/home-menu.html (p. 88)

Literature Resources for the High School and College Student http://www.teleport.com/~mgroves/index.shtml#Home (p. 12)

NetNovel http://www.netnovel.com/partners/index.html (p. 137)

Roget's Thesaurus http://ecco.bsee.swin.edu.au/text/roget/index.html (p. 24)

Screenwriters.com http://www.screenwriters.com/screennet.html (p. 62)

Screenwriters/Playwrights Page http://www.teleport.com/~cdeemer/scrwriter.html (p. 63)

Tales from the Vault http://www.rigroup.com/storyart/tales/message1.html (p. 138)

WRITING OPPORTUNITIES FOR STUDENTS

256 Shades of Grey
http://www.primenet.com/~blkgrnt/index.html
Clifford J. Kurkowski, publisher
- English, Literature, Writing
- 11, 12, AP

This 'zine offers an opportunity to read works by previously unpublished authors. If you are inclined, you may submit your own work. Featured are poetry, fiction, non-fiction, reviews, essays, lyrics, artwork, and translations. Links take you to Figments (poetry) and Footlights (fiction) to see what has been published.

Creative Nexus' Literature Site
http://tqd.advanced.org/3089/lit/lit.html
ThinkQuest
- English, Literature, Writing
- All

This site features poetry, short stories, essays and journalism from students. The offerings are limited at present with only 40 works available, but will grow once more students submit their own work.

The Diary Project: Kids' Diary Entries from Around the World
http://www.well.com/user/diary/
The Well
- English, Reading, Writing
- All

The inspiration for this site was *Zlata's Diary: A Child's Life in Sarajevo*. The journals included in this site allow young people to share their personal thoughts, feelings, and dreams. By the end of 1997, the sponsors hope to include a forum to make the Diary Project an interactive experience. The visitor may just enter the Diary or browse submissions by subject: drugs, tolerance, point of view, family, loss, racism, school, relationships, who am I?, friends, violence, feelings, parents, or stress. There are also links for submitting works and to KidPub and Kids on the Web.

For Young Writers
http://www.inkspot.com/young/
Debbie Redpath Ohi
- English, Indexes and Resource Lists, Writing
- All

This resource page has six sections. Feature articles provide inspirational information about writing. Market information tells you about magazines looking for stories. Useful sites provides an amalgam of sites to help you get started and network with other young writers. The forum offers ongoing communication from young writers. Classifieds gives very specific information from editors, magazines, and publishers looking for stories. There are also recommendations of other sources of interest to young writers.

English & Literature

The Global Campfire
http://www.indiana.edu/~eric_rec/fl/pcto/campfire.html

Allen Sylvester and Christopher Essex

- English, Writing
- All

This is an interactive story site. Read from several stories and add to them. The idea is to allow any number of people from many backgrounds to have an "around the campfire" experience of storytelling. Most importantly it gives everyone an opportunity to be a storyteller.

The Greatest Tale Ever Told
http://www.amazon.com/exec/obidos/subst/features/g/greatest%2Dtale/greatest%2Dtale%2Dhome.html/1603-7486006-421910

Amazon.com, Inc.

- English, Literature, Writing
- 11, 12, AP

This is a contest page. John Updike has begun a story and you are invited to add to it. If the judges like what they find, you may win up to $100,000.

i am smitten
http://www.allura.net/smitten.html

Allura Ellington

- English, Literature, Writing
- 11, 12, AP

This on-line journal is well-written and heartfelt. Here young people wondering what to write about their own lives will find answers. Linked to this Web page is a site called Open Pages, an on-line community of people who put their lives on line.

MidLink Magazine
http://longwood.cs.ucf.edu:80/~MidLink/index.html

MidLink Magazine

- Current Events, English, Geography, Literature, Math, Science (General), World History, Writing
- 9, 10

This site provides students from around the globe with an opportunity to share their thoughts on any number of issues. It also provides links to author pages and resource pages for teachers. An interesting link to book reviews includes a list of recommended reading and students' opinions about the books. There are special links to reviews from students in other countries, such as Canada and Australia. Every issue has a theme. A quick index provides links to sections on history and geography, science and math, recreation, culture, 3D projects, and stories.

✔ *World Wide Web Associates Top Ten Winner, A#1 Quality Award for Excellence, Best 500 Web Sites in the World, Magellan 4 Star Site.*

The Mighty Pen Online Magazine Home Page
http://pages.prodigy.com/FL/coolie/coolie.html

Young Writers Association

- English, Literature, Writing
- All

This site offers an on-line magazine for high school students written by members of the Young Writers Association. Featured are book/music reviews, poems, short stories, an interview, pictures, graphics, and more. You scroll from page to page for the contents. Also offered is a monthly contest—the one I checked was for a limerick—and a monthly market report. For the full impact, you can subscribe or submit your own work by—you guessed it—following directions.

✔ Coolie Online.

NetNovel
http://www.netnovel.com/partners/index.html

NetNovel

- English, Grammar and Style, Writing
- All

This site encourages participation by an entire class. The idea is to encourage creative writing by taking on a project with publication as the goal. There are opportunities for students, teachers, and administrators to get involved as writers, curriculum developers, and program hosts.

Shadow
http://metro.net/shadow/

Shadow Magazine

- English, Writing
- All

This site aims to provide a "collection of exciting fiction for teenagers." The only links are to subscribe to the printed version of the magazine, submit a story, join the mailing list, or read a representative piece of fiction.

Spark Magazine
http://www.teenhangout.com/spark/

Teen's Hangout International

- English, Writing
- All

This site is home to an on-line magazine for teens. Every three months new work by teenagers appears in these categories: essays and fiction, poetry, and reviews. Find out what other young people are thinking and writing about or submit something you've written.

Tales from the Vault
http://www.rigroup.com/storyart/tales/message1.html
The Rock Island Group
- English, Literature, Writing
- 11, 12, AP

This site contains stories subdivided by genre in ten "chambers," including science fiction, fantasy, humor, and poetry. Most categories are filled with stories completed in segments provided by visitors. The exception is chamber nine, which features complete stories. New Tales begin in chamber ten. A full-featured site, Tales from the Vault has links to a general information, guidelines and legal information, reviews and favorites, a chat area, and resources for writers.

✔ *Awards:* USA Today *Hot Site* and Omnivision Winner.

Young Canadian Voices: An Independent Literary Journal for Young Writers
http://www.ugalumni.uoguelph.ca/~ttsuchid/ycv.html
Young Canadian Voices
- English, Literature, Writing
- All

This site replicates on the Web the independent journal for young writers, *Young Canadian Voices*. The homepage lists the table of contents, biographies of the people whose work is included, a note from the editors, submission information, and buttons for previous issues. The journal is available twice a year, but there is an attempt being made to offer more writing and graphics throughout the year at this Web site.

✔ *Yahoo! Pick of the Week*

zeen
http://www.cyberteens.com/ezine/Issues.html
Mountain Lake Software and Cyberteens
- English, Writing
- All

This 'zine for people under 18 years old accepts and publishes short fiction, articles, poems and editorials; art, photos and comics; reviews of software, web sites and books; musical compositions; and Shockwave movies. The site offers links to back issues of the zeen. Check out the posts link to find out what's on the minds of young people from almost everywhere.

See Also

CYBER & WEB WRITING chapter (p. 139)

Bosnian Virtual Fieldtrip, The http://geog.gmu.edu/gess/jwc/bosnia/bosnia.html (p. 126)

Case, The: The Fun and Challenging Mystery Website http://www.thecase.com/thecase/ (p. 147)

Crayon — CReAte Your Own Newspaper http://crayon.net/ (p. 126)

Cyberteens http://www.cyberteens.com/ctmain.html (p. 139)

Kay E. Vandergrift's Special Interest Page http://www.scils.rutgers.edu/special/kay/kayhp2.html (p. 10)

Positively Poetry http://advicom.net/~e-media/kv/poetry1.html (p. 55)

Tangerine: Poetry Site Extraordinaire http://tqd.advanced.org/3721/ (p. 56)

Young Writers Clubhouse http://www.realkids.com/club.htm (p. 133)

CYBER & WEB WRITING

Amnesia Interactive Novel
http://www.bergen.org/AAST/Projects/Amnesia/
Joshua Ludzki and Josh Goldfond
- English, Writing
- 11, 12, AP

This page is the result of an idea at the Academy for the Advancement of Science and Technology. The premise: rather than depending on an author to make things interesting for a reader, how about giving the reader choices to determine where the story is going. A discussion area and voting privileges are built into the site.

✔ *Microsoft Network Pick of the Day, InfiNet's Cool Site of the Day.*

Bonebox, The
http://www.hway.net/netguru/bonebox/main.htm
Ryan Ferguson
- English, Literature, Writing
- AP

This site is for serious writers. It features poetry, fiction, and criticism, with opportunities for readers to submit both original works and criticism. Links take you to the people behind the Bonebox, updates, other information, and related sites.

Cyberteens
http://www.cyberteens.com/ctmain.html
Mountain Lake Software, Inc.
- English, Writing
- All

This site aims to create community among teens throughout the world. Cyberteens hopes to bring teens together through writing and other artistic activities, providing a forum for young people to discuss submissions and make contributions to the b-board. Among the features are interviews with celebrities and movie reviews. There are also links to a youth 'zine, art galley, young composers room, and other sites.

✔ *Shocked Site of the Day, Magellan 4 Star Site, Thumbs Up Award by Teenagers Circle.*

Hyperizons
http://www.duke.edu/~mshumate/hyperfic.html
Michael Shumate
- English, Literature, Writing
- 11, 12, AP

Some people may think this site foreshadows the future, and it very well might. Hyperizons is an exhaustive presentation of hyperfiction—meaning stories that take different paths depending on the choices you, as a reader, make by clicking on hypertext. You get links to an impressive index of original stories, reviews, theory and criticism, and bibliographies. Announcements provides notice of contests, in case you are inclined to submit something of your own.

✔ *GNN Best Net Winner.*

Hypertext and Hypermedia: A Select Bibliography
http://gwis2.circ.gwu.edu/~scottlib/hyperbib.htm

Scott Stebelman, George Washington University

- Computers, Indexes and Resource Lists, Writing
- 11, 12, AP

The increasing explosion of materials on the Internet makes this page a valuable one for students interested in this use of computers. The visitor will find a definition, hypertext FAQs, links to relevant journals, links to useful Web sites on hypertext, a timeline, bibliographical/literature reviews, and general resources. All students wishing to try their hands at this genre will find helpful background at this site.

Kairos: A Journal for Teachers of Writing in the Webbed Environment
http://english.ttu.edu/kairos/1.1/index.html

Alliance for Computers and Writing

- Computers, English, Literature, Writing
- AP

This newly inaugurated journal—it debuted Spring 1996—is concerned with technology in the teaching of writing, composition, technical communication, rhetoric, literature, and writing across the curriculum. It makes use of frames technology to allow for several contributors to take on a subject, such as pixelated rhetoric, make comments, and receive E-mail.

On-line Highbeam
http://www.en.utexas.edu/~daniel/309m/

Daniel Anderson, Computer Writing and Resource Labs, University of Texas

- Computers, English, Grammar and Style, Writing
- AP

This site calls itself "a computers and writing site" and concerns itself with Internet media, writing, and culture. There are links to leading on-line writing centers, search engines, style guides, and related resources.

Oz Project Home Page
http://www.cs.cmu.edu/afs/cs.cmu.edu/project/oz/web/oz.html

Carnegie Mellon University School of Computer Science

- Computers, Drama and Theater, English, Literature, Writing
- AP

This site is the home page for a university project to develop a computer system that would allow authors to create and present interactive dramas. Presently, the link to worlds and images provides a rudimentary example of an interactive drama using a character called Woggles.

A Ring of Her Own
http://www.geocities.com/~alliegator/ring/
Webring and New Dream Network
- English, Literature, Writing
- AP

This is a site that requires a password and a Web site of your own. It is for women only. Specifically, it is for women who write journals, as the "ring" provides a link to other women who write journals. Not very practical for school work, but for someone who is a writer and willing to explore her world, this could be a valuable site.

ThinkQuest
http://io.advanced.org/thinkquest/
Advanced Network and Services
- All
- All

This site offers an annual contest that challenges students ages twelve to nineteen to use the Internet "as a collaborative, interactive teaching and learning tool." The quest is to build Web pages to prepare students for the twenty-first century. The site offers a library of original and award-winning pages. This library is worth paging through to see the quality of the work being done. Awards begin at $25,000 for first place finishers to $500 for fifth place.

✔ Education World, Planet Science Award, NetGuide Gold Site, Scout Report Selection, ZIA Award, Family-Friendly Site.

Tree Fiction on the World Wide Web
http://www.cl.cam.ac.uk/users/gdr11/tree-fiction.html#Introduction
Gareth Rees
- English, Literature, Writing
- 11, 12, AP

This resource site concerns itself with a particular type of hyperfiction called "tree literature" (or "plot branching" or "choose your own fiction.") You'll find an essay, with links to terms and other essential information, discussing the merits of tree literature, providing examples of different methods of merging narratives, and links to prominent hyperfiction sites. Among the links are those to a style guide and short fiction sites.

Wacky Web Tales
http://www.hmco.com/hmco/school/tales/
Houghton Mifflin Company
- English, Writing
- 9, 10

Based on the "Madlibs" concept, this entertaining site allows students to insert words into any one of a dozen Web tales provided or access an archive of tales. Students are also given the opportunity to write their own Web tale and have it posted on the site. There is a listing of over sixty tales submitted by students from around the world, which can be read for ideas and amusement.

See Also

WRITING OPPORTUNITIES FOR STUDENTS chapter (p. 135)

Book Recommendations of Real Folks
http://www.best.com/~yylee/homespun/booktop.html (p. 143)

Introduction to Chicana/o Literature http://www.en.utexas.edu/~sheilac/chicana.html (p. 80)

VOID: PERFORMANCE http://www.voidp.demon.co.uk/index.htm (p. 64)

Wired Style http://www.hotwired.com/hardwired/wiredstyle/ (p. 25)

BOOKS & PUBLISHING

Academy of Achievement: Virtual Book Club
http://www.achievement.org/library/bookclub.html
Center for the Book, Library of Congress
- English, Literature
- All

The Virtual Book Club features works by members of the Library of Congress's Academy of Achievement. During each month, a contemporary writer who belongs to the academy is featured with a photo, a brief biography, and a list of his or her favorite books. At the end of the month, during which time you are encouraged to read the books, there is an open chatroom forum with the author. An interview and more information is forthcoming. As you search deeper and deeper into the page and the Academy of Achievement more resources unfold. Unfortunately, the number of writers invited to join the Academy of Achievement has been quite limited.

Banned Books Online
http://www.cs.cmu.edu/people/spok/banned-books.html/
John Mark Ockerbloom, Carnegie Mellon University Censorship Project
- Current Events, English, Indexes and Resource Lists, Literature
- 11, 12, AP

Almost anything you wanted to know about books that have been banned can be found here, including links to actual texts of banned books and transcripts from Supreme Court cases. The information is presented under categories such as books suppressed or banned by legal authorities, those considered unfit for schools and minors, and more information about censorship. Comprehensive, authoritative, and even entertaining, if you enjoy listening to James Joyce reading from one of his books.

✔ *Free Speech Online Blue Ribbon Campaign.*

Bibliomania, The Network Library
http://www.bibliomania.com/
Data Text Publishing Ltd.
- English, Literature, Reading
- All

This site allows visitors to read on-line or print their own copies of books. The categories given are Reference; Fiction, which included over forty classic novels listed by author and divided into chapters; Nonfiction; and Poetry. The most recent additions are listed separately and there is a U.S. mirror site available as well as a search engine.

Book Recommendations of Real Folks
http://www.best.com/~yylee/homespun/booktop.html
Y.Y. Lee and Marty Betz
- English, Indexes and Resource Lists, Literature
- All

Looking for a good book to complete that reading assignment? Find out what books other people feel strongly about, strongly enough to want to list them at this site. Some lists include comments; many do not. Read good books and contribute your own list to this site. Links from this page take you to a list of all titles. You can browse random lists, use the search button for a specific author or title, or click on the related sites for more lists.

English & Literature

Booklist: Books for Youth
http://www.ala.org/booklist/002.html

Booklist Magazine
- English, Indexes and Resource Lists, Literature
- All

Over 2,500 books for youth are listed and reviewed at this site, sponsored by the American Library Association's respected *Booklist* magazine. Choose older level—middle and young reader categories are listed also—and you'll find a formidable list of books. Further down this linked page you get the review. From the Books for Youth page, you can go directly to lists of fiction, nonfiction, features, archives and the *Booklist* Index. Features include YA Talk with subjects such as "The Challenge and Glory of Youth Adult Literature" or "Editors' Choices Revisited." Take control of your reading assignments by choosing books that interest you.

✔ HomePC *1996 Best Web Sites.*

BookTalks—Quick and Simple
http://www.concord.k12.nh.us/schools/rundlett/booktalks/

Nancy J. Keane
- English, Indexes and Resource Lists, Literature
- All

With more than 400 short book reviews and still growing, this site is primarily intended for teachers and librarians. But what works for them works for any student who is pressed for time to find a good book. The page provides links by author, title, and an author list. This is a nicely presented, efficient site.

✔ *Librarian Site du Jour, Top 1,000 World Sites.*

BookWire—The First Place to Look for Book Information
http://www.bookwire.com/

Bowker Book Information, Cahners Publishing
- Literature, Reading
- All

This site is bursting with information concerning books and related reviews. The visitor may choose to use the BookWire Navigator that displays a hierarchical view of all information or may Search the Book Info database. The content of the page changes but generally contains links to categories in BookWire. Features include numerous reviews of books in specialized areas; the BookWire Index, which includes thousands of book-related resources; and Inside the Book Business.

✔ *Magellan 4 Star Site, CNN Best of the Net Nominee,* Literary Market Place *Technical Achievement Award for 1995.*

BookZone
http://www.bookzone.com/

BookZone
- English, Literature, Indexes and Resource Lists, Writing
- All

Here you will find lists of books and descriptions for your next reading assignment or research paper (click on Literary Leaps, or on Super Catalog to go directly to a link for young adult literature). You can also find tips on writing (check the Resources button to find all about publishing, writer's agreements, etc.) and directions to the nearest bookstore to locate that hard-to-find book.

✔ *Cool Site of the Hour, Your WebScout Way Cool Site. EZConnect Best of the Net, Magellan 4-Star Site, POINTCommunications Top 5% Web Site.*

Chapter One
http://www1.psi.net/chapterone/
Dial-A-Book
- English, Literature
- 11, 12, AP

This site offers first chapters, tables of contents, and other excerpts from more than 360 books and ninety-two publishers. You can browse these contents for free and then order online. The books included fall into several categories: one is for books reviewed by the prominent *Atlantic Monthly* or *Foreign Affairs* magazines; another features books from university presses; another is for Newberry Award winners. There are also several categories for science books.

Children's Literature Web Guide
http://www.ucalgary.ca/~dkbrown/
David K. Brown, Doucette Library of Teaching Resources, University of Calgary
- English, Indexes and Resource Lists, Literature, Reading, Writing
- 9, 10

Among the most valuable links at this site is the list of best books from 1996. Click on it and get another list with subjects including best books for young adults, picks for reluctant readers, popular paperbacks for young adults, and selected films and videos for young adults. Back at the home page there are many links to author, teacher resources, and research links.

Crack Fiction
http://allrise.com/index.html
The All Rise! Network
- English, Literature, Reading
- 11, 12, AP

Call up this site and a fascinating graphic of a woman warrior on a red background emerges. Three links at the bottom of the page take you to hypertext versions of books by William Burroughs, Timothy Leary, Jack Kerouac, among others. You click on an icon and get a paragraph or two of a story with a few words hyperlinked. Click on a word, and rather than getting a definition, you get more of the story. In other words, in this introduction to hypertext publishing, you create your own storyline. There are also links to related sites, background information about the sponsor, awards, and such.

✔ Riot's Hot Spot, Illumination Award, Gold Star Award. Best Hang Out, Rancho DeNada Outpost of the Week.

Favorite Teenage Angst Books
http://www.echonyc.com/~cafephrk/angstbooks.html
Grouchy Cafe
- English, Indexes and Resource Lists, Literature, Reading
- All

4 5   5   4   5   4

Ever get stuck looking for a good book to read, but were afraid to ask? Here's the page for you. Teen angst—drug use, stuff about sex, out-of-it parents. All of that, and —let it be our secret—good literature, too. Award-winning writers who tell it like it is. Links to the Grouchy Cafe, pages of reader reactions about the recommended books, graffiti, and an on-line diary. Attractive, clever, and fun.

Reading By Teens For Teens

http://tqd.advanced.org/3412/

ThinkQuest
- English, Literature
- All

This site provides a means to determine which books are most popular with teens. You choose a category, such as nonfiction, and go to a survey page where you fill in information about a book you would like to recommend. At the bottom of each page there is a list of the top three selections.

Women's Books Online

http://www.cybergrrl.com/review/

Lee Anne Phillips
- English, Literature
- All

This extensive site reviews a wide range of books by women. Women around the world review the books, providing a breadth of perspective. The reviews are organized in several categories: New Reviews, Nonfiction, Fiction, Reviews by Reviewer, and Reviews by Date. Although the site covers many books, visitors can easily find a specific review by using one of the search formats offered.

See Also

American Studies @ The University of Virginia http://xroads.virginia.edu/ (p. 67)

Athena: Authors & Texts http://un2sg1.unige.ch/www/athena/html/authors.html (p. 1)

AwardWeb: Collections of Literary Award Information http://www.city-net.com/~lmann/awards (p. 21)

Background Readings on Female Coming-of-Age Stories http://www.scils.rutgers.edu/special/kay/ageback.html (p. 1)

Books in Chains http://www.uc.edu/~RETTBESR/Links.html (p. 2)

Book Lovers: Fine Books & Literature http://www.xs4all.nl/~pwessel/ (p. 2)

Books of South Asian Writers Writing in English
http://www.ntu.edu.sg/home/mdamodaran/sabooks.html (p. 80)

CM http://www.mbnet.mb.ca/cm/home/about.html (p. 4)

Electric Library http://www.elibrary.com/search.cgi (p. 5)

First Lines http://pc159.lns.cornell.edu/firsts/ (p. 147)

Hola! (Hello) Oh What a Book! Science and More!! http://tqd.advanced.org/3240/ (p. 41)

Internet Public Library http://www.ipl.org/ (p. 9)

Judy Blume's Home Base http://www.judyblume.com/home-menu.html (p. 88)

Kay E. Vandergrift's Special Interest Page
http://www.scils.rutgers.edu/special/kay/kayhp2.html (p. 10)

MidLink Magazine http://longwood.cs.ucf.edu:80/~MidLink/index.html (p. 136)

Mysterious Home Page http://www.db.dk/dbaa/jbs/homepage.html (p. 43)

Native Lit-L: A Mailing List for Native Literature http://www.uwm.edu/~mwilson/lit.htm (p. 73)

NetNovel http://www.netnovel.com/partners/index.html (p. 137)

North American Native Authors Catalog
http://nativeauthors.com/search/home.html (p. 73)

On-line Books Page http://www.cs.cmu.edu/books.html (p. 14)

Sixties Project and Viet Nam Generation, Inc.
http://jefferson.village.virginia.edu/sixties/ (p. 74)

Wiretap Electronic Text Archive http://wiretap.area.com/ (p. 17)

Young Adult Literature Library
http://www.uiowa.edu/~english/litcult2097/tlucht/lit-yalib.html (p. 19)

MISCELLANEOUS SITES

The Case: The Fun and Challenging Mystery Website
http://www.thecase.com/thecase/
Newfront Communications
- English, Literature
- 9, 10

This Web site offers mysteries in a compact format. The visitor can spend five minutes on Monday with a short mystery; on Wednesday a five-minute mystery is offered to be solved by the next Wednesday; on Friday the offering is a Mysterious Photo about which the visitor can write or read a short mystery. There is also a link to mysteries on TV.

Deciphering Old Handwriting
http://www.firstct.com/fv/oldhand.html
Sabina J. Murray
- Literature, Reading, U.S. History, World History, Writing
- All

This fascinating on-line tutorial will help students get the most from old documents and records that may be available to them. The further back we go, the harder records may be to read because of changes in the way letters are formed. This Web page teaches students the basics of deciphering old handwriting. Topics explored are old style abbreviations, marks, and numbers. There are also sections on proper names, places of birth, and occupations. There are two sample documents that students can attempt to decipher to solve a mystery. This site is fun, informative, and unusual.

First Lines
http://pc159.lns.cornell.edu/firsts/
John Dobbins and Mary Ochs
- English, Literature
- All

Even younger students may enjoy this site, which provides the first lines of books that must then be identified by the visitor. The categories begin with Story Time and include Books I Read at Recess, Jamestown High, Eng. Lit., Tome of the Brave, Voices of Women, Translation Please, The Way It Was, Who Done It, Periods Are for Sissies, The Prize, I Spy, Sci-Fi, Boo!, I Saw the Movie, It's True, and Cheer Up. Another area is broken down by decades, from the 1950s to the 1990s.

Good Quotations by Famous People
http://www.cs.virginia.edu/~robins/quotes.html
Gabriel Robins
- English, Literature, Reference (General)
- All

This page contains a long list of quotable quotes from famous people. It's fun to browse the list to see what people such as Einstein and Voltaire had to say. (Voltaire: "Anything that is too stupid to be spoken is sung.") There are no links from this page to other quotation pages, only back to the page sponsor's home page.

✔ *POINTCommunications Top 5% Web Site.*

Letters Magazine

http://www.signature.pair.com/letters/

Letters Magazine

- English, Literature, Writing
- All

This site is a unique magazine devoted exclusively to letters. Its scope includes manner of letters, including but not limited to those of famous correspondence. It also accepts letters on any number of subjects from readers, either letters the readers have composed or letters from relatives, dead or alive. You must give permission to print before publication. The content from back issues of the magazine provides a substantive look at the types of issues *Letters* tackles: coming out, last letters, Christianity, U.S. presidents and politics.

New Moon: The Magazine for Girls and Their Dreams

http://www.newmoon.org/

New Moon

- English, Writing
- 9, 10

This is the on-line site for *New Moon* magazine. It is every bit as professionally put together but not as attractive as the magazine. However, both are nicely presented. You get selected pieces from the current and back issues of the magazine. Produced by girls for girls, *New Moon* contains articles and stories from its international readers. Click on the guidelines button and get advice on how to submit your own letter, story, article, or art work.

Quotations

http://www.geocities.com/~spanoudi/quote.html

Steve Spanoudis, Geocities

- English, Indexes and Resource List, Literature, Reference (General)
- All

This resource page features links to thirty collections of quotations, everything from Shakespeare to Serious Sarcasm, from Stupid to the Best, from a quote for the day to children's songs. Search by author or topic.

✔ Magellan 4 Star Site, Yahoo Best of the Web Site.

The Quotations Page

http://www.starlingtech.com/quotes/

Michael Moncur

- English, Literature, Reference (General)
- All

This site offers both a quote of the day and quotes of the week. You can contribute a quote, view a random quote, search for a quotation, or link to other quotation sites.

✔ POINTCommunications Top 5% Web Site.

See Also

CyberSchool Magazine http://www.cyberschoolmag.com/ (p. 39)

Mighty Pen Online Magazine Home Page
http://pages.prodigy.com/FL/coolie/coolie.html (p. 137)

Index

Entries in bold are Internet Sites

11 Rules of Writing 33
17th Century Studies 6; Literature 42; Writers 42
18th Century Studies 4,6,18,44,124
19th Century London State: An Exploration 58
19th Century Woman's Place, A 38
19th Century, British Playwrights 58; Costume 60; Literature 77; Studies 7,12,38,45,68,94,96,112
20,000 leagues Under the Sea 121
20th Century, Authors 41; Literature 2; Studies
221B Baker Street: Sherlock Holmes 96
256 Shades of Gray 135

A

A Very Unofficial John Irving Page 101
A&E—Behind the Scenes 38
Aboriginal Literature, Poetry 50
Aboriginal Poetry Bibliography, The 50
About Poetry—Stuff from Don 50
Absurd Man, The 90
Academy for the Advancement of Science and Technology 139
Academy of Achievement: Virtual Book Club 143
Academy of American Poets 50
Achebe, Chinua 80,84
Acronym Lookup 24
Adams, Deborah 84
Advanced Grammar and Composition 30
Advice on Academic Writing 33
Aesop 17
Afghanistan 82
African American Autobiography: A Collection of Critical Essays 1
African American Bibliography at the University of Michigan 18
African American Literature 67
African American Mosaic at the Library of Congress 18
African American, Literature 1,18,67,68,69,81,88; Poetry 55; Studies 44,68; Women Authors 11,16,95,100
African Writers: Vocies of Change 80
African, Culture 99; Literature 80,82,109; Proverbs 28
After the First Death 92
Akhmatova, Anna 54,82
Albert Camus 90
Alcott, Louisa May 84
Alexander, William 51
Alexie, Sherman 73
Algonquin Hotel 67
Algonquin Round Table, The 67
Alice Walker—Womanist Writer 122
Alighieri, Dante 93
Alsop Review, The 38
American Drama 58
American Film Institute 58
American Indian Students Journal 71
American Library Association 144
American Literature 7,67,68,74; Minorities 71; Poetry 50,51,52,53,54, 56,58
American Literature Survey Site 67

American Scenes: Lorraine Hansberry 99
American Slanguages 27
American South, 19th Century 68
American Southwest 56
American Studies@ The University of Virginia 67
Amnesia Interactive Novel 139
An Unofficial E.E.Cummings Starting Point 93
Ancient Chinese Dragon Series 47
Andersen, Hans Christian 84
Anderson, Sherwood 84
Angela's Ashes 42
Angelou, Maya 18,55,84
Angers, Felicite 75
Animal Farm 109
Anniina'a Amy Tan Page 119
Anthropology 5,8,49,56,70,72,73,81
anyone lived in a pretty how town 93
Aquinis, Thomas 15
Archeus: Worksearch Resources 33
Arden John 59
Arlington, VA 127
Around the World in Eighty Days 121
Art 1,2,6,8,10,15,23,38,45,56,72
Art History 1,2,3,5,6,7,8,13,14,38,45, 48,78
Arthurian Studies 76,78
Artsedge 38
Ash Wednesday 96
Ashe, Geoffrey 78
Asian American, Drama 58;Literature 75
Asian Poets Page 50
Asian, Literature 80;Poetry 50
Asian-American Theatre Revue 58
Ask an Expert 14,30,63,133
Ask Miss Grammar 29
Astronomy & Space 41,56
Athena: Authors & Texts 1
Atlanta 27
Atlantic Monthly 18,51,52,73,126
Atlantic Monthly Poetry Pages 51
Atlantic Unbound—*The Atlantic Monthly* 126
Atlas of the World Wide Web 1
Atwood, Margaret 84
Auden, W.H. 85
Augustine 40
Auld Lang Syne 89
Austen, Jane 42,76,86
Australia 119,136
Australian Literature 82
Austria 82
Author's Pen 1
AwardWeb: Collections of Literary Award Information 21
Aztecs 81

B

Background Readings of Female Coming-of-Age Stories 1
Bacon, Francis 17,42
Baillie, Joana 18
Bait, The 95
Bakhtin Center 82
Bald Soprano, The 101
Banks, Russell 73
Banned Books Online 143
Bar Harbor, Me 27
Baragona's Chaucer Page 91

Barr's English Class 21
Barry, Elizabeth 62
Barry, Robertine 75
Bartleby Project of Columbia 125
Bartlett's Quotations 24,43
Basic Prose Style and Mechanics 34
Beach, Sylvia 71
Beat Generation 27,71,89
Beauvoir, Simone de 87
Beckette, Samuel 87
Behind the Bookcase 49
Behn, Apra 62
Bellingham High School 7
Belloc, Hilaire 91
Ben Okri Page 109
Beowulf 13,77,78
Berkeley Digital Library SunSITE 2
Bible 40; Swahili Translation 4
Bibliomania, The Network Library 143
Biography 2,6,7,11,12,13,15,17,31,38,41,42,44,47 5,51,59,62,63,67,68,69,70,72-75,77, 80,84-125,138,143; Aboriginal 50; African American16; American Poets 53;Canadian 3; Cowboy Poets 57; Irish Poets 52; Playwrights 65;Screenwriters 61;West Indian 82; Women 18,39,45,69,75,76,84,-88,91, 92,94,95,98-101,104-107,111,112, 117,119,122
Biology 23
Bishop, Elizabeth 87
Black Classic Press 68
Black Cultural Studies WebSite, A 68
Black Family Pledge 84
Blake Multimedia Project, The 87
Blake, William 42,87,88
Blok, Aleksandr 54
Blood of Others, The 87
Blue Web'N Applications: English References 2
Blume, Judy 19,88
Bogland 99
Bohemian Ink 27
Bohemian News Archives 27
Bonebox, The 139
Booge, Barnabe 51
Book Lovers: Find Books & Literature 2
Book Reviews 4,17,18,19,39,43,44,73, 75,81,110,118,119,121,136,144,146
Book Stacks Unlimited 1
Booklist: Books for Youth 144
BookRadio 39
Books in Chains 2
Books of South Asian Writers Writing in English 80
Books Recommended for Real Folks 143
Bookstores Online 1,2,23,27,43,80,101,103,131
BookTalks—Quick and Simple 144
BookWire—The First Place to Look for Book Information 144
BookZone 144
Boorstin, Daniel 42
Borges, Jorge Luis 41
Bosnian Virtual Fieldtrip, The 126
Bradbury, Ray 60
Bram Stoker Home Page 119
Branagh, Kenneth 61,105

English & Literature

Braun 60
Brazil, Theater 62
Brideshead Revisted 122
Brief Guide to the Romance Genre 39
Britain *see* United Kingdom
British Library 78; Literature 7; Poetry 51,53
British Poetry 1780-1910: A Hypertext Archive of Scholarly Editions 51
British Womens' Novels: A Reading List, 1777-1818 76
Broadway 62
Brooke, Rupert 53
Brooks, Gwendolyn 55,88
Brothers Karamozov 95
Brown University 21,45
Brown University Women Writers Project, The 21
Browning, Elizabeth Barrett 42,88
Bruderhof Community 40
Bulfinch's Mythology 47
Bulgaria 82
Burden of Proof, The 104
Burney, Frances 76
Burns—The National Bard 89
Burns, Robert 89
Burroughs, Edgar Rice 89
Burroughs, William S 71,89,145
Butterflies 108
Byron, Lord 90

C

CalRen Project, The 34
Calvin, John 40
Camelot Project, The 76
Camelot *see* Arthurian Studies
Campus Writing Program's Resources for Writers 30
Camus, Albert 90
Canada 3,33,37,72,75,136; Theater 62
Canadian Literary Archive Service 3
Canadian Literature 11,82,84
Canadiana—The Canadian Resource Page 3
Careers 38,64
Caribbean Literature 82
Carl Con's Slanguage of Swing 69
Carlyle, Thomas 90
Carnegie Mellon University 18
Carroll, Lewis 90
Carson, Rachel 91
Cartland, Barbara 76
Case, The 60
Case, The: The Fun and Challenging Mystery Website 147
Cassady, Neal 71
Castle, The: Joseph K's Franz Kafka Homepage 103
Casualty 99
Catcher in the Rye 113
Catcher in the Rye Campfire, The 113
Catcher in the Rye 21,113
Cather, Willa 91
Caulfield, Holden 113
Cela: A+ Research and Writing for High School and College Students 34
Celebration of Women Writers, A 39
Celestial Timepiece: A Joyce Carol Oates Home Page 109

Celtic, Culture 52,77; Literature 78
Censorship 88
Centaurian, The: John Updike Home Page 121
Centre for Reformation and Renaissance Studies 3
Chan, Karen Y 50
Chapter One 145
Charles Dickens 94
Charles Dickens, The Great Expectations Index 94
Chaucer, Geoffery 79,91
Chekhov, Anton 63,82
Chen, Jennifer Crystal 50
Cheney, Harriet Vaughn 75
Chesterton, Gilbert Keith 91
Chicago 27
Chicano Literature 80
Childe Harold's Pilgrimage 90
Children's Literature Web Guide 145
Children's Writing/Publishing Link 10
Chilean Literature 108
China, 13th Century 47
Chocolate War, The 92
Chomsky, Noam 92
Chopin, Kate 92
Christian Classics Ethereal Library 40
Christian Literature 40,91
Christian Resources on the Net 91
Christina Rossetti 112
Christopher Marlow (1564-1693) 106
Churchill, Caryl 59
Cinema Sites 59
Cinua Achebe: An Overview 84
Clarke, Austin 52
Classics 5,9,13,17,22,43,67
Classroom Connect 3
Clearances-3 99; *-5* 99
Clifton, Lucille 55
Clinton, William J 71
CM 4
Cochise 70
Coleridge, S T 18,42,51
Collected Works of Shakespeare/The Works of the Bard 114
Collector's guide to Regency Romances, A 76
Colloquia 97
Columbian Literature 106,107
Comedia 59
Coming of Age Fiction, Female 1,40; Male 42
Common Errors in English 30
Complete Collection of Rudyard Kipling 104
Complete Works of Edgar Allan Poe, The 111
Complete Works of William Shakespeare, The 114
Computer Writing and Research Lab 130
Computers 5,6,7,8,10,30,36,64,130,132,140; Dictionaries 24,25; in Theater 60
Con, Carl 69
Conan, Laure see Angers, Felicite
Confessions of Nat Turner 18
Congreve, William 62
ConnectED 4
Connecticut Yankee in King Arthur's Court, A 121
Conrad, Joseph 42

Constitutions, US 17; World 17
Contemporary Authors 38,39,42,44; Irish 77; Poets 52,53,54,56; Women 56,104
Contests 54,62,75,133,136,139,141
Cooke, Elaine 57
Cool School Tool —Literature and Rhetoric 4
Cool Word of the Day Page 27
Coolidge, Calvin 99
Cooper, James Fenimore 42,74
Corio, Ron
Cormier, Robert 92
Corso, Gregory 71
Courses *see* Lessons & Tutorials
Crack Fiction 145
Crane, Stephen 71,92
Crawfrod, Isabella Valancy 75
Crayon—CreAteYour Own Newspaper 126
Crazy Horse 70
Creative Nexus' Literature Site 135
Crime and Punishment 95
Crucible 63
cummings, e.e. 71,93
Curmudgeon's Stylebook: Contents and Index, The 130
Current Events 1,3,5,22,38,44,73,78, 92,114,126,127,128,136
Cushing, Eliza Lanesford 75
CyberSauner—Henry David Thoreau 120
CyberSchool Magazine 39
Cyberteens 139
Czech Literature 103

D

D.H.Lawrence 105
Dahl, Roald 93
Dakota Writers Project 37
Dallas 27
Dance *see* Music and Dance
Dante 42,93
Dante Alighieri on the Web 93
Darkness 90
Darsie, Richard 55
David Mamet 106
Davidson, Lucretia Maria 18
Dawe, James 85
Dead Poets Society 51
Debate 4,22,30,36,37,130,132
Deborah Adams 84
Deciphering Old Handwriting 147
Descartes, Rene 6
Detroit Journal 104
Detto d'Amore 93
Devereux, Robert 51
Devotions upon Emergent Occasions 95
Diary Project, The: Kids' Diary Entries from Around the World 135
Dickens Page, The 94
Dickens, Charles 12,94
Dickinson, Emily 42,51,94,95
Dictionary of Literary Terms 21,116
Digital Education Network Home Page 31
Discovery Channel 122
Division of Rhetoric and Composition 130
Documenting the American South 68

Index

Don Juan 90
Donne, John 40,42,51,95
Doris Lessing: A Retrospective 105
Dostoevsky, Fodor 42,82,95
Doublespeak 92
Dove, Rita 55,95
Downes, Stephen 36
Doyle, Sir Arthur Conan 96
Dracula 48,119
Drama & Theater 2,3,7,8,12,14,15,18, 19,21,38,41,45,58-66,68,74,78,99, 106,107,114-117,123,140; Agents 62
Dryden, John 62
Du Bois, W.E.B. 43
Dunbar, Paul Laurence 55,79
Durer, Albrecht 97
Dying Synagogue at South Terrace, The 52
Dylan Thomas 119
Dylan Thomas Society of Australia 119

E

e.e. cummings 93
Eclectic Writer, The 130
Eco, Umberto 41
Ecologues, The 93
Economics 3,14,15
Edgar Rice Burroughs: From Africa to Mars 89
Edith Warton 123
Edmund Spencer Home Page, The 118
Egyptian Book of the Dead 4
Egyptian Literature 105
Eighteenth Century Resources 4
Electric Library 5
Electronic Archives for the Teaching of American Literature 68
Electronic Beowulf, The 77
Elements of Style 33,43
Eliot, T.S. 71
Elizabeth Barrett Browning: An overview 88
Elizabeth Bishop 87
Elizabethan Times 116
Ellison, Ralph 96
Emancipation Proclamation 18
Emily Dickinson 94,95
Emma 38
Emmeline 76
Emory University Postcolonial Studies 80
Encyclopedia Hibernica Online 77
England *see* United Kingdom
English 102: Multicultural English Web Page 69
English as a Second Language 27,30,31,32,33,35
English Bards on Scotch Reviewers 90
English Contemporary Theater 59
English Language Resources 5
English Literature—Voices of the Shuttle 77
English Literature 12,77,99,105,124; Restoration 62,77
English Server 5
English Server at Carnegie Mellon 18
English Teachers' Web Site, The 6
Enlightenment 6,15
Environmental Studies 3,5
Epistle to Augusta 90
Epistrophy: The Jazz Literature Archive 69

Erasmus Text Project 97
Erik's Quick Style Sheet: Better Writing in Only Twenty Minutes a Day! 34
Ernest Hemingway Campfire Chat 100
Ernest M. Hemingway's Home Page 100
Essays 1,30,35,36,37,69
Essays on the Craft of Dramatic Writing 130
Eugene Ionesco (1912-1994) 101
Europe 3,6
European Enlightenment 6
Evelina 76
Evelyn Arthur St. John Waugh 122
Evergreen Review Reader 101
EXCHANGE 27
Existentialism 63,90
Exit the King 101
Exorcist, The 130
Expressionism 63
eZines: Ultimate Magazine Database 126
Ezra Pound (1885-1972) 111
Ezra Pound Poetry Award 111

F

F. Scott Fitzgerald Centenary 97
Fables *see* Mythology, Fairy Tales & Folk Tales 49
Fabulists Home Page 77
Face of Another, The 104
Fade 92
Faerie Queene 118
Faeries: Lore and Literature 47
Fairy Tales *see* Mythology, Fairy Tales & Folk Tales
Fairy Tales: Origins and Evolution 47
Falcon Education Link 116
Fall of Icarus 86
Famished Road, The 109
Famous Poets 51
Fantasy Fiction 40,41,43,138
FAQ Finder 6
Faulkner, William 71,97
Favorite Teenage Angst Books 145
Female Coming of Age Stories 40
Feminism *see* Women's Studies
Feminist Fiction: Feminist Uses of Genre Fiction 1
Feminist Science Fiction, Fantasy and Utopia 40
Ferlinghetti, Lawrence 71
Fiction *see* specific genre
Film Reviews 59
Film *see* Drama and Theater
Finland 82
Fire 101
First Lines 147
Fitzgerald, F. Scott 70,71,97
Flannery O'Connor Collection 109
Flappers 2 Rappers 28
Flea, The 95
Folk Tales *see* Mythology, Fairy Tales & Folk Tales
For Young Writers 135
Four Quartets 96
Frankenstein 48,117
Frankenstein: Mary W. Shelley 117
Freedom of Information Center 127

French 3,72,75
Frost, Robert 42,43,53,56
Fugard 63
Fundamentals of a Research Paper 35
Fyodor Dostoevsky 95

G

G.K. Chesterton 91
Gabriel Garcia Marquez 106
Gabriel Jose Garcia Marquez-Macondo 107
Gaelic and Galic Culture 77
Gaelic, Culture 77; Literature 78,79
Galileo 7
Games, Puzzles and Quizzes 12,27,28, 29,31,43,60,62,90,120,147
Garden of the Forking Paths 41
Gaskill, Elizabeth 12
Gender Issues in American Literature 69
Geography 3,5,10,24,25,49,56,72,81, 126,136
George Eliot 124
George, Dan 70
Georgia College and University 109
Get Shorty 60
Ghost Stories 48
Gibson, Mel 61
Gilman, Charlotte Perkins 69,74,97
Ginsberg, Allen 53,54,71,89
Glass Menagerie, The 124
Global Campfire, The 136
Globe Theatre 115,116
Glossary of Rhetorical Terms with Examples 22
Godey's Ladys Book Online Home Page 69
Goethe, Johann Wolfgang von 98
Goldberg, Rube 99
Golding, William 98
Good Quotations by Famous People 147
Gordimer, Nadine 80,81,98
Gothic Literature 1764-1820 78
Gothic Literature 48,78
Government Documents 17
Gower, 79
Graham Greene 99
Grammar & Style 2,6,8,10,12,13,23,24, 25,27,30-37,128,130-133,140
Grammar and Style Notes 31
Grammar Lady, The 31
Grammar Safari 31
Grapes of Wrath 118
Graves, Robert 98
Gravesiana 98
Grayford, James 57
Great Books Overview 22
Great Books *see* Classics
Great Expectations 94
Great Irish Famine of 1845-1849 107
Great Thompson Hunt, The 120
Great War *see* World War I
Great Writers 7
Greatest Tale Ever Told, The 136
Greece 48
Greek Literature 9; Mythology 47,48
Greek Mythology 47
Green Grow the Rashes, O 89
Greene, Graham 99
Groundhog Day 130

English & Literature

Guide ot the Works of John Donne 95
Guide to Christian Literature on the Internet, A 40
Guide to Classic Mystery and Detection 40
Guide to Theater Resources on the INTERNET 59
Gulliver's Travels by Jonathan Swift 119
Guttenberg Master Index 7
Gwendolyn Brooks Page 88

H

Haiku 55
Halloween USA 48
Ham, Paul 50
Hamlet 61,116
Hans Christian Andersen:Fairy Tales and Stories 84
Hansberry, Lorraine 74,99
Hard Boiled 60
Hardy, Thomas 51
Harlem Renaissance, 1919-1937 70
Harlem Renaissance, The 70
Harper's Magazine 73
Hart 71
Harvest Bow 99
Haworth, November 1904 124
Hawthorne, Nathaniel 42,99,107
Head, Bessie 80
Heaney, Seamus 52,99,133
Heart of the Matter, The 99
Hemingway and Fitzgerald 70
Hemingway, Ernest 41,70,71,100
Henry James Scholar's Guide to Web Sites 101
Henryson, 79
Herrick, Robert 51
High School English Resource Page 7
History of Costume 60
History, of Costume 60,65; of the Book 3; U.S.1,4,5,7,8,10,14,17,22,34,38,45, 60,67,68,70,72,73,92,117,127,132,14 7; World 1,3-8,10,13,14,15,17,18,22, 34,38,45,47,48,49,60,72,76,78,107,1 32,136,147
Hogarth 65
Hola! (Hello) Oh What a Book! Science and More! 41
Hollow Men, The 96
Holmes, 42
Holmes, Sherlock 96
Home Page of Theater 60
Homer 41
Homework Assistance 21,22,53,130
Homework Help 22
Horagai: Abe Kobo 104
Horror Fiction 48,96,97,103
House of Usher, The: Edgar Allan Poe (1809-1849) 111
Houseman 42,51
HTI American Verse Project 52
Huckleberry Finn 121
Hughes, Langston 69
Humanities Scholarship 7
HUMBUL Gateway, The 8
Hunger 107
Hunt for Red October, The 130
Hurston, Zora Neale 100,101
Hydra 53
Hyperbibliography to American Poetry 52

Hyperizons 139
Hypertext and Hypermedia: A Selected Bibliography 140

I

I am smitten 136
I Am the Cheese 92
Ice Man Cometh, The 130
Idioms *see* Slang
Improve Page, The 60
Improvisational Theater 60,65
Ina Dillard Russell Library 109
Inaugural Addresses of U.S. Presidents 43
Index of Web Sites on Modernism, An 8
India 81,82
Indian Literature 81
Indiana University 45
Indigenous People's Literature 70
Indispensable Writing Resources 131
Infomine: Scholarly Internet Resource Collections 8
Initiatives for Access: Beowulf Project 78
Injun Joe 74
Inkspot: Resources for Writers 131
Inkwell, The; In Appreciation of Writers and Writing 61
Inquirer's Guide to the Universe, An 41
Insomniac 84
Internet 1996 World Expostion 9
Internet Classics Archive, The 9
Internet Movie Database, The 61
Internet Poetry Archive, The 52
Internet Public Library 9,73
Internet Resources in Literature 9
Inter-Play 8
Introduction to Chicana/o Literature 80
Invisible Man 96
Ionesco, Eugene 63,101
Iran 113
Ireland 52,78
Irish Literature 78,82,102; Poetry 52,99,107
Irish Literature Mythology, Folklore, and Drama 78
Irish Poetry Page, The 52
Irving, John 101
Irving, Washington 74
Isaac Rosenberg's "Break of Day in the Trenches"112
Islam 113
Italian Literature 81
Italian, Literature 81; Poetry 93
Italian, The 76
Ivanhoe 38

J

Jack Kerouac (1922-1964) 103
Jack London Collection, The 105
Jackson, Mississippi 125
Jacobi, Derek 61
Jacobs, Harriet 69
James Bond 007 60
James Dawe's Jane Austen Page 86
James Joyce Web Page 102
James, Henry 42,101
Jane Austen Campfire Chat 86

Jane Austen Info Page 86
Japan 28,48,55,61,82
Japanese 104
Japanese Fairy Tales 48
Japanese Literature, Poetry 55; Proverbs 28; Theater 61
Jazz 69,71
Jesus Creek Mysteries 84
Jewett, Sarah Orne 74
Job Search 33
Johann Wolfgang von Goethe 98
John Hewitt's Writer's Resource Center 131
John Steinbeck 118
John's Nautical Literature Page 41
Johns Hopkins Guide to Literary Theory and Criticism 22
Johns Hopkins University Press 22
Johnson, Samuel 102
Jokinen, Anniina 1199
Jonson, Ben 51
Journal of Jazz and Literature, A 69
Journalism 1,2,3,5,10,15,78,100,126-131,133; Gonzo 120; Muckraking 117
Journalists' Resources List 10
Journey of the Magi, The 96
Journey to the Center of the Earth, A 121
Joyce for Beginners 102
Joyce, James 71,102,143
Judy Blume Homebase 19
Judy Blume's Home Base 88
Julius Caesar 115
Julius Caesar Web Guide 115

K

Kabuki for Everyone 61
Kafka, Franz 103
Kairos: A Journal for Teachers of Writing in the Webbed Environment 140
Kamath, Rekha 50
Kansas City Star 100
Kate Chopin Project, The 92
Katherine Mansfield, Short Story Writer 106
Kathy Schrock's Guide for Educators 10
Kay E. Vandergrift's Special Interest Page 10
Keats, John 43,44,51
Ken saro-Wiwa 114
Kerouac, Jack 71,89,103,145; Gap Ad 53
Khayyam, Omar 103
Kierkegaard 15
Kilgore Trout 122
Kimble, F.W. 121
King Arthur *see* Arthurian Studies
King Arthur: History and Legend 78
King, Stephen 103
Kipling, Rudyard 42,54,104
Kobo, Abe 104
Kurdish Literature, Proverbs 28
Kurt Vonnegut Corner 122

L

Lamott, Annie 104
Langland 79

Index

Lansdowne Local, The—Review of Southern African Literature 81
Lansky, Meyer 99
Lara 90
Last Christmas, The 49
Last of the Mohicans 74
Latino Literature Web Page 81
Latino, Culture 81; Literature 81
Laura Ingalls Wilder, Frontier Girl 123
Lawrence, D.H. 105
Lay, Eleanor 75
Layamon 79
Learning About Poetry 53
Learning Disabilities 5
Leary, Timothy 89,145
Leavitt, Henrietta 99
Lennon, John 99
Leprohon, Rosanna 75
Lermontov, Mikhail 54
Lessons & Tutorials 30,31,35,67,69,71, 132,147
Letters Magazine 148
Levine, Philip 52
Lewis Carroll Home Page 90
Librarians' Index to the Internet 10
Libraries Online 2,5,8,9,18,40,52,53,68, 72,73,74,78,82,109,143
Library of Congress 18,52,123,143
Libyrinth, The 41
Life and Works of Herman Melville, The 107
Life and Works of Jules Verne, The 121
Life of Pablo Neruda 108
Lightenings 99
Literary Gothic, The 48
Literary Kicks 71
Literary Managerie, The 11
Literary Resources—Ethnicities and Nationalities 11
Literary, Criticism 13,21,22,23,44,53, 68,71,73,74,82,84-125,139; Theory 14,22,23
Literature and Film 61
Literature and Language Arts Resources 11
Literature and Medicine 11
Literature and Poetry Page 42
Literature from Many Countries 82
Literature Hotlist 12
Literature in India: AnOverview 81
Literature Resources for the High School and College Student 12
Little House on the Prairie 123
Little Women 39
Logic 36
Loiusa May Alcott (1832-1888) 84
Lolita Effect 108
London, Theater 62,63,65
Longfellow, William Wadsworth 42,43
Lord of the Flies 98
Lorde, Audre 69
Los Angeles Film Festival 58
Lost Generation 71
Lost Minds' Christopher Pike Page, The 110
Lost Poets of the Great War 53
Louisaniana State University Libraries 12
Love Song of J. Alfred Prufrock 96
LSU Libraries Author Webliography 12

Luminarium 42
Lynch, Jack 14,32,33

M

Macavity: The Mystery Cat 96
MacBeth 116,117
MacBeth Plugged 117
Machar, Agnes Maule 75
Machiavelli 15
Magazines & Newspapers, Online 2,3, 8,9,12,19,28,31,39,40,59,62,71,74,80, 98,101,103,111,115,122,126,137,138, 140,148
Magical Realism 106,107
Malcolm X 18
Male Coming of Age Stories 42
Maltese Falcon FAQ, The 60
Mamet, David 106
Manjuro, Ichimura 61
Mansfield, Katherine 106
Many Voices: American Indian Students Journal 71
Margaret Atwood Information 84
Marge Piercy Homepage 110
Mariae Encomium 97
Marie, Erin 95
Mark Twain from the Mining Company 121
Mark Twain's Huckleberry Finn 121
Marlowe, Christopher 106
Marquez, Gabriel Garcia 106,107
Marquez-Macondo, Gabriel Jose Garcia *see* Marquez, Gabriel Garcia
Marx, Karl 15
Mary Shelley and Frankenstein 117
Mary Wollstonecraft 124
Masaoka, Shiki 55
Math 6,15,22,34
Matsuoka, Mitsuhara 12
Mautz, Nancy 14
Maxwell, Don 50
Maya Angelou Home Page 84
Maya Angelou Pages 84
Mayans 81
McCarthy, Thomas 52
McClure, Michael 71
McClure's Magazine 104
McCourt, Frank 42
McCrae, John 53
Me up at does 93
Meaning of Life 101
Medbh, Maghred 107
Medieval Studies 7,8,13,42,77; Women Authors 18
Meditation 17 95
Melville, Herman 42,74,107
Mending Wall 53
Mexico 81
MGM 99
Michigan State University 42
Michigan State University Celebrity Lecture Series, The 42
Middle English 79
Middle English Collection at the Electronic Text Center, University of Virginia, The 79
Middleton, Thomas 107
MidLink Magazine 136
Mighty Pen Online Magazine Home Page, The 137
Millay, Edna St. Vincent 43
Miller Arthur 58

Million Man March 84
Milosz, Czeslaw 52
Milton, John 108
Milton-L Home Page, The 108
Mining Company 121
Minority Literatures—Voices of the Shuttle 71
Minotaur, The 90
Mirriam-Webster OnLine 23
Mission Impossible 60
Mississippi 72,125
Mississippi Writers Page, The 72
Mitsuhara matsuoka's Home page (English Literature on the Web) 12
Model Essays 35
Modern and Contemporary American Poetry 53
Modernism 8
Mole and the Owl, The 49
Moore, Marianne 56
Morrison, Toni: 1931- 108
Mosley, Walter 68
Mothers Who Think: Word By Word—Annie Lamott's On-line Diary 104
Mount Everest 99
Mr. William Shakespeare and the Internet 115
Mrs. Gaskell 124
Mrs. Parker and the Vicious Circle 67
Ms. Smith's English Page 13
Multiculturalism 69
Musee des Beaux Arts 86
Music & Dance 3,4,5,9,14,15,23,38, 73,77
My Heart's in the Highlands 89
My Virtual Reference Desk 13
Mysterious Home Page 43
Mysterious Homepage 60
Mystery and Detective Fiction 40,43,96,147
Mythology, Fairy Tales & Folk Tales 47-49,78,81,84

N

Nabokov Sights 108
Nabokov, Vladimir 82,108
Nadine Gordimer: An Overview 98
Naguib Mahfouz Page, A 105
Napier University Library: War Poets Collection 53
Nathaniel Hawthorne 99
National Library of Canada 72
National Library of Scotland 79
National Poetry Month 50
National Writing Project, The 13
Native American Authors 72
Native American Indian Resources 72
Native American Literature Online 73
Native American, Literature 11,69, 70,72,73,74; Poetry 56; Studies 72,73
Native Lit-L: A Mailing List for Native Literature 73
Natural Language Playground, The 32
Nautical Literature 41
Nepal 82
Neruda, Pablo 108
NetNovel 137

English & Literature

NetSERF: The Internet Connection for Medieval Resources 13
New Moon: The Magazine for Girls and Their Dreams 148
New Orleans 27
New York City 67; Theater 62,63
New York Public Library Home Page, The 23
New Yorker, The 127
Newseum 127
Newspaper Archives on the Web 127
Newspapers Online *see* Magazines & Newspapers Online
Newsport 128
Nick Evans' Survey of American Literature 73
Nigera, Human Rights 114
Nigerian Authors 114
NM's Creative Impulse 14
Noam Chomsky Archive, The 92
Nobel Red Man 74
Nobel, Foundation 23; Museum 23; Prize Winners 7,23,52,87,90,99,105,107,108,118
Nobelstiftelson: The Nobel Foundation 23
Norris, David 102
Norris, Frank 74
North American Native Authors Catalog 73
Notions of the Americans 74

O

O'Connor, Flannery 109
Oates, Joyce Carol 109
Objectivism Resource Guide, The 43
Odyssey 43
Of Mice and Men 118
Okri, Ben 109
Old English Literature 5
Olds, Sharon 54
Oliver Twist 94
Olivier, Laurence 61
Omar Khayyam 103
On the Road 103
On-book: An Introduction to the Study of Literature 23
One Look Dictionaries: The Faster Finder 24
On-line Books Page 14
On-line Dictionary of Computing 24
OnLine English Grammar 32
On-line Highbeam 140
On-Line Literary Resources 14
Original Home Page of Robert W. Service, The 114
Orwell, George 109
Osborne, John 59
Other Literatures Written in English—Voices of the Shuttle 82
Other Places 81
Otway, Thomas 62
Owen, Wilfred 53
Oxford English Dictionary 5
Oxford University 112; Press 21
Oz Project Home Page 140
OzLit@Vicne—Australian Books, Australian Literature 82

P

Page Index for the Catcher in the Rye 113
Palestinian Literature, Proverbs 28
Papa Page, The 100
Paradigm Online Writing Assistant 35
Paregien 57
Pascal, Blaise 6
Pasternak, Boris 82
Pastor 79
Paton, Alan 80
Payne, Darwin 63
PBS 125
Percy Bysshe Shelley Home Page 117
Percy, Walker 110
Perseus Project, The 48
Personal Helicon 99
Phantasmagoria 103
Phelps, C.E.D. 104
Philadelphia 27
Phillippines 82,104
Philosophy 4,8,15,17,43
PHRASEOLOGY: A Catalog of Multilingual Resources on the Internet 28
Piercy, Marge 110
Pike, Christopher 110
Pitsco's Ask an Expert 14
Plath, Sylvia 110
Playbill On-Line 62
Plutarch 42
Poe, Edgar Allen 42,51,54,111
Poet's Park 54
Poetry 7,38,43,50-57,70,82,84,87,89,94,106,110,111,114,117,119,138; Cowboy 57; Forms 53,56
Poetry Archives, The 54
Poetry Lover's Page 54
Poetry On-line Project 90
Poets in Person 54
Polish 94
Political Science 3,5,6,8,14,15,17,25,92,127,132
Polwhele, Richard 18
Pope, Alexander 111
Porta Ludovica 41
Portland, OR 27
Positively Poetry 55
Postcolonial Studies 80
Postmodernism 63
Pound Journal 111
Pound, Ezra 71,111
Praise of Folly, The 97
Preludes 96
Pride and Prejudice 38
Project Bartleby 43
Project Gutenberg 24,114
Prometheus 90
Public Broadcasting System *see* PBS
Public Domain Modern English Studies 15
Public Electronic Library 82
Publishers & Publishing 10,40
Pulitzer Prize Winners 7,133
Pulp Fiction(film) 60
Pulp Literature 43
Pulp Page, The 43
Purdue Online Writing Lab (OWL), The 35
Purdue Online Writing Laboratory 30,32,33

Pushkin Page, The 112
Pushkin, Aleksandr 54,112
Puzzle Depot 27
Puzzles *see* Games, Puzzles and Quizzes
Pynchon, Thomas

Q

Quarterly Black Review, The 44
Quizzes *see* Games, Puzzles and Quizzes
Quotations 148
Quotations 24,28,40,42,63,99,102,147,148
Quotations Page, The 148

R

Rachel Carson Issues Forum, The 91
Radcliffe, Ann 76,78
Radin, Grace 124
Rage Against the Machine 92
Raisin in the Sun 99
Rand, Ayn 43
Rape of the Lock Home Page, The 111
Readers' and Writers' Resource Page 131
Reading 2,10,21,22,31,34,49,67,144,145,147
Reading By Teens for Teens 146
REAL McCoy African American Phat Poetry Page 55
Realists Wonder Society, The 49
Recommended Readings 16,19,22,33,40,41,69,73,80,131,136,143,145,146
Reference Shelf 24
Reformation Studies 3
Religion 3,4,6,7,8,14,15,40,45,47,56,81
Renaissance Studies 3
Reporters Network, The 128
Research Paper Assistance 8,34,35,36,67,115,133
Research Paper Page 36
Researching American Literature on the Internet 74
Resources for American Literature 74
Restoration Drama Homepage 62
Reverse Dictionary 32
Rhetoric and Electronic Arts Site 132
Rhetoric *see* Debate
Rhymes 24
Richard Wright—Black Boy 125
Richard's Poetry Library
Ring of Her Own, A 141
Rinoceros 101
Rita Dove Page 95
Roald Dahl Home Page, The 93
Roane State Community College On-line Writing Lab 36
Robert Graves Society Information Center, The 98
Robinson, Mary 18
Roget's Thesaurus 24
Roman Literature 9; Theater 60
Romance Literature 39,43; Regency 76
Romance Novels and Women's Fiction 44
Romancing the Indian 74

Index

Romanian Literature, Drama 101
Romantic Circles 44
Romantic Era *see* 18th Century Studies
Romeo and Juliet 116,130
Romeo and Juliet Web Guide 116
Ron's On-line ESOL Classroom 32
Rosenberg, Isaac 53,112
Rossetti, Christia 51,112
Rousseau, Jean-Jacques 6
Rubayyat 103
Ruden, Sarah 81
Rushdie, Salman 113
Russian 94; Culture 112; Literature 82,112; Orthodox Church 95
Russian Literature 82

S

Sailing Through 49
Salinger, J. D. 21,113
Salman Rushdie 113
Salon Magazine 104
Sameul Beckett 87
Samuel Johnson 102
San Diego 27
Sandburg, Carl 42
Saro-Wiwa, Kenule B. 80
Sartre, Jean-Paul 87
Sassoon, Siegfried 53
Satanic Verses 113
Schneider 60
Schrock, Kathy 10
Science 1,5,6,14,22-25,34,41,136
Science Fiction 15,16,40,41,43,64,121,122,138; Awards 21
Science Fiction Resource Guide 15
Scorcese, Martin 58
Scotland 79,89
Scots Wha Hae 89
Scottish Literature 79,82,89
Scottish Literature at the University of South Carolina 79
Screenwriters/Playwrights Page 63
Screenwritiers.com 62
Scripts 58,59,61,63
Seamus Heaney 99
Seeger, Alan 53
Selected Poetry of George Gordon, Lord Byron 90
Semantic Rhyming Dictionary, A 24
Service, Robert W.
Set Designs for the Crucible by Darwin Payne 63
Shadow 137
Shadwell, Thomas 62
Shakespeare Classroom, The 116
Shakespeare, William 41,42,51,60,114-117
Shakespeare's Globe Theatre 115
Shapiro, Karl 54
Shelley, Mary 117
Shelley, Percy Bysshe 43,44,51,117
Sherlockian Holmepage 96
Sherwood Anderson Page, The 84
Silent Movies 63
Silent Spring 91
Silko, Leslie Marmon 73
Simon, Neil 99
Simone de Beauvoir 87
Simpson, Erik 34
Sinclair, Upton 117

SIRS: The Knowledge Source: Arts and Humanities 15
Sixties Project and Vietnam Generation Inc, The 74
Skelton, John 51
Slang & Idioms 27,28,69
Slavery 68
Smith, Charlotte 76
Snagged Links: On Modern World Drama 62
Snyder, Gary 71
Social Studies 23,
Sociology 5,8,56
Song 99
Souls of Black Folks 43
South Asian American Literature 75
South Asian American Literature 80
South Asian Graduate Research Journal 80
Spanish 41,59,80,81,106,108; Civil War 53; Golden Age 59
Spanish American Literature 11
Spark Magazine 137
Speak Out! 44
Speech 22,36,38,132
Speech Writing 132
Speeches 1,73,92,104,132
Spenser Society 118
Spenser, Edmund 118
Spermatikos Logos 41
Spondee 56
St Petersburg, Russia 95
Stanton, Elizabeth Cady 69
Station Theater 60
Stein, Gertrude 53,71
Steinbeck Country 118
Steinbeck Research Center 118
Steinbeck, John 118
Stephen Crane: Man, Myth and Legend 92
Stephen King WebSite 103
Stephen's Guide to Logical Fallacies 36
Stetson University 63
Stevens, Wallace 56
Stevenson, Robert Louis 42,54,118
Still I Rise 84
Stoker, Bram 119
Strunk, William 33,43
Students Works, International 55
Study Guide for H.G. Wells: *War of the Worlds* 122
Study Skills 34
Submit Your Own 41,54,55,56,75,135-139,141
Sun Microsystems 1
Supreme Court Cases, Banned Books 143
Surrealism 63
Susie's Place—The Word Games Page 28
Swift, Jonathan 119
Sydney, Australia 102
Sylvia Plath 110

T

T.S.Eliot Page, The 96
Tales from the Vault 138
Tales of Wonder: Folk and Fairy Tales from Around the World 49
Tames, David 97
Tan, Amy 11

Tan, Annabel 50
Tangerine: Poetry site Extraordinaire 56
Tarzan 89
Ten Year Lunch, The (documentary) 67
Tennyson, Alfred 42,51
Texts and Contexts 15
Theater Performance Schedules 62
Theater *see* Drama and Theater
Theater Sites 64
ThinkQuest 141
Thomas Biggs Harned Walt Whitman Collection 123
Thomas Carlyle 90
Thomas Middleton (1580-1627) 107
Thomas Pynchon Home Page 112
Thomas Wolf Festival 124; Society 124
Thomas Wolfe (1900-1938) 124
Thomas, Dylan 119
Thomas, Edward 53
Thompson, Hunter S 120
Thoreau, Henry David 99,120
Thornton Wilder (1897-1975) 123
Tibbets, John C. 91
Tillman, Benjamin 104
To a Mouse 89
Tolkien Guide, The 120
Tolkien, J.R.R. 120
Tollund Man 99
Tolstoy, Leo 82
Tom Sawyer 74,121
Toomer, Jean 55
Treasure Island 118
Tree Fiction on the World Wide Web 141
Trilling, Lionel 99
Turgenev, Ivan 82
Tutuola, Amos 80
Twain, Mark 17,42,67,74,121
Twentieth-Century Poetry in English 56

U

Ultimate Science Fiction Web Guide, The 16
Ulysses for Dummies 102
Uncle Remus 67
United Kingdom 6,31
United States 3,9
University of California at Berkeley 1
University of Florida 65
University of Manitoba 3
University of Michigan 18
University of Missouri Press 95
University of North Carolina Chapel Hill 68,99
University of Pennsylvania 31
University of South Carolina 79
University of Texas 74
University of Virginia 51,73,79,130
University of Victoria Writer's Guide 36
Updike, John 121,136
Upton Sinclair 117
Urbana, IL 60
Useful Resources for Composition 37
Using Young Adult Fiction and Non-Fiction to Produce Critical Readers 16
Usual Suspects, The 130
Utopian Literature 40

V

Vandergrift, Kay E 10
Vandergrift's List of Young Adult Authors and Titles 10
Vassar College 16
Vassar CoolSchool: The Best Sites on the Web for Teens and Teachers 16
Vatican 3
Venezuela 82
Verne, Jules 121
Victorian Studies see 19th Century Studies
Victorian Web, The 45
Victorian Women Writers Project 45
Videomaker's Glossary of Terms 64
Vietnam Generation: A Journal of Recent History and Contemporary Culture 74
Vietnam War 74
Vintage Press 96
VIOD:PERFORMANCE 64
Virgil 7
Virginia Woolf 124
Virginia Woolf's the Years: The Evolution of a Novel 124
Virtual English 45
Virtual Presnetation Assistant 132
Virtual Reference Desk 25
Virtual Theater Project 64
Virtually react 128
Vision of Judgement 90
Voices from the Gaps: Women Writers of Color 16
Voices of the Shuttle 71,77,82
Vonnegut, Kurt 122
Voyage to Another Unviersi: 1994

W

W.H.Auden (1907-1973) 86
Wacky Web Tales 141
Wake Forest University 63
Walcott, Derek 42
Walden 120
Walker Percy Project, The 110
Walker, Alice 122
Walt Whitman Collection, The 123
War of the Worlds 122
Washington, D.C. 27,67
Wasteland, The 96
Waugh Newsletter 122
Waugh, Evelyn 122

WebCrawler Guide: Arts: Literature 17
Weblit 17
Webspeare 115
Webster's Dictionary 24
Wells, H.G. 122
Welsh Literature 82,119
West Indian Literature 82
Western Canon, The 17
Wharton, Edith 123
Where's That From? 29
Whitman, Walt 42,43,51,123
Wilcoxiana 124
Wilde, Oscar 43,51
Wilder, Laura Ingalls 123
Wilder, Thornton 123
Willa Cather Page 91
William Blake Archive, The 88
William Butler Yeats (1865-1939) 125
William Faulkner on the Web 97
William S. Burroughs 89
William S. Burroughs Files, The 89
Williams, Tennessee 124
Williams, William Carlos 53,56
Wilson, August 58
Windsor McCay 49
Wired Style 25
Wiretap Electronic Text Archive 17
Wolf, Thomas 124
Wollstonecraft, Mary 18,76,124
Women in Canadian Literature 75
Women Romantic Era Writers 18
Women Writers of the Middle Ages 18
Women, Authors 18,21,39,45,69,80, 122,141,146;in Literature 1,40,75; in Theater 65; Periodicals 69
Women's Books Online 146
Women's Studies 1,10,14,38,76,76,122
Woolf, Virginia 124
Woon, Yeap Yin 50
Word a Day, A 29
Work in Progress: A James Joyce Website 102
Works Online 1,2,4,5,8,10,11,12,14,15, 17,28,32,34,39,40,42,43,45,51,52,53, 59,63,67,69,72,73,74,77,79,84- 125,131,141,143,145
World Internet Directory: Drama 65
World Literature 2,4,11,14,49,70,80-83
World of London Theatre, The: 1660-1800 65
World War I 53

World Wide Web in the Classroom 140
Wright, Richard 125
Writer's Toolbox 132
Writers Free Reference Desk 133
Writers' Workshop, The: Online Resources for Writers 133
Writing 10,22,30,31,33,34-37,39,40, 41,43,44,45,53-56,62,63,64,67,69,78, 88,126-142,145,148; Online Centers 12,130,133,140; Resources 2,3,5,12- 15,19,21,23,24,27,28,32; Tips 6,25
Writing Argumentative Essays 37
Writing Black 18
Writing Process Handbook 133
Writing Resources 133
Writings of Henry David Thoreau 120
Wycherly, William 62
Wyoming Companion, The: Cowboy Poetry and Poets 57

Y

Yagi, Kametaro 55
Yahoo!Arts: Humanities:Literature: Authors 18
Yeats Society 125
Yeats, William Butler 43,125
Yellow Wallpaper, The 97
Young Adult Librarian's Help/Homepage 19
Young Adult Literature Library 19
Young Adult Literature10,16,19,88, 110,128,137,148
Young Adult Services 19
Young Canadian Voices: An Independent Literary Journal for Young Writers 138
Young Writers Association 137
Young Writers Clubhouse 133

Z

zeen 138
Zembla: The Nabokov Butterfly Net 108
Zlata's Diary: A Child's Life in Sarajevo 135
Zora Neale Hurston (1901-1960) 101
Zora Neale Hurston 100
Zuzu's Petals Literary Resource Homepage, The 19
Zuzu's Petals Quarterly 19